Far From the Land
New Irish Plays

At the Black Pig's Dyke
Vincent Woods

Language Roulette
Daragh Carville

Disco Pigs
Enda Walsh

Bat the Father, Rabbit the Son
Donal O'Kelly

Frank Pig Says Hello
Patrick McCabe

Hard to Believe
Conall Morrison

Foreword by Sebastian Barry
Edited and introduced by John Fairleigh

Published with the support of the Arts Council for
Northern Ireland and An Chomhairle Ealaíon and in
co-operation with the Stewart Parker Trust

Methuen Drama

This collection first published in Great Britain in 1998
by Methuen Drama
Methuen Publishing Ltd
215 Vauxhall Bridge Road
London SW1V 1EJ

Methuen Publishing Ltd reg. number 3543167

ISBN 0 413 72270 8

A CIP catalogue record for this book is available at the British Library.

Typeset by Deltatype Ltd, Birkenhead, Merseyside
Transferred to digital printing 2002.

DP/08

Far From the Land

New Irish Plays

For Brian Friel

Special thanks to the following in the preparation of this anthology:

Richard Froggatt, Phelim Donlon, Philip Hammond, Alan Reynolds, Tony O'Dalaigh, Fiach MacConghail, Tom Coughlan, Karin McCully, Judy Friel, Brian McManus, Declan McGonagle, John and Yvonne Speers, Peter Sirr, Philip Orr, Ciaran Carson.

Contents

Foreword

I received a BBC Stewart Parker Award in 1989 for my first play *Boss Grady's Boys*. It was the first time the award was given, and the first award I ever got, and I still remember the excitement of the train to Belfast and the long unfamiliar day of interviews and speeches. Since then the Trust has fished the length and breadth of Ireland and England for new playwrights, and the list of names is luminous and marvellous indeed.

It's sometimes said that there is a new theatrical resurgence going on comparable to the National Theatre movement, as orchestrated by Yeats and Lady Gregory in the 1900s. I think there is a comparable renaissance, but this time there is no controlling mind along the lines of the Yeatsian model, as one might say, and really the new playwrights are quite separate entities and do not strictly speaking form a group. This accidental fact has unexpectedly given it a unique strength and independence. The new Irish theatre is a moveable feast that moves quite naturally and lightly between Dublin, Belfast, London, New York.

Nevertheless, as writing itself is a solitary business and being an Irish person a challenging station, it is a deeply heartening thing that there is such a plethora of outstanding Irish writers for the theatre. Theatre is a nervy and taxing arena and when a playwright and a play comes through the fire unscathed and indeed as may be trailing clouds of glory, it is a sight to see and a fact to sing about. All the plays in this volume turned the heads of whatever cities of the world they played in, and all are – to put it simply and plainly – brilliant playwrights. They may not form a group beyond the fact that the Stewart Parker Trust has endeavoured to honour their achievements, but they certainly form a collection to lift the top of the head and make a person sit back in wonder and thanks.

Sebastian Barry
October 1997

Introduction

Much of the story of Irish literature is about the artist taking off to find sanctuary and appreciation elsewhere. Once safely in exile, home thoughts from abroad can turn to sentimentality or, just as likely, distance and time may stir venom into recall of the native land. But much has changed in the Ireland of the 1990s and its relationship with its own creative talent. Within no more than a few years the place has remade its own image to become the essence of a modern European state, with the artist being warmly embraced as confirmation of the country's new dynamism and diversity. This enthusiasm is expressed at government level by the funding of Aosdána, something like a national academy which gives a guaranteed income for life to a core of established artists, and the apparent commitment of all political parties to increasing levels of financial support for the arts. And in the media and in the talk when people get together, the artist would seem to be considered not so much an adornment as at the core of national life; admit to strangers in an Irish pub that you are a writer and they will respond to you not as a work-shy drop-out but as a useful person who deserves another drink.

The Irish playwright has shared in this general surge in appreciation of the arts. The Abbey [Theatre, Dublin] on its main and Peacock stages has continued its traditional role of nurturing the writer, but there have also appeared in the capital and in towns around the country, dozens of companies of actors and directors which exult in presenting new work: companies with names like Rough Magic, Passion Machine, Pigsback and Co-Motion in Dublin, Druid in Galway, Red Kettle in Waterford, Mad Cow and Tinderbox in Belfast and Bickerstaffe in Kilkenny. The evidence of this enthusiasm is that something like half of all theatrical productions each year in Ireland are premières; a fair proportion of these are explorations of texts by first-time writers. As companies seek out and encourage the writer as the seed of their own creativity, in turn their reputation with the public and with funding bodies such as the Arts Council is enhanced.

An irony, perhaps, is that while the dynamism within Irish theatre and the other arts has been used in the construction of the new and positive image that the country has of itself, the common achievement of the artist is, of course, to undermine this comfortable façade. Playwrights might not see such exposure as their primary intention, considering their texts as public exploration of private territory; yet the measure of a play is not only how it moves an audience, but the critical evaluation of how it interacts with its own time and its perceived success in peeling back the deceptions which society layers around itself. Even the youngest of the writers now having their plays produced in Ireland have in their lifetime seen seminal changes which have left individuals scarred and many broader social conflicts unresolved. Suddenly, and defying any easy analysis as to its inherent cause, the economy is developing at one of the fastest rates in the European Union, creating conflict between traditional community life and a new and more ruthless individualism. The battle between moral fundamentalism and individual choice continues, though the joint lock of church and state on areas of personal morality such as divorce and sexual orientation has been broken to the extent that candidates in the 1997 Presidential election had to take quick action to defend themselves against charges of being too close to Catholic orthodoxy. And the righteous indignation of the old enmity with Britain, with some residual toleration of force as a legitimate element of political change, has yet to give way to an accommodation of all the differing versions of history within the island. It is such continuing irritants beneath the skin of the 'Celtic Tiger' which must concern anyone living in Ireland in the 1990s, no less the writers represented in this volume.

All six plays were premièred during the past ten years, not in Dublin's major production houses but in the independent sector of younger and regional companies which continually feeds new writers and fresh production styles into the mainstream of Irish theatre. Many important texts by established writers were presented in the same period and will be recorded in any comprehensive theatrical history of the times; what distinguishes the plays included here is that each marked the launch of a new writer with the originality and force to make an impact on the theatrical scene both in Ireland and beyond.

Vincent Woods' *At the Black Pig's Dyke* and Conall Morrison's *Hard to Believe* confront one of the most urgent and unresolved issues in contemporary Irish life – the incipient violence that counterpoints the cultivated national stereotype of *bonhomie* and blarney. Woods depicts a group of mummers in the borderland between North and South, blending their rituals of death with the all-too-modern assassins going about their awful task; the stories of the past interlocking with current acts of revenge expose a continuity of guiltless killing in the Irish countryside. Morrison's investigation of the roots of violence centres on one man, and how his moral disorientation relates to the sectarianism of his Irish past. The single actor stands on stage and invokes his Protestant preacher grandfather and his turncoat father who married a Catholic and thereafter denied his background. Out of this union comes the protagonist, an agent for British army intelligence, so far retreated from reality that he is bemused rather than repulsed by schemes of death. In both of these pieces, a past denied or unresolved carries through to distort the moral judgements of the present.

Patrick McCabe's *Frank Pig Says Hello* can also be interpreted as an investigation of violence. His target is not the brutalisation of history, but the sullen ungenerosity of a rural community towards an innocently simple young man, provoking him into a wild acting-out of his hurt; it is meanness that sears the soul and creates the monster.

Donal O'Kelly's *Bat the Father Rabbit the Son* explores the loss of spirit in the passage between one generation and the next. In a tussle between father and son, the usual status-relationship is reversed with the father being gentle and unambitious while the son is thrusting and conventionally successful. Beneath his anger at the father's unworldliness, the son is reluctantly envious of his expressiveness and contentment. It is a powerful personal story, but also broadly symbolic of a society in transition.

Enda Walsh's *Disco Pigs* and Daragh Carville's *Language Roulette* are firmly set in the sub-culture of youth; tough, fast-talking and street-wise, the young people are Irish but quintessentially urban. In *Disco Pigs* two friends, bonded in their fantasies and shared baby-talk, face into Cork city on their seventeenth birthday and the intimacy of their old relationship falters. In *Language Roulette*, a group of young people in Belfast come together for a reunion, and the underlying atmosphere is anger and revenge. For both Carville and Walsh it is not a very supportive or generous society, North or South, in which they place their characters; severed from traditional loyalties and values, all would seem to be adrift in the new Ireland.

These plays, the product of six talents with distinctive life experiences, together explore some of the most important issues to be resolved in contemporary Ireland and beyond. Whether their focus is the inescapable interface between history and the present, the search for the origins of violence or the psychological danger of concealing the truth in human relationships, what they share is courage to challenge the deceptions which block the healthy functioning of individuals and societies.

In theatrical style, the plays vary from Vincent Woods' invocation of ancient rituals in *At the Black Pig's Dyke* to Daragh Carville's linear and literal narrative of one drunken evening in *Language Roulette*. Taken together, they defy predictions from the 1970s and 80s that to engage an audience bred on the documentary style of film and television, theatre could thrive only by delivering slices of life; these plays address the most contemporary of problems, but are not afraid to draw on some of the oldest elements of Irish culture – mythology and fantasy, story-telling and exultation in extravagant language. By reworking these traditions and entrusting them to the imagination and the attention of a contemporary audience, this new generation of Irish playwrights manage to reinvigorate theatrical form while forthrightly addressing the problems of their own time.

John Fairleigh
October, 1997

At The Black Pig's Dyke

by Vincent Woods

At the Black Pig's Dyke was first performed at the Druid Lane Theatre, Galway on 30 September, 1992. This script is the text used in the first production. The cast was as follows:

Lizzie Boles	Stella McCusker
Young Lizzie	Diane O'Kelly
Sarah Boles	
Elizabeth	
Jack Boles	Brendan Laird
First Hero in the Mummers	
Hugh Brolly	David Wilmot
Second Hero in the Mummers	
Michael Flynn	Ray McBride
Captain Mummer	
Frank Beirne	Peter Gowen
Doctor in the Mummers	
Tom Fool	Frankie McCafferty
Miss Funny	Deirdre O'Kane
Beelzebub	Brendan O'Regan
Musician	
Butcher	Cora Smyth
Musician	

Directed by Maeliosa Stafford
Set and costumes by Monica Frawley
Lighting by Stephen McManus
Music composed by Brendan O'Regan
Choreography by Ray McBride

Setting

Leitrim and Fermanagh, past and present.

Act One

Prologue

Set should capture a sense of interior and exterior. There's a cradle, a chair, maybe a table. Neither interior nor exterior should be dominant or over-defined.

Enter **Lizzie Boles** *carrying a half-made straw wren and a knife. She sits by the cradle, rocks it gently, then begins to hum the air of 'The Enniskillen Dragoons'. The following rann is delivered as if she is about to tell a story to her granddaughter* **Elizabeth**, *the baby in the cradle.*

Lizzie It was a long time ago, Elizabeth, and it was not a long time ago ... It was a time when to go east was to go west, when to go south was to go north, when people sang songs at a wake and cried when a child was born. It was in a land where the sun never rose and the sun never set, where the dead prepared shrouds for the livin' and straw people walked the roads.

Three loud knocks are heard. **Lizzie** *turns towards the sound.* **A Man***'s voice is heard.*

Man's Voice Any admittance for Captain Mummer and his men?

As **Lizzie** *stands staring in the direction of the sound* **a Woman***'s voice is heard singing.*

Woman's Voice
  The wren, the wren, the king of all birds
  On St Stephen's night was caught in the furze.

Out of darkness — suspended in light at a higher level — the adult **Elizabeth** *is seen. She is wearing a white coat with a poppy in her lapel and a clutch of poppies in her hand. The effect is ghostly, unreal.*

Elizabeth It was not a long time ago at all and it was not far away. It was in a land where the black pig had furrowed an endless tunnel under the earth and where it ran still, trapped and frantic beneath the ground.

At that time there was a Strange Knight on the road. He met
a woman with a riddle. How many people were in the world
before the world was made? How many graves did it take to
bury them? What way were they laid – facin' north, south,
east or west? And did they rest or not from then till now? He
said he'd answer any riddle in three parts but not in four. So
she rose her hook to kill him – but if she did he shot her
first, through the heart with a golden bullet.

The Strange Knight went on till he arrived at a fair where
two men were havin' a dispute over a piece of land. He said
he could settle it and offered a fine price to whichever of
them would sell it to him. One man said he'd sell it that
minute, the other said he wouldn't sell it for love or money.
So the Strange Knight said to the second man, 'You're the
owner, it's your land.' Then he shot the two of them and had
the land for himself.

Act One

Scene One

Exit **Lizzie** *and* **Elizabeth**. *Enter* **Tom Fool** *and* **Miss Funny**
who cavort and play-act as they deliver their joint speech.

Tom Fool *and* **Miss Funny**
A midwinter's play for a widwinter's night.
A mummers' play all right. You know the stuff:
"Room room, gallant boys, give us room to rhyme
All silver, no brass; bad money won't pass."
Auld guff that had them in stitches
Every Christmas or midwinter.
Catholic, Protestant and Dissenter
Sittin' back to watch the crack.
The Captain leadin' in his pack,
Meself tight up to his backside.
And the others, Beelzebub or Devil Doubt
Sweepin' good luck in or out.
The Butcher carvin' up his pig.
The stragglers in to dance a jig.
And then, the Heroes, now they'd differ.
From Antrim down to Drumaliffer:
Copper-nosed Cromwell might be in,
Sir Patrick the foe to strike his chin;
The Turkey Champion and Prince George
Might come to blows – the cause?
Oh, some word or insult thrown about.
Sure as shootin', not a doubt
But they'd be at it hell for leather –
Sword and steel and whitest feather.
The Tsar, Lord Nelson, Dan O'Connell,
Impostors, Red Coats, Hugh O'Donnell,
Wellington, Napoleon, Grand Signors,
Fought their corners, evened scores.
And one was killed – it all relied
On the tradition, the tribe, the side
Of the household where they played – or fought.

Either way, the doctor wrought his miracle
When called; he brought the Heroes back to life
And all shook hands.
Then came a wife for me –
Miss Funny – with a box to catch the money.

Both

And then we'd dance and play and sing
Around the kitchen, in a ring and out.

Miss Funny

We'd dance the house around about . . .

Three knocks are heard, then a man's voice.

Captain Mummer   Any admittance for Captain Mummer
and his men?

Tom Fool *and* **Miss Funny**   Come in and welcome . . .

Enter the **Mummers**, *the* **Captain** *at their head. They may carry a
straw wall. They perform the First Mummers' Play.*

Scene Two

Captain Mummer

Here come I, Captain Mummer and all me men;
The door was on the latch and so we entered in.
Room, room, gallant boys, give us room to rhyme,
And we'll act out our activities for this is actin' time.
We'll act the young, we'll act the age
We'll act what was never acted on any stage.
We'll dance without, we'll dance within,
We'll dance your arse around your chin.
And if you don't believe in what I say,
Enter in the Butcher and he'll soon clear the way.

Butcher

Here come I, the Butcher, with me steel,
I can cut any living creature from its head to its heel.
I can strip the fat from sinew, I can strip the fat from bone
And leave nothing of a carcass except the horn and thoin.

And if you don't believe in what I say,
Enter in Beelzebub and he'll soon show the way.

Beelzebub

Here come I, Beelzebub,
On my heart I carry a club
And on my rear I carry a heart

Tom Fool

So there's always room for a rhyme there too!

Beelzebub

I'm otherwise known as Devil Doubt
And I chew the fat around about,
The fat the Butcher cuts for me –
A frying pan to start my tea.
And if you don't believe in what I say,
Enter in a Hero Brave and he'll soon show the way.

First Hero

Here come I, an Orange Knight, a Hero Brave,
From England I have come:
I have cleared the fields and houses
And cut down the native scum.
I've conquered nations, I've conquered seas,
My deeds of valour are sure to please.
Show me the man who dares me stand
And I'll dispatch him with my right hand.

Second Hero

I'm the man who dares you stand:
A Green Knight, a Hero Grand.
I've defended ditches, gripes and drumlins
From foreign tyrants and their foreign mumblin's.
I rode an ass, I beat a goat
And cut many's the dirty stranger's throat.
And I'll do the same with you right now
And leave your entrails for the sucklin' sow.

First Hero

Take out your sword and fight, sir!

Second Hero

I'd see you up to your eyes in shite, cur!

First Hero

Impostor! Liar! Upstart!

Second Hero

Feel this blade run through your black heart.

The two **Heroes** *fight, egged on and supported by various of the other* **Mummers**. *Finally the* **First Hero** *is struck and falls.*

Captain Mummer   Doctor, doctor! – Is there a doctor in the house?

Doctor

Here come I, a Doctor good, a Doctor pure
There's no disease that I can't cure.

Captain Mummer   But are you the ten-pound doctor?

Tom Fool   There is no ten-pound doctor.

Captain Mummer   Then send for the twenty-pound doctor.

Tom Fool   Call the twenty-pound doctor.

Doctor

Twenty pound is not a lot
For a doctor who's travelled from bed to pot,
And back again from pot to bed
To cure the living and the dead.
It's not a lot for one who's seen
The whole of England and the Queen,
Who's travelled Scotland, Wales and France
Attendin' weddin', wake and dance.
Double the fee and then I might
Find the medicines to restore his sight.

Captain Mummer   And what medicines do you use?

Doctor

The fillicee fee of a bum bee
And the thunder nouns of a creepie stool.
Boiled up in a wooden, leather, iron pot,
Poured into a ditch and left to rot.

Captain Mummer   And what other potions do you use?

Doctor
Fishes' feathers, Lourdes water,
Babies rescued from the slaughter;
Spiders' elbows, flags from graves,
Hearts fresh off the sharpest staves;
Certain hairs from randy goats,
Giblets out of overcoats.
Stir all up in a cat's behind –
Forty days to cure the blind.
The dead need certain extra measures
This bottle here contains me treasures –
The broom's left foot, a midge's thigh,
A sparrow's fart, a graveyard's sigh.
Made into a mixture,
Hocus, Pocus, Sally Campaign,
Rise up dead Hero and fight again.

The **Doctor** *stoops down, puts the medicine in the* **First Hero***'s ear.
The* **First Hero** *rises to the great delight of the others.*

First *and* **Second Heroes**
We'll shake hands
And fight no more
And pretend to be brothers
As we were before.

Captain Mummer
Pigs squeal in Ulster, echoed all round
Strike up the music to block out the sound.

The **Musicians** *strike up a jig which is danced by the others. At the
end of the dance* **Tom Fool** *steps forward.*

Tom Fool
Here come I, Tom Fool,
With me bladder and staff in me eye;
I didn't come here to make you laugh,
No, I come to make you cry.

Other **Mummers** *mutter angrily.*

Captain Mummer   That's wrong, Fool. Say it right.

Tom Fool *retreats, then comes forward again.*

Tom Fool
Here come I, Tom Fool,
With me bladder and me staff.
I didn't come here to make you cry,
No, I came to make you laugh.
I'm as happy as the day is long,
I'm as happy as a lord.
But I need a wife with a soft scabbard
In which to rest me sword.

Miss Funny *comes forward.*

Miss Funny
And here come I, Miss Funny,
The very one:
Me oven ready for a bun.
It's babies I want
And babies I crave
And babies I'll have
Till I'm stretched in the grave.

Tom Fool (*removing his mask*)   And I'm the man for ye . . . (*To the audience.*) I had fourteen children born in the one night and not two in the same townland.

Miss Funny *also removes her mask and the two fall on each other lustfully. They simulate intercourse front stage right while the others look on.*

Captain Mummer
That's not what's meant to happen,
Nor what he was to say,
But it's close enough,
So good luck, good health,
We must be on our way.

Miss Funny (*lying on her back straddled by* **Tom Fool**)
And the money . . .
Don't forget the money:

That's what I want,
That's what I crave,
And if I don't get it,
You're all for the grave.

Captain Mummer *and the remaining* **Mummers** *are standing in a line centre stage. They hit the ground with their sticks creating a rhythm for the next lines.*

Captain Mummer
Fifteen, sixteen, seventeen . . .

Tom Fool
Pounds, shillings, pence . . .

First Hero
Pints, half-pints, whiskey . . .

Second Hero
With an e, without an e, Black Bush . . .

Beelzebub
Irish, Scotch, Parliament . . .

All
Here's to you, Tom Browne . . .

All now bow to the audience, as if at the end of a performance; then take off their masks, wipe sweat away and relax.

Scene Three

First Hero (*singing*)
Here's to you with all our hearts
We'll have another drink or two
This night before we part
Here's to you, Tom Browne.

Captain Mummer (*holding aloft a lantern*)   Shush! (*He listens.*)
The storm is over boys – the night is fair. And we promised
Lizzie Boles we'd call back if there was light. We can't let her
down. On yer feet now. Come on . . . Ready for the road.

Scene Four

The **Mummers** *form a line with the* **Captain** *at their head. They march in procession, complete a circle or two, then stop.* **The Captain** *holds up a lantern and raps on the ground with his stick. The other* **Mummers** *have formed a circle.*

Captain Mummer   Any admittance for Captain Mummer and his men?

Silence from the circle. **Captain Mummer** *raps again three times.*

Captain Mummer   Any admittance for Captain Mummer and his men?

Silence.

Captain Mummer   It's only the mummers come back to ye ... Are ye all right inside? Lizzie, Sarah – are ye all right?

Silence.

Captain Mummer   There's something wrong inside. Stand back – I'm goin' in.

The **Captain** *raps his stick on the ground, swaying as if he were trying to shoulder open a door. The circle of* **Mummers** *sways to the same rhythm and on the fifth rap the circle of* **Mummers** *scatters to reveal the bodies of* **Lizzie** *and* **Sarah** *on the ground*

Sarah   Men with masks ... Men with guns ... Butchers of men ...

Captain Mummer *cradles* **Sarah***'s body in his arms.*

Captain Mummer   Where's the child, Sarah? Where's Elizabeth?

Sarah   Safe. Hugh gone ...

Sarah *slumps dead in* **Captain Mummer***'s arms.*

Captain Mummer   For Christ's sake – somebody go for help. Someone phone for the doctor quick.

Exit **Tom Fool**. **Captain Mummer** *closes* **Sarah***'s eyes. The* **Mummers** *take up a sort of chorus.*

Miss Funny
All dead – the two.

Beelzebub
Lizzie Boles who was Lizzie Flynn.

First Hero
And Sarah her daughter who married Hugh Brolly.

All
Shot this midwinter's night when the mummers were jolly.

Miss Funny
Lizzie Flynn who married Jack Boles.

Doctor
Jack Boles who was killed in a fight.

Second Hero
Killed for love, killed for hate, killed for spite.

All
All dead – but the child . . .

Captain Mummer, *who has walked to the cradle, holds the lantern up and sees the sleeping child.*

Captain Mummer   Elizabeth! She's alive, the wee thing. Sleepin' – none the wiser.

He turns from the cradle back towards the bodies.

Captain Mummer   But these two are dead and won't be brought back. And a track of blood like a small river in their wake.

Captain Mummer *now turns his attention to the* **Mummers** *standing around, pointing at each one in turn, accusing, questioning.*

Captain Mummer   Is there anybody here knows anything about this? Is there any of ye had a hand in it?

Do you know anything?
Or you?
Heroes?
Doctor?

And you, Miss Funny?
And what about him who's gone for help?
What do I know myself?

Captain Mummer *returns to the bodies, stoops and closes* **Lizzie***'s eyes.*

Captain Mummer   Lizzie Boles: as fine a woman as you'd meet in a lifetime's travellin'. Dead and no cure. No Hocus Pocus Sally Campaign to bring them back to life.

Captain Mummer *points to one of the* **Musicians/Mummers**.

Captain Mummer   Play the tune – play the tune that was her favourite. And make a good job of it, for the last time . . .

The **Musician** *plays part of the air of 'The Enniskillen Dragoons'. Enter* **Tom Fool**.

Tom Fool   She's comin' – the Doctor.
'Who's dead?' she said.
'Two,' says I.
She didn't believe me – but she's comin' anyway. Oh – and more police to fiddle while Rome burns.

Captain Mummer   Shut yer trap, Fool.

Tom Fool *retreats.*

(*To* **Musician**.) Play on – she'd want it.

The **Musician** *plays on. Exit* **Lizzie Boles** *and* **Sarah**. *The* **Mummers** *may exit or remain.*

Scene Five

Miss Funny
   That's a fine start to a play.
   Two dead; men made of hay
   Or straw – what does it matter?
   Better keep back, mind your place,
   Better watch the face beside you –
   You never know, in the latter end
   What's what, who's who, what will happen.

Tom Fool

Who am I? Tom Fool – you know well,
Don't be lettin' on. The rule is
There's one in every village, townland,
Every band of boyos has one.
I'm the one that knows nothing and knows all:
The fall guy, wise guy, fly as Bejasus.
I'd steal the eye out of your head, the clothes
Off your line, the cross off an ass's back.
I lack – oh, an ounce or two up here – was queer
From birth – but mirth I tell you comes
As natural as pissin'.

Miss Funny

And in every other department
Nothin' missin'.

Tom Fool

Tom the Fool – John Thomas the Fool.
But no – no talk of sex – I wouldn't like
To vex the decent people.

Miss Funny

Forgive the Fool, Forgive poor Tom.

Tom Fool

Better to talk about a bomb
In a creamery can, a van in a ditch,
The two dead: swingin' the lead
Is no idle occupation around here.
Am I clear as muck? Well, fuck
The lot of them. From a height.
Shite is too good for their sandwiches.

Miss Funny

Bite the bullet, Tom, shut your mouth.
The play is what we're here about.
Not the rantings of a fool about
The bomb, the gun and foreign rule.
Play your part, Tom, play it right –

Tell the people what's to come
Or your nose will kiss your . . .

Tom Fool
All right. So them's the mummers that you saw.
But who knows what's behind a straw man.

Miss Funny
Or a straw woman. There's more to all
Of this than mummin'.

Tom Fool
I'd watch them all if I were you –
I'd watch them for the slightest clue
Of badness, evil, malice, hate,
Of poison hidden in a trate
Or old acquaintance not forgot.
A border never stopped a shot
That set its target years before.

Enter **Lizzie Boles**.

Tom Fool *and* **Miss Funny**
And found it – oh
Not much more than hours ago.

Miss Funny
But say no more now, Tom, sing dumb.
She's goin' back a while to – oh,
A rum enough time . . .

Tom Fool
When Jack Boles . . .

Enter **Jack Boles**.

Miss Funny
Courted Lizzie Flynn . . .

Enter **Young Lizzie**.

Tom Fool
And a cock was a cock.

Miss Funny
    And a hen was a hen.

Exit **Tom Fool** *and* **Miss Funny**.

Scene Six

Older Lizzie   What can you see on the lake, Jack?

Jack   I can see us in a boat – it's a fine boat like the *Lady Spencer*. We're sailin' along to the south, past the Holy Island, Lizzie, and the old jetty; past the town where it's Sunday mornin' and the bells of the two churches is ringin' – mine up on the hill and yours below in the hollow. We sail on down the length of the Shannon – through Lough Ree and Lough Derg; through Athlone and on to Limerick. We sail on out to sea, Liz, and keep goin' till we meet the ship from Cobh. And we keep on to the south – into the sun – to the new world.

Older Lizzie   Are we happy, Jack?

Jack   Happier than anyone could ever ask to be. Happy as heroes, Lizzie, comin' home after a great victory.

Young Lizzie   Have we a flag up so?

Jack   Aye, we have. The white hand of nowhere. A nice, neat, white hand. The pirates will never take it down.

Young Lizzie   Go on out o' that. No, I think we'd better have a few flags with us. A green one – and an orange one in case the wind changes. And I suppose German and American too. We could sleep under them when it gets cold.

They embrace, kiss. **Jack** *stands behind* **Young Lizzie**, *covering her eyes with his hands.*

Jack   Right, Miss Flynn. What do you see now on the lake?

Young Lizzie   I see us in a boat too – but it's not like the *Lady Spencer*. It's Harry White's fishin' boat that he brought with him from Lough Neagh. And we're castin' for eel, Jack – but we hook a water horse as black as the pit face and eyes on him like embers. He sinks the boat – but we mount on his back and set off like the hammers of hell.

Jack   To where, Lizzie – where are we goin'?

Young Lizzie *stands, whirls around and takes* **Jack**'s *hands, forcing him to swing.*

Young Lizzie   To Dublin – for the coronation!

Older *and* **Young Lizzie** (*singing*)
   Up de Valera, you're the champion of the fight,
   We'll follow you to battle 'neath the orange, green and
      white!
   And we'll tackle Eoin O' Duffy and we'll roll him in the
      shite,
   And we'll crown de Valera King of Ireland!

Jack   You have a fierce wicked tongue in ye.

Young Lizzie *sits staring out ahead of her.*

Young Lizzie   But I'm only coddin', Jack – that's not what I see at all.

Jack   What is it you see then?

Young Lizzie   I see . . . what happened. I see the fishin' boat and the two men in it. There's a shout and one of them is standin' up. They're strugglin' now – and the boat is overturned. They're gone under – but they're up again – their heads. One holdin' on to the boat – one strikin' for shore – swimmin' strong. But the other – his companion – has the oar now. He's puttin' him down – he's pushin' him down by the shoulder – leverin' with the boat. The people is runnin' from the hayfields – shouting. But they're gone – the two of them – swept down the lake. The two of them is drowned.

That's what I see, Jack – out there – straight forenenst us where it happened.

Jack   What is this, Liz? What drownin'?

Young Lizzie   Lord Leitrim's nephew Clements – and John Brolly his manservant. Master and boy, Jack – that's the drownin'.

Jack   William Clements and Brolly. I only ever heard the names and that their boat went down. There was more to it so?

Young Lizzie   There was a lot more to it. Clements drowned Brolly because he couldn't swim himself and he couldn't bear to see his servant survive. His boast was there wasn't enough water in the lough to drown him.

Jack   But they were strugglin' in the boat, you say, and the people saw it. What were they fightin' about?

Young Lizzie   I don't know for sure. The old people used to say there was some – matter of honour, some promise broken. I know Brolly had a sister Mae – and I think maybe she had a child – Clements' child. I'm not certain.

Jack   What's the cause you're tellin' me this now? What are you tryin' to get across to me?

Young Lizzie   You asked me what I saw on the lake. That's what I saw. And that's what some will see if the two of us gets married. Master and servant, Protestant and Catholic, Boles and Flynn. They still see it, Jack – after near a lifetime – they still remember every little thing.

Jack *turns away from* **Young Lizzie**, *stares off.*

Young Lizzie   Jack – what's wrong?

Jack   'Every little thing.' Do they, Lizzie? Or is it just what suits them to remember? Do you know what I see a lot of the time? What I mind of? Me brother Tom's face half gone from a gunshot and me father's corpse bleedin' like a pig inside in the shop ... It's only twenty years ago, Lizzie – but how many cares to remember that?

Young Lizzie   I care to – and so does me father. He was in the town that day and he's told us so often it'll never leave my memory. I swear, Jack – so long as I live I'll never forget it.

Older *and* **Young Lizzie**   It was a blustery May day at the height of the raidin' and shootin'. And he was beyond in the

forge with Jim Boles and a good few others. The shop was a'
raidin' every few weeks before that; and this day didn't
someone come runnin' over to tell Jim there was another raid
on.

Older Lizzie *takes up the narrative while* **Young Lizzie** *and* **Jack**
sit quietly.

Older Lizzie   Damnee, he lifted up a big lump of an iron
bar and said, 'It'll be the last raid ever they'll make' – and off
with him across to the shop. The men in the forge heard the
shootin' and ran over. The gunmen were gone – out the back
– and Jim was lyin' on top of the bag of provisions they were
fillin' to bring with them. Be the time they moved him the bag
was full up with blood and everything in it – bread and tay
and sugar – was saturated right through. Young Tom was dead
out in the back yard; he must have chased them and pulled the
mask off one of them – for there was a white hankie on the
ground beside him. Most of his face was gone from the shot.

Jack   I was ten and they didn't let me see Tom's body. But
that didn't stop me imaginin'. I used to dream about him
nearly every night – and that was worse. Me father's corpse
was laid out on a plank in the shop and the people came in to
see him before he was brought up the stairs. I swore then that
I'd never use a gun or shoot any livin' thing so long as I lived.

Young Lizzie *takes Jack's hand, comforts him.*

Older Lizzie   I never did forget me father talkin' about it
. . . about how the Boleses were the finest people about the
place and all the sympathy in the world he had for Minnie
Boles and her son Jack. He was as happy as could be when I
went to work in the shop: 'You couldn't ask for better
employers, Lizzie – you be as straight with them as they are
with you and ye'll be all right.'

Young Lizzie   And so I was.

Older Lizzie   And so I was.

Young Lizzie   Do you remember the first day I came to
work for ye? I'd only ever seen you before and I was a bit shy.

Jack   And I must have been walkin' around with me eyes closed. For when I saw you it was like – a haze liftin' off that lake – like gettin' me sight back.

Young Lizzie   The shopgirl cured the blind.

Jack   Well, weren't you born around Christmas. You're bound to have some powers.

Young Lizzie   Not enough, Jack. I can't do much for me father's health – *an diabhal le* Flanders. And I can't turn Frank Beirne into a pillar of anything only the thick shite that he is.

Jack   I thought he'd given over botherin' you.

Young Lizzie   He has not. He was in the shop yesterday pesterin' me about the fools' weddin' tonight. He's goin' in straw – though God knows you'd deck the turn of his heel anywhere.

Jack   He won't come near you tonight. If he does he'll have me to contend with.

Young Lizzie   Stay out of it, Jack. I can mind meself. The likes of him has done enough to you already. And they'd have your shop in the mornin' too if they could.

Jack   They're as entitled as the next to bid for it – if I sell up. I have a fair good idea what the Beirnes have done, Lizzie – but I have no proof and never will. Pointin' the finger isn't so different to pointin' a gun.

Young Lizzie   Then you won't mind Frank Beirne tonight.

Jack   Not if he doesn't bother you. He wouldn't be at you if we were married. Give me your answer, Liz, once and for all. Is Fermanagh new world enough? As God is my witness if you marry me you'll never know want or disfavour. I'll put bread on the table and meat in the pot. I'll play tunes for you and bring you dancin'. We'll make a better life of it around Enniskillen.

Older *and* **Young Lizzie** (*singing*)
Fare thee well Enniskillen, fare thee well for a while,
And all around the borders of Erin's green isle.

And when the war is over we'll return in full bloom
And we'll all welcome home our Enniskillen Dragoons.

Young Lizzie   Me father's song since the war. The
Connaught Rangers he was with.

Jack   The Devil's own.

Young Lizzie   And the Devil's own war – no more than this
one. I'd better go, Jack – he'll be home soon from the town.

Jack   Is he master of ceremonies again tonight?

Young Lizzie   He is – and ye'd think it was Master of Red
Russia he was to be . . . He'll have a few on him now . . .

Jack   As usual . . .

Young Lizzie   Now! (*Kissing* **Jack**.) I'll see you tonight.

Exit **Young Lizzie**.

Jack (*to himself*)   The next weddin' will be ours, Lizzie. I don't
care where it is or who's there. Our weddin' is next.

Jack *rises, walks stage right, stops and looks out.*

Older Lizzie   And our own weddin' was next. Not that long
after in the registry office in Enniskillen. The shop in Leitrim
was put up for sale and we left without a word to anyone.
Jack's mother was a good while dead be then. I think she knew
the way things were between us though she never said a hate.
Only once she asked me to say grace at the table. And when I
was finished she looked straight at me and said:

Older Lizzie *and* **Jack** (*looking at each other*)   'You'll do.'

Exit **Older Lizzie**. *Enter* **Tom Fool** *and* **Miss Funny**.

Scene Seven

Tom Fool *and* **Miss Funny**   'You'll do.' 'You'll do.'

Miss Funny   Well, she won't do at all.

Tom Fool   Forgettin' the best bit – our weddin'.

Miss Funny   Aye, jumpin' the gun – and no call to forget.

Tom Fool   That day, remember, a neighbour on the road met Frank Beirne with a hard glint in his eye.

Miss Funny   'Are ye for the weddin' tonight?' says the neighbour.

Tom Fool   Says Frank, 'Is a pig for a sty? Damnee I am; and me own might be next, for betwixt this and Easter I'll have Lizzie Flynn on a halter, the altar'll be the next stop.'

Miss Funny   'Troth then,' says the other, 'Jesus, ye'd better watch her tight, there's others might have the same notion.'

Tom Fool   'What?' says Beirne, 'I'll fight and beat any cunt: there's not enough blood in beast or human to keep me from what I want.'

Miss Funny   A nice boyo to have on your tail.

Tom Fool   A nice fellow. I'll go bail there's none like him.

Miss Funny   But he came in straw – no law against it.

Both   To our weddin'.

Tom Fool   The daftest match ever was made.

Miss Funny (*producing a straw hat and putting on* **Captain Mummer**'s *head*)   And Lizzie's father – Lance-Corporal Michael Flynn – Blind drunk.

Tom Fool   And the speech that he gave – ye wouldn't find its equal in . . .

Michael Flynn   In Borneo. I'm the wild man from Borneo and I'll have you all know this is the finest speech I ever gave.

Enter the **Mummers** *to create the* **Fools'** *wedding scene. Enter* **Young Lizzie**. **Tom Fool** *and* **Miss Funny** *are groom and bride.* **Michael Flynn** *delivers the wedding speech.*

Scene Eight

Michael Flynn
 Ladies and gentlemen, cousins and friends,
 Neighbours with rushes and bushes and whins;
 'Tis bigger than Yankee Land, better than Rome,
 Warmer than Africa, safer than home.

 There's more tay than in China, despite the auld rations,
 There's poteen in plenty and porter in lashin's;
 And tobaccey and snuff – as much as a wake,
 Soda bread, boxty and lots of sweet cake.

 And diversion with music and dancin' and crack,
 Stories to raise up the hair on your back;
 Not forgettin' our kind and most generous host,
 And to him and his family I now raise a toast:

Glasses are raised etc.

 May yer cattle all prosper, yer crops double or more,
 May harm and all badness not darken yer door;
 May yer hens lay gold eggs, may yer butter be swate,
 May ye live to see sturdy grandchilder ate mate.

 And as for the marriage – well, never a pair
 Was more suited to love – and less suited to care;
 On the longest of journeys, now where would you find
 Such an elegant couple – more sight to the blind.

 Here's Tom, God bless him, a hero of Erin,
 Who stood up to the Tans and him dauntin' and darin';
 And the part that he played in our nation's brave fight
 Will be talked of and wondered at be day and be night.

 A more suitable mate for such a fine man;
 Could you ever find better than sweet Mary Anne?
 If medals were given for sharpness of mind
 She'd be laden in front – aye – and laden behind.

 By which – no offence – was it Virgil who said
 That beauty is all in the shape of the head?
 And under Mary Anne's ringlets of red and of gold
 There's a shape that the devil would pay to behold.

Michael Flynn *interrupts his speech to 'marry' the* **Fools**.

Michael Flynn   Right, do ye two want to get married?

Tom Fool   Oh, we do.

Michael Flynn *throws his stick on the floor and directs the* **Fools** *to jump*

Michael Flynn   Right so. Jump.

They jump over the stick.

Michael Flynn   Right. Ye're married.

There's a short dance of celebration, then **Michael Flynn** *resumes his speech.*

Michael Flynn

> Their childer, no doubt, will be sturdy and strong,
> At sums they'll excel – oh, they'll never be wrong;
> They'll bring laughter and fun to auld Liosnasidh,
> And ne'er a one ever will sail 'cross the sea.
>
> Before I conclude, let all present here vow
> They'll remember for ever the night as it's now;
> To the couple I pledge a hundred years' health,
> Praties and childer, bonhams and wealth.
>
> We'll be strawboys again, there'll be weddin's galore
> And plenty of chances to dance on the door;
> But let it be said, and I'm sayin' it straight
> The weddin' that's in it will never be bate.
>
> Now we the strawboys will light up a fire
> On a hill that's adjacent – or on something that's higher;
> To inform them in Leinster and in Munster likewise,
>   And in Ulster – THAT AN EVENT OR ENORMOUS SIGNIFICANCE
>   HAS JUST TAKEN PLACE IN CONNAUGHT!

The general merriment and dancing that follows the speech is interrupted by **Frank Beirne** *who has been standing at some distance from the others.*

Frank Beirne (*calling loudly*)

> Here's to the hand
> That made the ball
> That shot Lord Leitrim
> In Donegal.

The disgruntled **Dancers** *move off the floor, sit down, stand around.*

One of the Men   Ah, leave it, Beirne.

Frank Beirne   Come on, Lance-Corporal Flynn. Ye drank to the King in his day – and took his shillin'.

Another of the Men   Keep politics out tonight – can ye not be silent for once?

Frank Beirne   For whose sake will I be silent – whose honour?

Michael Flynn   For whose honour? If a country was good enough to work in . . .

Frank Beirne   . . . it was good enough to fight for. I heard that shite before.

Michael Flynn   A lot ye know . . . England gave me a good livin'. It put clothes on my family's backs and mate on their bones. And what did I get when I came home?

Frank Beirne   What did ye want? A hero's welcome?

Michael Flynn   Hero's welcome, me arse. I got a pack o' bastards stickin' a gun in me back and tellin' me I was lucky I wasn't shot for fightin' with the enemy.

Frank Beirne   And right they were too.

Michael Flynn   The fuckers – I never had an enemy only poverty and want. I had to cut the buttons off me army jacket – and it the only jacket I had – so some young *amadán* the likes of you wouldn't take it into his head to shoot me for a collaborator . . .

Frank Beirne   And what do ye want – sympathy?

Michael Flynn   And a mile up the road there was John Tom Frank swankin' it around like a lord in his Yankee uniform and drawing his army pension. And he was the hero and the soldier and the great man.

Frank Beirne   Well, at least he didn't take the shillin' . . .

One of the Men   Come on, Beirne – no more politics – leave it and have a drink.

Frank Beirne   I will not then. Where there's still planters there's politics . . . Will we be silent for them?

Where there's still them as owns half the place and goes north for the Twelfth there's still politics.

And while there's still them that'd glawn our women and have their pick of the best of them – I'll drink to the hand that made the ball.

Michael Flynn   Close yer trap, ye young pup, or will I have to close it for ye?

Frank Beirne   Would ye listen to him? You wouldn't close a windy gap and the cut of ye . . .

Frank Beirne *mimics* **Michael Flynn**'s *dancing.* **Flynn** *advances to fight him but is restrained by* **Young Lizzie** *and* **Others.** **Young Lizzie** *confronts* **Frank Beirne.**

Young Lizzie   Quit at him. You're only out to rise trouble.

Scene Nine

Exit **Young Lizzie.** **Frank Beirne** *begins to sing the ballad 'Barbara Allen'.*

Frank Beirne
 Near hand the town where I was born
 There was a fair maid dwellin'
 I picked her out for to be my bride
 And her name was Barbara Allen.

Young Lizzie *re-enters. Exterior wedding scene.*

Frank Beirne
 I courted her for seven long years
 Till I could court no longer
 Then I fell sick and very sick
 And they sent for Barbara Allen.

Tense silence.

Frank Beirne   You were with him today. I seen ye.

Young Lizzie   And what if I was? I work in the shop.

Frank Beirne (*mimics*)   'What can you see on the lake, Jack?'
Why didn't ye tell him the full story?

Young Lizzie   You followed me . . .

Frank Beirne   The full story, Lizzie . . . Of how you'll end
up if ye're not careful. With child – like Mae Brolly – and
promised the lot. That he'll marry ye. But he'll not marry you.
He'll be like Clements – only he'll be cuter and won't drown.
He'll find one of his own – and you'll be left high and dry with
a brown-eyed bastard. And you have no brother like John
Brolly to fight yer corner.

Young Lizzie   You know nothing about Jack . . . Not the
first thing.

Frank Beirne   I know enough about him and his kind. But
it's not him I want to know, Lizzie. We were friends before –
we can be friends again.

Young Lizzie   The same way ye're a friend to me father . . .

Frank Beirne   Ah, yer father's all right. That was only a bit
of sport. Ye look lovely the night, Lizzie.

Young Lizzie   Don't! Haven't I told you to leave me alone.

Frank Beirne   I'd be kind to ye, Lizzie . . . Kinder than he
is – not have ye slavin' away behind a counter.

Young Lizzie   I'm a slave to no man – and won't be to you
. . . When are ye goin' to get it into yer head: I don't want ye,
I don't like ye, I don't want ye comin' near me . . .

Frank Beirne *advances till he's standing very close to* **Young
Lizzie**.

Frank Beirne   Just one kiss, Lizzie. I'd be kind to ye.

Young Lizzie   Don't! (**Frank Beirne** *stops*.) I want to go
back inside . . . Let me pass . . . Please.

Frank Beirne *stands aside as if to let her pass but grabs her by the wrist as she walks by him.*

Frank Beirne   One kiss, Lizzie. Only one.

Young Lizzie *(struggling)*   Let me alone. Let me alone . . .

Enter **Jack Boles**.

Jack   You heard what she said, Beirne. Let her alone now.

Frank Beirne   The day is long gone when I have to take orders from the likes of you . . . If ye want her – come and fight me for her.

Young Lizzie   There's no one takin' me – and no fightin' over me.

Jack   I could fight him if I wanted. But it's all right. He's goin' to do what he's told.

Frank Beirne   Would you listen to him givin' orders. Do ye tell yer wee shop girl what to do? *(Mimics.)* 'Right, Miss Flynn – a kiss.'

Frank Beirne *tries to kiss* **Young Lizzie** *who breaks free and restrains* **Jack** *who is about to fight* **Beirne**.

Young Lizzie   Leave it, Jack – leave it – for my sake.

Jack *and* **Young Lizzie** *face* **Frank Beirne** *together.*

Jack   See this woman, Beirne. Look well on her now. She's to be my wife. For better or worse. If she kissed you, I'm certain she'll get over it.

Frank Beirne   A damn sight better than she'll get over you. The shopkeeper that can't keep his hands for his own breed, but has to go after our women – the same as all the fuckers before him. D'ye know what they should do to you? The same as was done with Lord Leitrim up at Manor Vaughan – or with Colonel McNeill. *(Miming a castration.)*

Jack   Right, so now we have the straight talk. Tell me so – did they do it? Did your father and brother kill mine?

Frank Beirne   How would I know? How would I know who

shot them? Maybe it was the Tans; they shot a lot. What matter anyway – didn't you fall into everything.

Jack   Did they get their pensions for it yet?

Young Lizzie   Leave it, Jack – come on back into the dancin'.

Exit **Jack** *and* **Young Lizzie**.

Frank Beirne   Aye – go on back into the dancin'. And take a good step out of it while ye're at it . . . (*Calls after* **Jack** *and* **Young Lizzie**.) Will ye take her sailin' on her honeymoon? Out on the water. Will ye give her the oar and let her row? The way Lord Leitrim's lot gave it to Brolly.

Frank Beirne *sings a verse of 'The Ballad of Lord Leitrim' with obvious threat.*

Frank Beirne
  The polis then like bagles
  Gathered round this dirty baste
  And the devils all, both great and small
  They had a sumptuous faste.
  He was dissected like a bullock
  At Manor Vaughan's Hall
  And the devils ate him rump and stump
  That night in Donegal.
  With me whack fal the deroo
  Whack fal the day . . .

Scene Ten

A dance tune strikes up. Enter **Older Lizzie, Jack** *and* **Young Lizzie**. **Young Lizzie** *dances at the centre of the wedding group.* **Older Lizzie** *watches and speaks as the music stops and the dance dwindles to a strange slow motion.*

Older Lizzie   I was dancin' like I had five legs and a heart like a daisy. But there was a knife of fear inside me for all me gayness. It kept twistin' and cuttin' at me – jabbin' at the edge of me heart or me soul. There was pigs' ribs goin' round and I

minded of the day I saw Frank Beirne's father killin' pigs in the
market yard. Most of the men used a hook and they stuck it in
the pig's mouth and out through his jaw so they'd be able to
do the job quick. But auld Beirne flung the pig down and
kicked him on the head with his hobnailed boot; and he held
him down with his own weight before he cut his throat . . . I
was lookin' at those boots with spatters of blood on them – and
I knew as well as everyone else that they were stolen out of
Boles's shop the day they shot Jim Boles and his son for being
Protestants and shopkeepers and decent people. They stole the
ledgers so there'd be no trace of the money they owed – and
all the credit the Boleses gave them that kept food in their
mouths.

Jack *and* **Young Lizzie**, *who have danced away from the others
embrace and face the audience.*

Older Lizzie   We slipped away from the fools' weddin' and
went back to our spot by the lough. There was a high moon
flickerin' in the water and light enough to keep the odd bird in
limbo . . . We lay down together on the slope near the old
nunnery and that's where Sarah was conceived.

Theme music plays. They turn and look out over the audience.

Young Lizzie   Look, Jack – the strawboys goin' home.
They're a quare sight all the same.

Jack   You'll see plenty of straw in Fermanagh too. There's
great mummin' country.

Young Lizzie   Are we goin' so? To the other side of the
Black Pig's Dyke.

Jack   We're goin'. It'll be our new world, Lizzie. For better or
worse . . .

The Mummers *don their masks again and with the straw wall
slowly form a circle into which* **Young Lizzie** *and* **Jack** *retreat.*

Older Lizzie   So we did go: not in the mornin' but a
fortnight after. I didn't let on to me father but left him a note
he'd be able to read. 'I'm gone to Fermanagh to marry Jack
Boles. Say a prayer for us and I'll pray for you.' There were no

strawboys for our weddin' – only Jack's Uncle Bob and his wife Hannah for our witnesses. The place in Leitrim was put up for sale and we had the farm bought and were well settled when you were born, Sarah . . .

Young Lizzie – *now* **Sarah** – *steps out of the circle of straw. She's dressed in simple, child's clothes. She runs to meet* **Older Lizzie** *who puts her arms around her.*

Older Lizzie   . . . the dead spit of meself in that hard January at the height of the war. They were the tough years after. Thin harvest and long winters. Cold springs and short summers. There were soldiers goin' the road and army camps about the places. A good trade toin' and froin' across the border. Word of death comin' back to this house and that. Numbers down in the chapel and up in the graveyards . . .

Jack was about with the mummers them few winters – Captains and Heroes doin' the rounds . . .

Aye, daughter – them times, no more than now, ye'd never know what would be abroad at night.

Scene Eleven

The **Mummers'** *voices are heard as a threatening chorus.*

Captain Mummer
  Here come I, Captain Mummer and all me men.

Butcher
  Here come I, the Butcher with me steel.

Beelzebub
  Here come I, Beelzebub.

Second Hero
  Here come I, a Hero bold.

Doctor
  Here come I, a Doctor pure.

Tom Fool
  Here come I, Tom Fool.

Miss Funny
  Here come I, Miss Funny.

The group of **Mummers** *fold the straw wall around* **Jack** *so that it looks like a sheaf. They stand in a large circle around it and sticks are handed out. As* **Older Lizzie** *delivers her speech,* **Frank Beirne***'s voice is heard singing another two verses of 'Barbara Allen' from within the circle.*

Frank Beirne
  Slowly, slowly she came up
  And slowly she came nigh him
  And all she said when e'er she saw
  Was 'Young man I think you're dyin'.'

  'A dyin' man is what I am
  But one kiss from you would cure me.'
  'One kiss from me you never shall have
  Though your poor heart lie breaking.'

Older Lizzie   Men with masks, men with sticks, men with their mouths full of rhyme, men with their hearts full of hate, men with their minds stained with blood. Men to dance at a wake, men to cry at a birth, men out searchin' for their own shadows ... Men in gangs, men in a line, men to cut sticks, men to break bones, men to set, men to reap, straight men, crooked men, broken men, ment men, boyos of men, lads of men ...

Sarah *has wandered away and is smearing berries on her face and lips. She sings in a child's voice.*

Sarah
  The wren, the wren, the king of all birds
  On St Stephen's night was caught in the furze.

Mummers' Chorus
  The man, the man, the king of all men
  Slept with a cock and woke with a hen.

The rest of **Lizzie***'s speech is punctuated by each* **Mummer** *jabbing a stick into the straw sheaf with an ugly grunting sound.*

Older Lizzie   Men with their heads soft from beatin', men with their hands raw from work, men with their best limb limp from nothing at all. Men with their feet that would walk by themselves for a day and a night and a week and a year and end up nowhere . . . Butchers of men.

The **Mummers** *withdraw the sticks with a harsh, violent sound.* **Jack** *stumbles forward from the sheaf and falls on the ground close to* **Lizzie** *and* **Sarah**.

Lizzie (*screaming*)   Jack!

Sarah (*in innocent, child's voice*)   Daddy?

Lights to black.

Curtain.

Act Two

Prologue

The same set, with an unfinished chess game. The adult **Elizabeth** *is seen as in Prologue, Act One.*

Elizabeth The Strange Knight walked on again till he came to a castle. There was a rook perched on the rampart with blood on its beak. The Knight asked whose blood it was and the rook said, 'It's the King's blood. The people have killed the King and his body is in pieces in the courtyard inside.' So the Knight thanked the rook and went inside to the people. He told them they had done a wonderful thing and he wanted to be their leader. So they elected him their leader and that night held a great banquet where he set one half of them against the other; and they fought till there was no one left alive but the Strange Knight.

And he was happy then: to have evaded answering the riddle, to have the piece of land for himself and to have the castle without King or people to bother him.

Act Two

Scene One

Enter **Tom Fool** *and* **Miss Funny**.

Tom Fool That's another fine sight to behold . . .

Miss Funny A wan with a poppy. . . ?

Tom Fool A story well told . . .

Miss Funny Of a Knight and a riddle? – Pure shite . . .

Tom Fool (*quietly*) Ye're right . . .

Now miming the playing of a fiddle on his left arm.

This is the way
Me father showed me
How to play the fiddle:
Up, down, up, down,
And bang in the middle.

The **Fools** *confront the audience with the next lines, then sit to play chess.*

Miss Funny What do you think it's about?

Tom Fool War . . . Here . . . North . . . South. . . ?

Miss Funny Is that it? Well, ye know what Thought did.

Tom Fool
Stuck a feather in the ground
And thought he could grow chickens . . .

Miss Funny
Stuck a feather up his arse
And thought he could fly to America . . .

Both Ye thought, ye thought, ye thought . . .

Miss Funny Well, ye ought to know better.

Tom Fool There's more comin' up . . .

Miss Funny   As the farmer said, strokin' the cow's leg . . .

Tom Fool   Aye, more up ahead . . .

*The **Fools** stand up, step back a few paces.*

We can't forget them that was dead at the start.

*Enter **Lizzie**.*

Miss Funny
Lizzie Boles, who was Lizzie Flynn . . .

Tom Fool
. . . And Sarah her daughter who marries Hugh Brolly.

*Enter **Sarah** and **Hugh Brolly** who sit and begin to play chess.*
Lizzie *sits weaving the straw wren.*

Tom Fool *and **Miss Funny**   Now the scene is midwinter.

Tom Fool
   Tis the season to be jolly
   Tra la la la la, la la, la la . . .

Miss Funny
   Stuff the turkey's hole with holly
   Tra la la la la, la la, la la . . .

*The **Fools** pause and listen elaborately.*

Tom Fool   The mummers are abroad . . .

Miss Funny   And we're sick of rhymin' for ye . . .

*Exit **Fools**.*

Scene Two

Silence and near stillness for a moment in the remaining scene, as
Lizzie *works on the straw wren and **Sarah** and **Hugh** concentrate*
on the chess game.

Lizzie   It was long ago. It was not long ago. It was a time
when to go west was to go east, when to go north was to go
south. When people sang songs at a wake and cried when a

child was born.

Sarah   It was in the land of the black pig.

Hugh   At that time there was a man on the road. He was doin' nothing at all. The King's soldiers were goin' the road in a lorry. They saw the man who was doin' nothing and they shot him dead. Then they closed the road to the south and went back to their own land where they're livin' still – and where they will live.

Lizzie   Time doesn't heal. Don't let anyone say it does. Time only puts a thin skin on the wound but you can always see the blood underneath. The same as on the baby's head. I do often think that was the wound in Christ's side – the stab of betrayal, not the mark of a sword.

Hugh   You're soundin' like the Salvation Army tonight.

Lizzie (*chanting*)
  Salvation Army without sin
  Went to heaven
  In a corned-beef tin.
  The bottom came out
  And down they fell,
  And instead of goin' to heaven
  They all went to hell!

She laughs.

God forgive me . . .

Silence again as **Sarah** *and* **Hugh**, *with an evident tension between them, concentrate on the game.*

Hugh   The mummers are abroad. I passed them at Cutlers on the way home.

Sarah   And not a word till now. You're a fine husband, Hugh Brolly.

Lizzie   They'll be up to us so, before night . . .

Sarah *moves a chess piece, defeating* **Hugh**. *She pushes the board away from her and stands up.*

Sarah   Put away that game – I have ye beaten anyway.

Lizzie   Ye'd better put a bit of cheer on this place, Sarah.

Sarah   Aye, it's sore in need of it . . . (*To* **Hugh**.) It would suit you better to be out with the mummers like you to . . . But 'you have to work on again'. Well, I'm sick of it.

Hugh   And I'm sick being jibed at. Ye know well it's always like this comin' up to Christmas.

Sarah   Well, it must have been Christmas this month so.

Lizzie (*to the baby in the cradle*)   The season of goodwill, Elizabeth – and they haven't a civil word for each other . . .

Sarah   All I'm sayin' is there's no point in broodin' on the past. It's not goin' to bring Seán back . . . This one night and you can't stay at home.

Sarah *goes, takes the baby from the cradle, walks her around for a few moments in silence.*

Sarah   I suppose ye're not even goin' to come to the weddin'.

Hugh   Small blame to me if I don't want to.

Sarah   Oh, Hugh – they had nothing to do with it . . .

Lizzie   Aye, the Stuarts are good neighbours – and so is Jim, for all he is a policeman. I'd not miss that weddin' if I had to walk on red coals to it.

Hugh   Am I imaginin' it – or am I always wrong recently in this house?

Sarah   I don't know what ye're imaginin' recently.

Lizzie *holds up the straw wren that she has just finished making.*

Lizzie   For the season that's in it – me father used to make them.

Sarah   A robin?

Lizzie   Are ye blind or what? That's no robin – it's a wren.

Hugh   Wee shit of a thing.

Lizzie   If you can't be civil, be silent.

Hugh   Aye – be silent about Seán. Be silent about everything. Keep yer mouth closed. Do what ye're told. Go out with the mummers. 'Any admittance for Marilyn Bloody Monroe and all her men?' Wish them all a Happy Christmas and a prosperous new year . . .

Sarah   When are you goin' to stop feelin' sorry for yerself? You're not the only one's lost somebody.

Hugh   Nobody else was my brother.

Exit **Hugh**.

Sarah (*singing*)
  The wren, the wren, the king of all birds
  On St Stephen's night was caught in the furze.

Lizzie   You remember that?

Sarah   I remember it . . . Daddy singin' it to me. I remember his eyes . . . Hugh's eyes have changed since Seán was killed. I don't know him any more.

Bodhrán-beats or music off signals the approach of the **Mummers**.

Lizzie   All I know is what I see about me. Now isn't the time, daughter. We'll have to throw a shape on ourselves for the mummers. Here, help me clear the floor and make room.

The two **Women** *prepare for the* **Mummers**.

Lizzie   We'll have to have a few coppers for them. Sarah, you'll have to put a face on it in front of the mummers – we'll try to enjoy ourselves like we used to. There's plenty of time for talkin' after.

Three knocks are heard, then **Captain Mummer***'s voice.*

Captain Mummer   Any admittance for Captain Mummer and his men?

Lizzie   Come in and welcome . . .

Scene Three

Enter the **Mummers**. *They perform the* **Second Mummers'
Play**.

Captain Mummer
Room, room, gallant friends
Give us room to rhyme.
We've come to show activity
At this deep winter-time.
Acts of age and acts of youth,
Tales of lies and tales of truth:
And if you don't believe in what I say
Enter in the Butcher and he'll soon show the way

Butcher
Here come I, the butcher with me knife,
I can take any living creature
And cut away its life.
I can cut the heads off cattle,
I can cut the feet off hogs,
And leave nothing of a carcass
But bones to feed the dogs.
And if you don't believe in what I say
Enter in the Devil Sweep and he'll soon show the way

Devil Sweep
Here come I, the Devil Sweep,
A card in me hand to make you weep,
A card at me arse to make you cry,
A pan in me hand to start the fry.
And when the fat it hits the pan
We'll laugh for woman and laugh for man
And if you don't believe in what I say
Enter in a Hero Bold and he'll soon show the way.

First Hero
Here come I, a Hero Bold:
I've made my foes to tremble
And my enemies to quake
And I massacred a gander

Coming home from Paddy's wake.
Show me the man who dares me sit
And I'll carve his head to improve his wit.

Second Hero
I'm the man who dares you sit:
A Hero Brave, a Hero Fit.
Just try, Bold Knight, to carve my head
And this vorpal sword will leave you dead.
Contrive, conspire, to improve my wit
And your sour entrails my blade will split.

First Hero
Put up your sword and fight then!

Second Hero
I'll cut off your head and foreskin!

First Hero
Impostor! Liar! Jack Ass!

Second Hero
Feel my steel perform a bypass!

The two **Heroes** *fight.* **First Hero** *is struck and falls.*

Captain Mummer   Doctor! Doctor! – send for the twenty-pound doctor.

Doctor
Here come I, a Doctor good, a Doctor pure . . .

All the Mummers   Oh, we all know that ye silly hoor!

Captain Mummer   But are you the twenty-pound doctor?

Doctor
Thirty quid or I'm away,
If you want the cure, you'll have to pay!

Captain Mummer
Quit your guff and do the trick:
You'll get your fee – then cut your stick.

Doctor (*prompting*)   And what can you cure?

Captain Mummer   Oh . . . And what can you cure?

Doctor
    I can cure all things:
    The plague within, the plague without,
    The pox, the palsy and the gout.
    If there's nine devils in I can knock ten out.
    I have lotions, potions, ointments and unctions
    To speed up all the bodily functions,
    To open the sluice gates on badness and bile
    And send cripples and Christians leppin' over the stile.
    And I have here my little bottle
    To pour down any dead man's throttle;
    Called Hocus Pocus Sally Campaign,
    Rise up, fine Hero, and fight again.

The **Doctor** *stoops down, puts his medicine in* **First Hero***'s mouth, who then rises.*

First *and* **Second Heroes**
    We'll fight again,
    But not just yet.
    First shake hands
    And dance a set.

They mum a tune and dance a brief, ridiculous set. **Tom Fool** *pushes forward, breaking them up.*

Tom Fool
    Here come I, Tom Fool,
    With me bladder and me staff;
    I'm otherwise known as Jack Straw
    With a riddle to make you laugh:
    Such a man you never saw,
    Jack Straw Stree Striddle,
    I'm the man that kicked the devil
    Through a rock, through a reel,
    Through an old spinning wheel,
    Through a grain of pepper,
    Through a miller's hopper,
    Through a sheep's shank bone,
    Such a man was never known.

And if I was the wren
I'd have a different rhyme:
'The wren, the wren, the king of all birds
On St Stephen's night was caught in the furze,
Although she is small, her honour is great,
Rise up old landlady and give us a trate
And if your trate be of the best,
We hope in heaven your soul will rest;
But if your trate be of the small
It won't agree with the boys at all.'

Miss Funny *comes forward.*

Miss Funny
Aye, it won't agree with the boys
And it won't agree with Miss Funny.
Cough up your fill or we'll break your till,
We've a need and a cravin' for money.

All the Mummers
All silver, no brass,
Bad money won't pass.

Lizzie *and* **Sarah** *put money in* **Miss Funny***'s collection box.*
Lizzie *and* **Sarah** *applaud.*

Captain Mummer   No, nor bad dancin'! Come on, Lizzie,
'The Coast of Leitrim'! And you, Sarah, come on, don't have
to be coaxed.

All dance 'The Coast of Leitrim'. *The* **Mummers** *remove their
masks, drinks are poured.*

Captain Mummer   Ye never forgot the steps, Lizzie.

Lizzie   Indeed I didn't. Oh, that was great altogether. Ye'll
have a drop.

Captain Mummer   Only a quick drop, so – we've good
ground to cover yet the night.

Sarah   You'll cover it all the quicker with a warm drink
inside.

Glasses are handed around.

Lizzie   Come on everybody, help yourselves now. D'ye know, I haven't enjoyed the mummers so much since I don't know when ... (*She raises her glass.*) Yer health ... And a Happy Christmas.

The **Mummers** *toast.*

All   Good luck ... Good health ... Happy Christmas.

Captain Mummer (*to* **Sarah**)   I hope we didn't waken the wee one with all the racket.

Sarah   If she sleeps through that, she'll sleep through anything.

Captain Mummer   How is she comin' on anyway?

Sarah   Oh, she's thrivin' ...

Captain Mummer   And Hugh? We met his van there at the bridge. It's late enough he's headin' south ...

Lizzie   It's north he was goin' – or so he told us.

Sarah   We mustn't have heard him right ... (*Holds up straw wren.*) Look what Mother's making for Elizabeth.

Captain Mummer   The straw wren – it's a long time since I saw one of them. Do you know the story of the wren?

Sarah *shakes her head.*

Captain Mummer   Well, the way I heard it, it was the wren betrayed St Stephen and him hidin' on the Roman soldiers in a field of corn ... The bird flew up and gave away his hidin' place and ever after he was hunted and killed for a traitor.

Some of the **Mummers** *have been nodding their heads in agreement; others shaking their heads in obvious disagreement. Of the latter,* **Tom Fool** *and* **Miss Funny** *are the most vehement.*

That's my version of it – though I know some of ye heard different.

Tom Fool *and* **Miss Funny**   No, no, no, the way we heard it was ...

Tom Fool   It was the wren betrayed a regiment of Billy's men at the Battle of the Boyne . . .

Miss Funny   They were creepin' up on a gantry of the others that was asleep . . .

Tom Fool   And didn't the wren fly up and waken them . . .

Miss Funny   They routed Billy's men and killed every last one of them . . .

Tom Fool   That's why the Orangemen kill the wren the same as everybody else. Isn't that right?

Miss Funny   That's right . . .

Captain Mummer   Isn't that a good one? The same wee bird in a field of corn in the east and in a battlefield in this whelp of a country.

Lizzie   Sure, whatever – here's to the wren. (*Raising her glass.*)

All   To the wren – the king of all birds.

Captain Mummer   And to us all – long life.

Tom Fool   As the bicycle lamp said to the battery.

Captain Mummer   I hope ye'll all be comin' on Tuesday. Jim'll be vexed if ye don't.

Lizzie   I wouldn't miss the weddin' for anything – it's more entertainment we need. Come on, boys – ye'll give us a song before ye go.

Captain Mummer   We'll do better than that – we'll give ye Jack's favourite.

Lizzie   Ah, 'The King' . . .

Silence for a moment, then **Lizzie** *strikes a note and the company sings the old Christmas song.*

All
  Joy, health, love and peace
  Be all here in this place

By your leave we will sing
Concerning our King

Our King is well dressed
In silks of the best
In ribbons so rare
No King can compare

We have travelled many miles
Over hedges and stiles
In search of our King
Unto you we bring

We have powder and shot
To conquer the lot
We have cannon and ball
To conquer them all

Old Christmas is past
Long time did it last
And we bid you adieu
Pray joy to the new

Silence for a moment after the singing.

Captain Mummer   God rest Jack Boles ... (*Pause.*) Right,
men – ready for away.

The **Mummers** *prepare to leave, putting down glasses, putting on
masks etc.*

Lizzie   Will ye be finished yer round tonight?

Captain Mummer   Well, barrin' the houses havin' shifted
a few mile we should get done.

Lizzie   Well, call by if there's a light on when ye're goin'
home.

Captain Mummer   We'll do that.

Sarah   We'd be glad of the company.

Exit the **Mummers** *to form a line, facing the audience, holding the
straw wall.* **Tom Fool** *and* **Miss Funny** *stand or sit at a distance.*

Scene Four

Lizzie   I have all locked up. It's freezin' out – not a night to be drivin' far.

Sarah   'We met his van at the bridge, headin' south.' I wanted to believe him, Mother, I wanted to believe he was workin' on. But he lied to me. I saw him – with Seán's friends – in the town. When I put it to him he said he was drivin' all that day and I must have been mistakin' someone else for him . . . Where is he, Mother? Where's the man I married?

Lizzie   You know well where he is, Sarah. Open your eyes . . . Unless I'm greatly mistaken, like his brother before him, he's out risin' the black pig . . .

Scene Five

Tom Fool
   Riddle me, riddle me, rye:
   Two fat cheeks and one blind eye.
   Riddle me that.

Miss Funny   Me arse.

Enter **Hugh Brolly**. *He stands behind the line of* **Mummers**.

First Mummer   Call to the back of the shop. Collect the stuff. Take the back road home by the dyke.

Hugh   He promised it'd be the last time.

Second Mummer   Don't worry – he never breaks a promise.

Hugh   What time?

Third Mummer   Ten o'clock. Not too early. Not too late.

Fourth Mummer   We can't botch this one.

Hugh   Don't tell me nothin'. I don't want to know . . . So long as it's the last time.

Fifth Mummer   I told you – he wouldn't break his word.

First Mummer   Good night.

Exit **Hugh**.

Scene Six

Miss Funny
Riddle me that.

And riddle me this:
There was a butcher with his knife
Who wanted Lizzie for his wife.
He stabbed her husband and he ran
And asked again to be her man.
And she refused and so he said
He'd live his life to see her dead.

Tom Fool
There was a husband, name of Hugh
Who knew the butcher
Oh, he knew a lot.
And got more than he bargained for.

Tom Fool *and* **Miss Funny**   In the end . . .

Miss Funny   And the end's comin' up . . .

Tom Fool   As the farmer said, kissin' the sheep . . .

Miss Funny   Comin' up fairly fast. And a storm too, if you wouldn't mind. Not a night to be a blind dog on the road.

Tom Fool   Or a half-blind man, or a wren – being hunted.

Tom Fool *and* **Miss Funny** (*singing, but speaking the last two words*)
The wren, the wren, the king of all birds
On St Stephen's night was caught in the furze.
Up with the kettle and down with the pan
And give us a penny to bury – *the man.*

Scene Seven

Lizzie *takes the baby from the cradle, paces with* **Elizabeth** *in her arms.* **Sarah** *sits at the table, resting her head in her hands. There's a sense of waiting.*

Lizzie (*singing*)
Where are the eyes that looked so mild
Haroo, haroo.
Where are the eyes that looked so mild
Haroo, haroo.
Where are the eyes that looked so mild
When my poor heart you first beguiled?
Why did you skedaddle from me and the child?
Johnny, I hardly knew ye . . .

Sarah   Stop that!

Lizzie   Oh, he'll be back all right. But ye'll not know his eyes again.

Sarah
'When my poor heart they first beguiled . . .'

I always imagined his eyes were the same as Daddy's. I had it in me head since I was a child that father's eyes were brown. I remember sittin' on his knee and starin' at them – tryin' to make him blink. And Hugh's eyes – though they were different – they were like his. When I told him – it was a Sunday and we'd driven over to Leitrim, up to the Dawn of Hope . . . He got annoyed first and then he laughed a bit and he told me how his grandfather had one blue eye and one brown.

Lizzie   And he told you where that mix came from.

Sarah   Brolly and Clements. Brown eye and blue.

Oh, he told me it all . . . How his grandfather with the two different-coloured eyes was the child of May Brolly and Clements – the man who drowned her brother. Can you imagine what it was like for that woman? Dragged up to the Big House and left pregnant and then promised the lot – that

he'd follow her on and marry her if she'd go to America.
Then nothing and nothing again till she got word he was
drowned on the lake and John, her own flesh and blood,
drowned with him.

Lizzie   Put down with the oar. A matter of honour.

Lizzie puts the baby back in the cradle.

Sarah   I said to him, 'I wouldn't blame you if you were
bitter.' He said he wasn't. But he said, 'Me brother Seán now
– he's the one for history.'

Lizzie   Seán wasn't doin' nothing on the road that day. He
was on look-out. But there was no call for them to shoot him.

Sarah   Hugh's eyes changed after that – they weren't like
Daddy's any more. They were forever looking at something
out past me – out beyond us all.

Lizzie   Revenge is the longest road. Revenge doesn't know
when to stop. And there's some don't want it ever to stop.
There's some men and they're only happy if there's a smell of
blood on the wind . . .

From the line of **Mummers Frank Beirne**'s *voice is heard – low,
drifting, singing 'Barbara Allen'.*

As she was crossin' o'er the field
She met the funeral comin'
Oh, lay him down ye six young men
That I may gaze upon him.

Lizzie   Dear Jesus . . . That song – I could choke on it.

Again **Frank Beirne**'s *voice is heard from the* **Chorus.**

The more she gazed the more she laughed
The more she slighted of him
Until her friends cried out for shame
Hard-hearted Barbara Allen.

Lizzie   Frank Beirne . . .
He wanted me. He always wanted me and I was soft with
him at the start because I was afraid and because he was

handsome enough. He'd catch hold of me any chance he got
and grip me so hard I'd bruise from the dent of pressure.
That was the song he used to sing whenever he saw me –
and it was like a knife pointin' at yer throat.

It was August it happened. Jack went out as usual that
mornin' to the hayfield. It was a late summer that year and
the big meadow was still down. The child was out playin' and
before I knew it the clock was strikin' noon. I prepared his bit
of lunch and I didn't put too much wonder in his not comin'
for it – I thought he must be workin' on while the weather
held up.

It held till three and the sky opened then with rain that would
rival the flood. I thought, 'He'll be in any minute now,' but
he didn't come. So I thought, 'he's shelterin' in the old
pighouse and he'll be down as soon as it stops.' It stopped
about half past four and I sat waitin' for him to come in. I
sat for an hour and I knew then there was something terrible
wrong. I took Sarah by the hand and we walked up the hill
to where he was workin'.

I didn't find him straight away. I walked the length and
breadth of the meadow and called, 'Jack, Jack – where are
ye?' There was no answer – only the echo of my own voice
comin' back from the outhouses . . . I walked up the lane
towards them same buildings. There was a bush of redcurrants
just before you turned in on the flags and I stopped and took
a fistful for Sarah. I don't know why I did.

He was lyin' in a puddle of water outside the byre door – his
face from me – and the water near as red as the berries on
her lips. He'd been stuck in the neck like a pig; and his hands
– his hands that played the melodeon – were slashed to
ribbons like he'd tried to ward off the blows of a knife.

Dead for certain. Dead and no cure. Jack Boles that I ran
away with. Jack Boles that I lay with the night of the fools'
weddin'. Jack Boles my husband . . .

Enter **Frank Beirne**.

Lizzie   He came back, ye know. More than a year later, he came back. I heard his car in the lane and his step outside on the flag. Too well I knew the sound.

Frank Beirne   I'm sorry for yer trouble, Lizzie Flynn.

Lizzie   Lizzie Boles is my name – and you're not one bit sorry for any trouble of mine.

Frank Beirne   I came here to make amends. I said I'm sorry – what more do ye want?

Lizzie   I want none of it. I only want you out of this house – and out of my sight for as long as I have eyes to see with.

Frank Beirne   We don't always get what we want, Lizzie – leastways not without a fight.

Lizzie   But ye got Jack's shop – so yer father must be cheerin' in his grave. Ye finally got yer hands on it. Well, much luck may it bring ye – for it was no fair fight that won that shop for ye. No fair fight – but butchery, Frank.

Frank Beirne   Words, Lizzie. You know nothin'. There was a war on. Things had to change, don't ye see. Things had to be done . . .

Lizzie   Like killin' my husband . . .

Frank Beirne   How could ye accuse me of that? We had our differences but I'd not do that. How could you accuse me of it?

Lizzie   I don't have to accuse. I know in me heart and soul ye did.

Frank Beirne   Then you know more than the constabulary. Let me tell ye, our own defenders of the peace beyond asked me a few questions. And they're satisfied I hadn't hand, act or part in the killin' of Jack Boles.

Lizzie   You know fine well that even if ye walked home, even if ye crossed the dyke soaked in his blood for all to see, ye'd never be sent here for trial.

Frank Beirne   Ye're wrongin' me, Lizzie, and ye're wrongin' yer country. What you're sayin' to me is hurtful. I came here in good faith and didn't expect this welcome. The past is the past – and I'm not to blame for what me father might have done. Can't ye forget that and listen to me?

Lizzie   What do ye want?

Frank Beirne   I came here to make a fair offer. Ye know I was always fond of ye, Lizzie. I want ye to come back with me to yer own people. I'll marry ye – and I'm prepared to take the child. Ye shouldn't be over here on yer own. Let bygones be bygones. We'll put our differences behind us and make a go of it – together . . .

Lizzie   O Jack . . .

Frank Beirne   What do ye say, Lizzie?

Lizzie   Did you see the dunghill on the way in? Well, I'd sooner eat shite from that than marry you. I'd let me daughter go in rags and beg the length of the country before I'd have you set a hand on her. I'd no more set foot in that shop than I'd sell me soul. For that's what it'd be. Get back over the border – back over the Black Pig's Dyke. Go back to yer slaughterhouse and yer shop and yer killin'. Get out of this house – and don't ever come near me or my daughter again. (*Grabbing knife from beside straw wren on the table and stabbing blindly at the air.*) Or by Christ if you do I'll sink this blade so deep in your hide that whoever pulls it out will have to choose which side to pull it from.

Sarah   Stop!

Exit **Frank Beirne**. **Lizzie** *drops the knife* **Sarah** *comforts her.*

Lizzie   Revenge is an endless road.

Scene Eight

Enter **Hugh Brolly** *through the line of* **Mummers**.

Hugh   They'll be after me.

Sarah *rushes to him, shakes him, slaps him.*

Sarah   Hugh, what's happened?

Hugh   Tonight was to be the last time – I swear that's the truth.

Sarah   What's goin' on? What the hell is goin' on, Hugh?

Lizzie   Let him have his say. Where were you tonight, Hugh Brolly? And what work have you been at these past months?

Hugh   What I was doin' tonight I've been doin' – since they killed Seán. Delivery work. Small things first – I didn't always know what. Tonight was to be a pick-up in the yard like I always did. They promised me it'd be the last run. There was no sign of anyone when I drove in, so I went up to knock on the back door. I could hear them inside, talkin' . . . What I was bringin' over tonight – the stuff I was collectin' – it was to be used on Stuart's weddin' on Tuesday. They're bound to have known half the country would be there.

Lizzie   And when did the like of them ever care about people . . .

Sarah   Jim Stuart's weddin' . . .

Hugh   I didn't let on a thing, but collected the lot. I drove the back road like they said, but I stopped, south of the dyke, and I dumped the lot in the lough there – into the deepest spot at the Long Point.

Sarah   Is that it? Is that all ye did?

Hugh   No. I stopped again, over this side, at the loneliest phone box I could find – and I rang the police. If anyone lifts a finger at that weddin' they're behind bars or dead.

Lizzie   O Jesus . . .

Sarah (*hysterical, hitting, slapping* **Hugh**)   Why didn't you tell me before now, Hugh? You should have told me.

Hugh   After Seán – something gave in me, Sarah. Not you, not the child, nothing – nothing could stop it. I could hear two sounds in me head – an oar on water and a volley of shots.

And then they were at me: he was a hero – what was I? What kind of strange brother was I?

Lizzie So ye gave in . . .

Hugh I could see the side of his face where he was hit – his eyes . . .

Sarah *moves away from* **Hugh**. *He follows, pleads with her.*

Hugh It makes no difference now. If I don't get away I'm a dead man. But I might get away, Sarah . . .

Lizzie An endless road, Hugh – and they're huntin' each side of it for the wren that flew up and betrayed them.

Hugh I didn't want to hurt you.

Lizzie No time. There's no time, Hugh . . . Go. Run. They'll be out for ye now. Get away from here.

Hugh *exits.*

Sarah Remember after we met Hugh – and we went on that drive across over the Black Pig's Dyke. We looked out over the lake where your ancestor was drowned by Clements and sat by the old nunnery where we could see out to the Holy Island. Remember the place we went to – with the view out over all the counties – the Dawn of Hope.

Lizzie I've barred the door. You'd never know who or what would be abroad this night.

Exit **Lizzie** *and* **Sarah**.

Scene Nine

The **Mummers** *form a large semicircle. Enter* **Hugh Brolly**. *The* **Mummers** *surround him.*

First Mummer Are ye dry now, Hugh?

Second Mummer Was yer tongue well oiled by the police?

Third Mummer It's Hocus Pocus Sally Campaign, Hugh.

Fourth Mummer Traitor.

Fifth Mummer Collaborator.

Sixth Mummer Informer.

First Mummer Grasser, squealer.

Second Mummer Dirty bastard.

Third Mummer Double dealer.

Remaining **Mummer** *removes his mask to reveal* **Frank Beirne**.

Frank Beirne Judas fuckin' Iscariot.

Frank Beirne *and the* **Mummers** *interrogate* **Hugh** – *they may use sticks.*

Frank Beirne Pigs squeal, Hugh. Do you know what I do with pigs? I cut their throats. You squealed, Hugh. Are you a pig? Come on, squeal for us.

Hugh *is moving, terrified, around the semicircle, pleading.*

Frank Beirne You squealed for others. If you squealed for them, squeal for us. The pig has lost his tongue. It's not all pigs lose, Hugh. How would your Sarah like that?

Did you tell them, Hugh? Lizzie Boles and Sarah?

Did you squeal to them too?

Hugh I didn't, Frank . . . I swear I didn't.

Frank Beirne What did he say, boys?

All He said he did . . .

Some make grunting, pig noises.

Hugh No, no, I didn't.

Frank Beirne It's all right, pig, we heard you the first time. Don't worry yer head about yer family – they'll be looked after . . .

First Mummer Informer.

Second Mummer Grasser.

Third Mummer   Squealer.

Frank Beirne *and* **Other Mummers**
The man, the man, the King of all men
Slept with a cock and woke with a hen

Frank Beirne   Yer brother must be turnin' in his grave, pig – to have a Judas fuckin' Iscariot in his litter.

Frank Beirne *produces a gun, shoots* **Hugh** *in the head; his body falls to the ground.*

Frank Beirne   Here's to you, Hugh Brolly. He had bad blood in him. Mixin' like that breeds informers.

The six **Mummers** *kneel, three at each side of* **Hugh***'s body, masks bent inwards across it, heads lowered.* **Frank Beirne** *stands at* **Hugh***'s head.*

Frank Beirne   There's things has to be done.

Enter **Lizzie***. She sits by the cradle.* **Frank Beirne** *sings.*

When he was dead and laid in grave
Her heart was filled with sorrow
O mother, mother make my bed
For I shall die tomorrow.

Lizzie *hums the last verse of 'The Enniskillen Dragoons' and rocks the cradle as in the opening scene.*

Lizzie   It was a long time ago, Elizabeth, and it was not a long time ago. It was a time when to go east was to go west, when to go south was to go north, when people sang songs at a wake and cried when a child was born. It was in a land where the sun never rose and the sun never set, where the dead made shrouds for the livin' and straw people walked the roads.

Frank Beirne *bangs on the ground three times with his stick stage right.*

Frank Beirne   Any admittance for Captain Mummer and his men?

Lizzie *stands slowly – as in the Prologue to Act one, and turns towards the voice.* **Frank Beirne** *raises the gun once more and another shot is heard.* **Lizzie** *drops the straw wren from her grasp and slumps – but remains standing.* **Frank Beirne** *sings the final verse of* 'Barbara Allen'.

> Farewell, she cried, ye maidens all
> And shun the fault I fell in
> Henceforth take warning by the fate
> Of cruel-hearted Barbara Allen.

Frank Beirne *and the* **Mummers** *kneel by* **Hugh***'s body.* **Elizabeth** *is seen as in the Prologues to Acts One and Two.*

Epilogue

Elizabeth   The Strange Knight remained in his castle. He watched from the ramparts and no one came. The land around him grew rancid from the decay of bodies in the ground.

He ordered a banquet but there was no food; a ball but there were no musicians; a duel but there was no one to fight. He posted orders that a beautiful woman be brought to him to sire an heir: all night he lay alone, naked, in his bed.

And the Strange Knight grew lonely and came to be filled with sorrow. He walked back along the road he had travelled till he came to the place where he'd met the woman with the riddle. He fell to the ground and begged to be forgiven. His tears fell like rain on the soil and the water soaked down, down into the heart of the dead woman.

And out of her heart grew a flower – a blood-red poppy. And the Strange Knight plucked it and when he did it fell asunder. (**Elizabeth** *lets the poppy petals in her hand drift to the ground.*) Petal after petal drifted to the ground and out of each sprang a dozen women with hooks and seeds and implements to sow and harvest. They yoked the Strange Knight to the plough and so began the endless task of restoring the land to life and the beginning of happiness.

Elizabeth *scatters the final petals of the poppy and stands still as the lights fade, very slowly, into darkness.*

Final Curtain.

Vincent Woods was born in County Leitrim in 1960. He was a journalist with RTE before giving up full-time work in 1989 to write and travel. He lived in the United States, New Zealand and Australia before returning to Ireland a few years ago. As well as writing plays, Vincent is a poet and has published a collection of poems entitled *The Colour of Money*. In 1991 his two one-act plays *John Hughdy* and *Tom John* were performed at the Galway Arts Festival. *At the Black Pig's Dyke* was first performed by Theatre Druid and won a Stewart Parker Award in 1992. This was followed by *Song of the Yellow Bittern* also performed by Theatre Druid and widely toured. His radio play *The Leitrim Hotel* won a P. J. O'Connor Award.

Language Roulette

by Daragh Carville

Language Roulette was first performed by Tinderbox Theatre Company in association with the Old Museum Arts Centre, Belfast, on 27 May, 1996. The cast was as follows:

Colm	Alan McKee
Ollie	Thomas Lappin
Sarah	Maria Connolly
Joseph	Peter O'Meara
Tim	Peter Ballance
Anna	Emma O'Neill

Directed by Tim Loane
Designed by Terry Loane
Lighting Design by Aidan Lacey
Sound by Jules Maxwell

For the revival of *Language Roulette* in February–May, 1997, which toured Ireland and played at the Bush Theatre, London and the Traverse Theatre, Edinburgh, the part of **Joseph** was played by Patrick Lennox.

Scene One

It is late 1994. Pound-for-a-pint night. The stage is set throughout to represent a Belfast pub, but in the opening scenes this doubles as **Colm***'s house in Belfast. An untidy living-room. One door to the outside in the back wall, another in the wall on the right heading off to the kitchen. A sofa and an armchair, a low table, scattered cups and cans and ashtrays. TV on with the sound down.*

The opening music is 'Sabotage' by the Beastie Boys.

Colm*, barefoot, in jumper and jeans, circulates with a waste-paper basket, trying to put the place in order.* **Ollie** *slouches in the armchair,* **Sarah** *lies on the sofa. Both are eyeing the TV, drinking beer from cans. They are in the way but apparently unaware of it.*

Colm *goes off for the hoover, comes back on and sets it down. Carries on tidying.*

Ollie   Drinks her own piss, you know.

Sarah   What?

Ollie   She drinks her own piss.

Sarah   Who does?

Ollie   Your woman.

Sarah   What woman?

Ollie   Your woman out of *Ryan's Daughter*.

Sarah   Sarah Miles?

Ollie   Yeah. Sarah Miles drinks her own piss. That's a well-known fact.

Sarah   You need help.

Ollie   Hey, I didn't say I drank my own piss. I said Sarah Miles drinks her own piss. Doesn't she, Colm?

Colm *tuts and ignores him; continues tidying.*

Ollie   She does, though. Swear to God.

Sarah   Why?

Ollie   Supposed to be good for you.

Sarah   You're a sick individual. What are you?

Colm *gives up tidying and approaches them stormily.*

Colm   Are youse still here?

Ollie   No.

Colm   I thought youse were going out.

Ollie   There's no hurry.

Colm   Yes there is.

Sarah   Why, are you expecting someone?

Colm   *Yes. (As if he's telling them for the hundredth time.)*

Sarah   Who?

Colm   Never you mind.

Ollie   Come on.

Pause.

Colm   A friend.

He bends to pick an empty pizza box off the floor. **Ollie** *snatches it away from him.*

Ollie   I haven't finished that!

Colm *(exasperated)*   OLLIE!

Ollie *bites into a pizza crust and hands the box back to* **Colm**.

Colm   Thank you.

Ollie, *obviously bored, picks up the remote control and zaps from channel to channel on the TV. Puts up the volume. The closing theme music of 'UTV Live'.* **Ollie** *raises the volume to an unbearable level.*

Sarah   Ollie.

Ollie *switches off the sound, and tosses the remote to* **Sarah**.

Ollie   You choose, then. The anus is on you.

Sarah Thank you. (*Zaps through the channels.*) There's nothing on.

Ollie Doin' much ridin' this weather, Col?

Colm Give over, will you.

Ollie I'll take that as a no.

Sarah (*to* **Colm**) Were you working today?

Colm Of course I was.

Ollie Did you get bullied?

Sarah You must be shagged.

Colm Yes, I bloody am.

Ollie Are we in the way, Col? We wouldn't want to be in the way. (*No reply.*) Would we?

Sarah No, we wouldn't. We wouldn't want to be in the way.

Ollie You're not ashamed of us, are you?

Colm Yes. (*He carries on with his tidying.*)

Sarah You're not afraid we'll let you down in front of your visitor, are you?

Colm Yes.

Sarah We promise we'll be on our best behaviour, Col. Don't we?

Colm Look, will youse just go. You said you were going out.

Ollie Oh, that's nice. That's very nice. Getting kicked out of my own house.

Colm It's *my* house.

Ollie I pay my rent, don't I?

Colm No. You're on housing benefit.

Ollie Well? I still have tenants' rights.

Sarah   Tennant's Extra!

Ollie   Exactly!

Colm   Look, Ollie, I don't want to argue about this. Sarah – I appeal to you –

Sarah   No, you don't.

Ollie   Boom boom!

Colm   Oh, for fuck's sake.

The doorbell rings.

Ollie (*blandly*)   Is that the door?

Colm   Shite!

He grabs shoes and socks and fumbles to put them on. **Ollie** *and* **Sarah** *watch with some amusement.*

Ollie   He looks lovely, doesn't he?

Sarah   He's gorgeous.

Ollie   Your mammy would be proud of you.

An exasperated **Colm** *signals for them to be quiet, then moves through and opens the door. It is* **Joseph***, wearing a suit, and holding a bottle of wine. An awkward pause.*

Colm   Well, stranger –

Joseph   Peace be with you –

Colm   And also with you.

A moment as they look at one another. They they hug, spontaneously, genuinely, but with much clumsiness. Laughter and relief. Meanwhile **Ollie** *and* **Sarah** *listen in.*

Colm   Come here till I see you. God, you're looking very cosmopolitan.

Joseph   Well, one has to try.

Colm   Oh yes, one does, doesn't one? Where did you get the suit?

Joseph   Rome.

Colm   You flash bastard. You flash bastard. Come on in. You know the others, don't you, Joe?

Colm *doesn't expect an answer.* **Joseph**, *however, doesn't remember* **Ollie**, *and has never met* **Sarah**. *Some hesitancy.*

Sarah   Hi.

Ollie   Well, Joe.

Joseph   Hello.

Colm (*overcompensating nervously*)   Och, how the fuck are you, Joe?

Joseph   . . . I'm fine. Fine. (*Composing himself.*) And how the fuck are you?

Colm   Not three bad, Joe. You know me.

Joseph   You're looking well.

Colm   Ah, you know –

Joseph   Yes, indeed. Here. (*He holds out the bottle.*)

Ollie   Excellent!

Joseph   A peace offering.

Colm   Eh?

Joseph   Well, a ceasefire offering, then. It's not peace yet, I suppose.

Colm (*taking the bottle*)   What is it? French?

Joseph   It's not Buckfast at any rate.

Colm   Aw now, Joe. God bless those hard-working monks.

Colm *blesses himself with the bottle. An old familiar joke.*

Should I open it?

Joseph   Now what do you think?

Colm   I think I'll open it.

He goes off to the kitchen to search for a corkscrew.

Sarah (*to* **Joseph**)   Why don't you sit down? (*To* **Ollie**.) Why doesn't he sit down.

Joseph   Thank you.

But with **Sarah** *still stretched out on the sofa, and* **Ollie** *in the armchair, there is nowhere to sit.* **Joseph** *looks around.*

Ollie *stands up and signals for* **Joseph** *to take his place.*

Joseph   Oh no, no. Stay where you are.

Ollie   Go on ahead. I insist. I mean, if that's going to be your bed the night.

A moment, and **Joseph** *takes the seat.*

Joseph   Thank you.

Ollie *remains standing, weighing up the newcomer.*

Ollie   You'd hardly remember me, Joe.

Joseph   Erm . . .

Ollie   I was the year under you at the college. Ollie Kearns. Do you remember?

Joseph   Oh, yes. Yes, of course I remember.

Ollie   Long time ago.

Joseph   Mmm.

Pause.

Joseph   So, are you two living here?

Ollie   I live here. She just comes round because she can't resist my charm.

Sarah   Aye, right.

Ollie   Seriously. Can't get enough of me.

Sarah   Dream on.

Joseph   I didn't know Colm had let out the room. Have you been living here long?

Ollie   Two years.

Joseph   God, is it that long already? That's amazing.

Sarah   *That's Amazing*, featuring Barry Sheene, Kenny Lynch and the lovely Suzanne Danielle.

Pause. **Joseph** *is bemused.*

Joseph (*calls to* **Colm**)   Any word of Tim, Colm?

Colm   What's that?

Joseph   I said any word of Tim.

Colm   Aw shite!

Joseph   What's the matter?

Colm *comes back in from the kitchen, holding the bottle and a corkscrew.*

Colm   The cork broke.

Joseph   Oh, dear.

Ollie   Here, give me it.

He takes the bottle and puts his thumb into its mouth.

I can push it through.

Joseph   No! Give it to me.

A moment, then **Ollie** *gives the bottle to* **Joseph**. **Joseph** *uses the corkscrew to remove what's left of the cork.* **Ollie** *moves to* **Sarah**.

Ollie   Here, move your arse.

Sarah *wiggles her arse, giggles, and makes space.* **Ollie** *slouches down with her. At some point during the following,* **Joseph** *hands the bottle back to* **Colm**.

Colm   What were you saying?

Joseph   I was asking about Tim.

Colm   Oh. Well, he's coming round.

Joseph   Are you sure?

Colm   Aye. I called him yesterday.

Joseph   And you told him I was home?

Colm   Yeah yeah yeah. Hang on, I'll just get some glasses.

He goes back to the kitchen to search for glasses.

Joseph (*slumped, absently*)   Christ.

Then, aware again of **Ollie** *and* **Sarah**, *he collects himself.*

Do you two know Tim?

Sarah   Everybody knows Tim.

Joseph   Yes, of course.

Sarah   He's a very useful man to know.

Ollie   Actually Tim's a very good friend of mine.

Sarah (*nudging* **Ollie**)   Here, shut up and skin up, Ollie.

Ollie   Oh yes. Your wish is my command.

Ollie *produces the necessary stuff and begins to skin up.*

Joseph   Do you need a hand, Colm?

Colm (*popping his head out from the kitchen*)   Sit your ground, Joe. You're our guest. You're *my* guest. I just have to wash a couple of glasses.

He dons a pair of bright pink kitchen gloves, and begins to sing.

'Now hands that do dishes
can feel soft as your face . . .'
Hold on, Mrs Smythe, we're going in . . .

He disappears back into the kitchen.

Joseph (to **Ollie** *and* **Sarah**)   Excuse me – do you have any idea when he's supposed to come?

Ollie   Who?

Joseph   Tim.

Ollie   I didn't know he was coming at all. News to me.

Sarah   Are youse going out or something?

Joseph   I think so. We're supposed to be –

Ollie   Of course they're going out. It's pound-a-pint night. Where are youse going?

Colm (*returning with glasses*)   Never you mind, Ollie. You're not coming. (*Setting down two glasses.*) One wee drink and that's it. Me and Joe have a lot to talk about.

Colm *heads back to the kitchen.*

Ollie   Mother-fucker. Are you still at the writing, Joe?

Joseph   Sorry?

Sarah (*to* **Joseph**)   Are you a writer?

Joseph   Yes. Well . . . let's say I had a stab at it. Ended up stabbing it to death. For all the good it did me.

Colm (*returning with more glasses*)   Away o'that, Joe. (*To* **Sarah**.) He's going to be famous. He'd a play put on in London. Didn't you, Joe? (*Distributing glasses.*)

Sarah   Really? What was it called?

Joseph   *Piss Artist.*

Ollie   Sarah Miles drinks her own piss. Did you know that?

Colm   Shut up, Ollie.

Joseph   I find that very hard to swallow.

Ollie   So does she!

General laughter.

Boom Boom!

Joseph *starts to relax.* **Ollie** *lights the joint.* **Colm** *perches on the end of the sofa.*

Joseph *pours drinks for everyone and raises his glass in a toast.*

Well, here's to you, Joe boy. Welcome home.

Joseph   Thank you.

They drink.

Colm (*to* **Ollie** *and* **Sarah**)   I suppose youse will be off now?

Ollie   Eh?

Colm   I suppose youse will be off now?

Ollie   Where to?

Colm   I don't know. You said you were going out.

Sarah   Who did?

Colm   You did.

Sarah   Did I?

Colm   You said you were going out for a drink.

Ollie   Good idea. Come on and we'll go out for a drink.

Colm   Not us. You two.

Sarah   So youse aren't going out?

Ollie   You just said you were.

Joseph   Perhaps we could all go together.

Ollie   Now you're talking.

Sarah   Yeah!

Colm   No. Me and Joe have a lot to talk about.

Ollie   Please yourself.

Colm   So are youse going out or what?

Sarah   Definitely what.

Ollie   Sarah, I know – stare you out.

Ollie *and* **Sarah** *lock into a close-stare competition.*

Colm   Pair of reprobates.

Pause.

I just wanted to say, Joe –

Joseph Yes?

Colm It's good to see you back, boy.

Joseph Thank you.

Colm When did you arrive?

Joseph I've been back for a while.

Colm Where've you been hiding yourself?

Joseph Oh, at home. You know.

Colm With your ma?

Joseph Yes.

Colm How is she?

Joseph Same as always.

Colm Tell her I was asking for her.

Joseph I will.

Colm How long are you staying?

Joseph I don't know yet. I might ... I don't know –
(*Looking at* **Sarah** *and* **Ollie**.) Are they all right?

Colm As long as they're quiet I'm not complaining.

Joseph Mmm ... So, what about you? Are you working?

Colm Yeah.

Joseph Teaching?

Colm Yeah. Key Stage Two.

Joseph What does that mean?

Colm P5s and up, basically.

Joseph So how's it going?

Colm It's great. Great.

Joseph That's good. You've landed on your feet then.

Colm   Yeah, I suppose so. I was lucky to get it. The kids are brilliant though. There was one wee boy today who thought an isoceles triangle was called a sausages triangle.

Joseph *laughs. A pause.*

Joseph   And what about Anna?

Sarah   Moved.

Ollie   No, I never.

Sarah   Yes, you did. You rolled your eyes when he said 'Anna'.

Ollie   I *so* didn't!

Sarah   You *so* did. Do you give up?

Ollie   Fuck it. Let's get really pissed.

Sarah   Yeah, let's get really pissed.

Colm   Well, youse can get pissed on your own. You're not coming with us.

Sarah   Ah lighten up, Col.

Colm   Look – I haven't seen Joe for years.

Ollie   Sure you don't mind us tagging along, do you Joe? I'm sure we've got an awful lot to talk about. (*To* **Sarah**.) I haven't seen him for years either. (*To* **Joseph**.) So where have you been? How've you been keeping?

Joseph   I've been abroad.

Ollie   You've had a sex change?

Joseph   No. I've been on the Continent.

Ollie   Do you have to wear those special pants?

Sarah   Where were you?

Joseph   Mostly France. I moved around a lot.

Sarah   In France?

Joseph   No, not just in France. I spent some time in Poland.

Ollie   Poland.

Joseph   And Italy.

Ollie   You don't say.

Sarah   He does, you know.

Ollie   And tell me this, Joe. Of all the lovely countries you have visited in your travels, which would you say is your favourite?

Joseph   Oh, France.

Ollie   Really?

Joseph   Without a shadow of a doubt.

Ollie   Then what the *fuck* are you doing in Belfast?

Joseph   I –

Ollie   If you don't mind me asking.

Colm   He's here to see *me*, Ollie.

Ollie   Temper temper.

Colm   Look, just drink up and piss off the pair of you.

Sarah   Aw –

Colm   I'm serious.

Joseph   Colm –

Sarah (*to* **Joseph**)   Aw please, mister, let us come with you. We haven't got any friends of our own.

Ollie   Oh yes, please let us come out to play.

Colm (*getting up*)   Come on, Joe, are you right?

Joseph   What about Tim?

Colm   He knows where to find us. He can meet us down there.

Ollie   No, don't leave us.

Sarah   Don't leave us here all alone!

Colm   I've no intention of leaving youse here. Get your coats on and get the fuck out.

Ollie   Oh, marvellous –

Joseph (*getting up*)   Listen, Colm, why don't we all go together?

Sarah   Oh yes sir, thank you sir, thank you, thank you.

Colm   No.

Joseph   Why not? The more the merrier.

Colm   Joe –

Joseph   Really, Colm, let's all go.

Ollie   Yes, let's!

Ollie *and* **Sarah** *jump up to join* **Colm** *and* **Joseph**.

Colm (*to* **Ollie** *and* **Sarah**)   Well, youse better bloody behave yourselves.

Ollie (*to* **Joseph**)   God bless you an' keep you, sir.

Sarah   To be sure.

Ollie   To be sure.

Joseph   My pleasure ... (*To* **Sarah**.) I'm terribly sorry, I don't think I caught your name.

Sarah   You don't have to be terribly sorry. I'm Sarah.

Ollie   *Our* Sarah. Not Sarah Miles. She doesn't drink piss or anything.

Joseph   Quite. Well, I'm Joseph. So, shall we go?

Ollie   Yes, shall we?

Joseph   Are you going to leave the TV on?

Colm   Yeah. Anti-burglar device.

Ollie   Burglars are scared of television. That's a well-known fact.

Colm *returns some glasses to the kitchen.* **Ollie** *helps himself to more wine. Business with coats etc.*

Colm   Are we right?

Tim *enters. Pause*

Tim   It's gonna be a dark night the night, boys and girls.

Blackout.

Music – Intro to 'Tourettes' by Nirvana.

Scene Two

An exact reprise of the end of Scene One. A small skip back in time.

Tim   It's gonna be a dark night the night, boys and girls.

He comes in, seemingly at home, sits on the sofa and flicks at the TV channels with the remote control.

Ollie   Well, Tim.

Tim   Well, smell.

Sarah   How are you, Tim?

Tim   I'm gorgeous. (*Taking the wine bottle and drinking.*) Gorgeous.

Colm   It's about time you showed up. We were about to go.

Ollie   Funny enough, I was looking to talk to you, Tim.

Tim   Later.

Ollie   OK. No problemo.

Colm   Tim –

Ollie   You know our visitor, don't you, Tim?

Sarah   The writer.

Ollie   Piss artist.

Tim *looks up. Pause.*

Tim   Well well, and if I might add, well.

Joseph   Hello, Tim.

Tim (*to* **Colm**)   What's he doing here?

Joseph   Didn't Colm tell you I was home?

Tim   No. No, as a matter of fact he didn't.

Joseph   Well. Here I am.

Tim   Yes. Here, as you so rightly say, you are.

Ollie   One big happy family.

Sarah   It's sweet, isn't it?

Ollie   It's like on *This is your Life* when they bring in somebody's granny from New Zealand.

Sarah   Youse could get on *Richard and Judy*. It's like something off *Richard and Judy*.

Tim (*to* **Colm**)   What's all this in aid of?

Colm   Well, you know, I thought we could all get together and –

Tim   – celebrate –

Colm   – yes –

Tim   – the homecoming.

Colm   Yes.

Tim   Talk over old times. Is that it?

Ollie   *Plus* – it's pound-for-a-pint night.

Sarah   Get pissed for peace!

Pause.

Tim (*turning back to the TV, flicking with the remote control*)   What's on TV tonight?

Colm   Och come on, Tim.

Tim   Shh! It's *Telly Addicts*!

Colm   Well, we're going to the pub.

Tim   Shhh!

Colm   Are you coming?

Tim (*pointing at* **Ollie** *and* **Sarah**)   With those two?

Sarah   Joseph said we could come.

Tim   Bully for you.

Ollie   Us and Joe are big mates, aren't we, Joe?

Pause.

Tim   You know what I hate?

Colm   What?

Tim   Gigs where people wave their lighters in the air.

Colm   Eh?

Tim   All that fucking Phil Collins crap.

Colm   What's that got to do with it?

Tim   It's pound-for-a-pint night. What are youse going to do, wave your lighters in the air?

Colm (*making light*)   We're just going down the pub.

Tim   Away youse go, then.

Pause.

I'll let myself out.

Colm   You can't stay here.

Tim   Why, do you not trust me?

Joseph   Come on, Tim. Just a drink. On me.

Tim   Such generosity.

Joseph   I want to see you, Tim. I want to talk to you.

Tim *ignores this and lights a cigarette.*

Colm   Look, Tim, there's supposed to be a ceasefire on. Can't we have a ceasefire, just for one night?

Tim *raises his lit lighter and waves it in the air.*

Tim   Phil fucking Collins.

Pause.

Colm   Well sod you, then. Come on, Joe.

Joseph   Tim –

Tim   Night night.

Joseph   Well. You know where we'll be.

They leave, **Joseph** *and* **Colm** *tight-lipped,* **Ollie** *and* **Sarah** *full of energy, singing 'What a man, what a man, what a man, what a mighty good man'.*

Tim *is left alone on-stage. He switches off the TV. Sits staring for some time. Then takes out a mobile phone and dials.*

Tim   It's me.
Tim.
All right. Listen. Joseph's back.
I've just seen him. They're away to the pub.
Colm's.
What? I can hardly hear you. What?
No, I'm on the mobile. Fuck away off.
I don't know. He must have just got back.
The usual place.
No listen, stay where you are.
All right, I'll come round.
No, I've some business.
Stay put till then. OK. See you.

He clicks off the phone and pockets it. Lifts the remote control and turns off the television.

Music – 'Supersonic' by Oasis.

Blackout.

Scene Three

Music fades.

A snug in a Belfast pub. The pub is probably busy, but the audience need only see **Colm** *and* **Joseph** *for the moment. They raise their glasses.*

Colm   Right.

Joseph   Cheers.

Colm   *Sláinte.*

They drink. Music down.

Joseph   Do you remember the day at school when you and I had a fight?

Colm   Yeah. Christ.

Joseph   And I was holding you down on the ground, kneeling on you, with my knees on your shoulders –

Colm   Ye big bully ye.

Joseph   And you were screaming –

Colm   Oh, you bastard.

Joseph   And I spat –

Colm   Bastard!

Joseph   And it went right down your throat!

Colm   Christ, I'm going to puke just thinking about it.

Joseph   I've always meant to apologise for that.

Colm   Well, go on then.

Joseph   I'm sorry, Colm.

Colm   About bloody time.

Joseph   I'm sure you forgive me.

Colm   *You* used to pick your nose and eat it.

Joseph   I did *not*!

Colm   You did. Swear to God. In Biology class. You used to pick your nose and eat it.

Joseph   No, I used to pick my nose and *flick* it. I'll grant you that. I used to pick my nose and *flick* it. But I'd rather die than pick my nose and eat it.

Colm   You did though. You were a dirty wee shite.

Joseph   And Tim was just as bad.

Colm   If not worse. And he hasn't changed much either.

Joseph   Oh, I'm sure he has.

Colm   Hang on. Shite.

Ollie *and* **Sarah** *arrive, with as many pints of Guinness as they can carry.*

Ollie   Ulster says Yo!

Sarah *squeezes in with* **Joseph** *and* **Colm**.

Sarah   Did you keep my place warm for me?

Joseph   Absolutely.

Ollie   Hang on one momento, boys and girls. There's more, much much more where that came from.

He disappears back to the bar.

Colm (*to* **Sarah**)   You found him, then.

Sarah   Aye. No getting rid of him.

Joseph   Anyway, talking of Tim –

Sarah   We weren't.

Joseph   Sorry?

Sarah   We weren't talking of Tim.

Colm   *We* were talking of Tim.

Sarah   Oh. Well, don't let me interrupt you.

Joseph . . . Has he been working?

Colm Well . . .

Sarah He's been keeping himself busy.

Colm He's been on telly.

Joseph Really?

Sarah He's on all the time.

Joseph That's great.

Sarah He's in an advert. For dog food.

Colm Cat food.

Sarah Are you sure?

Colm Definite.

Sarah I think it's dog food.

Colm There's a cat in it. Why would there be a cat in a dog food commercial?

Sarah Maybe it's ironic.

Ollie *returns, again carrying as many pints as possible.*

Ollie (*sings*) 'Hold me close, don't let me go . . .'

Colm Fuck me, Ollie, what are you at?

Ollie It's pound-a-pint. And I've twenty pound.

He returns to the bar. The others look at the stacked table.

Colm Christ Jesus.

Joseph I was just going to say –

Sarah Before you were so rudely interrupted –

Joseph Colm, do you remember the night when a certain person, who shall remain nameless –

Colm i.e. Tim.

Joseph – came back to the house pissed out of his mind,

and I think Anna was in the bath, so –

Colm   Oh Christ, yeah.

Joseph   So he went into the kitchen –

Both **Colm** *and* **Joseph** *laughing.*

– and he – oh, God – he shat in the sink!

Sarah   He wha'?

Joseph   He shat in the sink. And he just left it there.

Colm   No, no, if you remember, he tried to get rid of it.

Sarah   How?

Colm   He turned on the hot tap and tried to melt it.

General disgust and hilarity.

Joseph   Do you still see Anna?

Sarah   Oh God, here we go. I need a drink. (*Takes one.*)

Joseph   I'm sorry, I –

Colm   No, don't worry, Joe. I see her from time to time. It's fine.

Joseph   What are you going to do?

Colm   What do you mean?

Joseph   I mean are you going to get a divorce, or what?

Colm   Well, I can't, can I?

Joseph   Well, I don't know, I mean –

Colm   I can't, because of the job.

Joseph   I see.

Colm   I'm going to try and get it annulled. You can do that in some cases.

Joseph   Right.

Pause.

Sarah   Well, you know how to put a downer on an evening, don't you, Joe?

Joseph   I'm sorry.

Colm   Never worry, Joe.

Ollie *returns with the last of the beers, and a packet of crisps dangling from between his teeth. The table is now completely packed.*

Joseph (*briskly, changing the subject*)   All right, Ollie, how much do we owe you?

Ollie   Youse don't owe me anything. These are all for me.

Sarah   Oh, cheers.

Ollie   Cheers.

He raises his glass and begins to drink. Also munches crisps.

Colm   Fuck this for a game of soldiers.

He takes a beer. **Sarah** *and* **Joseph** *follow suit.*

Joseph   It would be a shame to let it go to waste.

They drink. **Ollie** *munches.*

Ollie   So what's the crack?

Joseph   We were just reminiscing about schooldays.

Sarah   Were youse at school together?

Joseph   In the dim and distant past.

Colm   Primary school and then the college.

Joseph   And on to Queen's. But we first met –

Colm (*laughs*)   Oh, Jesus!!

Joseph   We first met during a peeing contest.

Sarah   A what?

Joseph   A peeing contest. You stood in line and competed to see who could pee the highest.

Sarah   Who won?

Joseph   Well, I had a head start.

Colm   No way! You were playing with a handicap.

Laughs.

Ollie   Aye, we used to play that in our school as well. But I never won.

Joseph   Really?

Ollie   Nah. There was this girl at our school was really good at it.

Laughter. They drink.

Ollie   God, I love beer.

Colm   Me too.

Sarah   Me three.

A moment.

Joseph   Me four.

They drink.

Ollie   See me? I'm on the pull tonight.

Joseph (*to* **Sarah**)   You'll have to keep an eye on him, then.

Sarah   Why?

Joseph   Well, to see he doesn't get into any trouble.

Sarah   I don't give a shite.

Ollie   I *am* gonna get into any trouble. I'm gonna get out of my head and pull some bird.

Joseph   . . . I'm terribly sorry, I hope I haven't put my foot in it. I thought you two were –

Sarah   What?

Joseph   Seeing one another.

Ollie   *Seeing one another?*

Sarah   I've never seen him before in my life.

Joseph   I'm sorry. I must have got the wrong end of the stick.

Ollie   Joe – do you like see food?

Joseph   Well, yes. Yes, I do.

Ollie *opens his mouth wide, showing* **Joseph** *the crushed crisps inside it. Chorus of laughter and 'bleughs' subsides after a time.*

Colm   What about you then, Joe?

Ollie   Yeah, how's the old love life?

Joseph   Oh, my God!

Sarah   Are you 'seeing' anyone?

Joseph   No no no. I was. But not now.

Colm   What was her name?

Joseph   Virginie.

Ollie   Virginie?

Joseph   It was in Paris.

Ollie   Oh, Virginia. I knew a Virginia once. They called her Virgin for short – but not for long.

Joseph   You're talking about the woman I like, Ollie.

Ollie   *Terribly* sorry. Listen, just between you and me – did sexual intercourse take place?

Joseph   Just between you and me?

Ollie   No, just between you and her.

Joseph   That's a very personal question.

Ollie   Well, let me put it another way – was she a donor?

Joseph   A what?

Ollie   A donor. Did she give freely?

Sarah   Now, now, Ollie, don't be rude.

Colm   You're getting on my wick, Ollie. Again.

Ollie   What?

Colm   You're getting on my wick.

Ollie   It's a long time since anyone got on your wick, Colm.

Colm   Funny man.

Ollie   How long is it now, Col?

Colm   Shut up.

Ollie   No, seriously. How long is it since you last had a shag?

Colm   You see, Joe, this is the level of humour I have to put up with.

Joseph   The long winter evenings must just fly by.

Ollie   Top comedy action!

Colm   Shut up, Ollie, you're not funny.

Ollie   I'm funnier than you.

Colm   What?

Ollie   I'm funnier than you.

Colm   No, you're not.

Ollie   I fucking am. (*To* **Sarah**.) Aren't I?

Sarah (*deadpan*)   You're hilarious.

Colm   Prove it.

Ollie   What?

Colm   Prove it.

Ollie   Right. Let's have a funny contest.

Sarah   A funny contest?

Ollie   A fucking funny contest.

Ollie *and* **Colm** *roll up their sleeves and adopt kung-fu style positions, ready for the funny contest.*

Joseph   All right, calm down, everyone.

Colm   What do you mean calm down?

Joseph   We shouldn't be fighting. We should be celebrating.

Ollie   What?

Joseph   We should be celebrating.

Ollie   Yes. *What?*

Sarah   Joseph's homecoming.

Joseph   No, the ceasefire. That's the most important thing. Come on, let's have a toast. To peace.

He raises his glass. The others join in with varying degrees of enthusiasm.

Colm   Peace.

Sarah   Cheers.

Ollie   Bollocks.

They drink.

Sarah   So.

Ollie   So.

Colm   So.

Sarah   What's it like to be home, Joseph?

Joseph   It's – strange.

Ollie   Strange.

Joseph   I mean it's familiar and unfamiliar at the same time.

Ollie   Pants.

Sarah   It must be a big change after Paris.

Ollie   Big pile of pants.

Joseph   Well, yes. But it's not just that. It's very different from the way I remember it.

Colm   Well, things have changed.

Joseph   Yes, of course –

Colm   Thanks be to God.

Joseph   The strange thing is, though, a lot of the things I associate with home have gone. Like the helicopters. There aren't so many helicopters. They used to be buzzing round all the time when I was growing up.

Ollie   Yeah. No helicopters. You've never had it so good.

Sarah   Peace in our time.

Joseph   And I've hardly seen any soldiers since I came home. I haven't been stopped or searched. It's bizarre.

Sarah   Therese Bazaar.

Colm   What?

Sarah   Therese Bazaar. Do you remember her?

Ollie   Who was she?

Sarah   She was in *Dollar*.

Joseph   But you know the strangest thing is just the way people talk.

Colm   What do you mean?

Joseph   Well, the accents, for one thing. I'd forgotten the way people talk here.

Colm   You've lost your accent.

Joseph   Do you think so?

Sarah   Yeah, you have, definitely.

Colm   And how would you know?

Sarah   I just do.

Ollie   Bollocks. He hasn't lost his accent. He's just putting on another one. A bloody poncey accent.

Joseph   I'm not putting it on. But I can understand you thinking that.

Ollie   Oh good.

Joseph   Sometimes I become aware of the way I'm speaking and it doesn't sound right at all. Do you know what I mean?

Ollie   Do you mean your balls have dropped?

Joseph   The thing is, I'm really not used to being with English speakers at all. I've been a foreigner for years. The people with whom –

Ollie   With whom?

Joseph   Sorry?

Ollie   You said 'with whom'.

Joseph   Yes.

Pause.

Ollie (*blessing himself*)   'Blessed be the fruit of thy whom.'

Sarah   Amen. Probably.

They drink.

Joseph   Where was I?

Sarah   France.

Colm   You were saying about being a foreigner –

Joseph   Yes. Well, it's just strange being back here where there's really only one language and we all more or less understand each other. It gives you an advantage when you have another language to hide behind. You can't do that here.

Colm   You don't need to do it here.

Joseph   Yeah. Listen, there's a game the ex-pats play in Paris. It's called Language Roulette.

Sarah   How do you play it?

Joseph   Well, the idea is to go into a public place, where there are crowds, like in the métro, and you choose somebody you don't like the look of, and then you – abuse them.

Colm   Abuse them?

Joseph   In English.

Ollie   Not sexually, then.

Joseph   No, it has to be in English. It's called Language Roulette because there's just a chance your victim will be able to understand. And if he does – you get your head kicked in!

Ollie   Excellent! What kind of things do you say?

Joseph   Anything. You can be as nasty as you like.

Ollie   Mother-fucker?

Joseph   No. They'd be sure to understand that. It's in all the films.

Ollie   What about Cock-sucker? Could you say Cock-sucker?

Joseph   Possibly.

Ollie   Wank-stain?

Joseph   I suppose so.

Ollie   Arse-wipe? Fuck-finger? Pish-flaps?

Colm   Shut up, Ollie.

Ollie   What an excellent game! (*Shouts.*) Cock-sucker! Wanker!

Colm (*panicky*)   Shut up, for fuck's sake, you'll get us chucked out!

Joseph   That's not the idea, Ollie.

Sarah   More like Language Suicide than Language Roulette in here.

Joseph   You have to use a particular tone of voice so that the person won't know what kind of thing you're saying. For instance, you could say, (*Close to* **Ollie**, *smiling, charming.*) 'You know you really are extremely ugly.'

Pause. **Ollie** *not sure whether to feel insulted or not.*

Sarah   Did you play this game, Joe?

Joseph   Sometimes. It's just a way of relieving the tension. One girl I knew went into a post office in Paris, and the woman behind the till was being extremely rude and difficult, so this girl said, 'Can I have two stamps – Est-ce que je peux avoir deux timbres – and a pint of your blood please?' And she got away with it.

Sarah   Cool.

Ollie   What an excellent game! I can't wait to go on holiday and try it.

Sarah   What, in Donegal?

Ollie   Donegal my arse. Come on, here's to Language Roulette!

They drink, and as they do, **Tim** *arrives, accompanied by* **Anna**.

Tim   Greetings.

Blackout.

Music: 'How Soon is Now' by the Smiths.

Scene Four

The pub snug, as before – **Ollie**, **Sarah**, **Joseph**, **Colm**. *Exact reprise of the end of Scene Three.*

Tim   Greetings.

Anna   Well, I never did.

Tim   Did you not?

Anna   Well, just the once.

Colm   Anna, what the fuck?

Anna   What the fuck what?

Colm (*standing*)   What are you at, Tim?

Anna   He told me Joseph was back.

Tim   Joseph! Me old mate, me old mucker! How the *devil* are you?

Colm (*to* **Tim**)   Is this some kind of joke?

Tim   I just fancied a night out with old friends, that's all. A stroll down memory lane. You know how it is. (*He sits.*) Have a seat, Anna.

Anna *and* **Colm** *remain standing.*

Colm   Look. I don't want any hassle.

Anna   Neither do I. I just came out for a drink. Really.

Tim   What are you scared of?

Colm   I'm not scared.

Tim   Well, sit down then.

Pause.

Will youse sit down the pair of youse.

Anna   Please, Colm.

A moment, then **Colm** *sits. Then* **Anna**. *Now, in the snug, round from left to right, are* **Tim, Ollie, Sarah, Joseph, Colm** *and* **Anna**.

Tim   Isn't this nice?

Ollie   Help yourselves to drinks there.

Tim   That's very kind of you. I don't mind if I do. (*Takes a pint.*) Anna?

Anna   No, thank you.

Joseph   Would you like me to get you something from the bar?

Anna   Just a Club Orange thanks, Joseph.

Joseph   Ice?

Anna   Please.

Joseph *heads to the bar. All drink, except* **Anna**.

Ollie (*quietly, hinting*)   Tim –

Tim (*loud*)   Yes, Ollie. What can I do for you?

Ollie   Any luck?

Tim   Excuse me?

Ollie   Any luck?

Tim   What exactly do you mean?

Ollie   You know what I mean.

Tim   No, I'm sorry. I'm afraid I don't. Come on, Ollie, spell it out.

Ollie   It's private.

Tim   No secrets among friends, Ollie.

Ollie   Forget it.

Tim   If you have something to say –

Ollie   Just forget it.

Tim   Consider it forgotten.

Joseph *returns with a Club Orange for* **Anna**. *They all drink.*

Well, now that we're all together at last – why don't we play a wee game?

Colm   What are you on about now?

Tim   Why don't we all play a game?

Anna (*deliberately cheery*)   Good idea. Let's play a game.

Tim   What do you think, Joseph?

Sarah   . . . What kind of game?

Tim   A fun game. A top-fun game. (*To* **Ollie** *and* **Sarah**.) Are youse on, you two?

Sarah   I'm always game for a game. What'll we play? Tig?

Ollie   We could play Celebrity Bowl.

Tim   No, we're going to play a special game.

Sarah   Celebrity Bowl is a special game.

Tim   We're not playing Celebrity Bowl.

Sarah   Why not?

Tim   You need a bowl to play Celebrity Bowl. We don't have a bowl.

Sarah   There's an ashtray.

Tim   Well, we're not playing Celebrity Ashtray, right?

Anna   Well, what will we play then?

Tim   A top-fun game. OK?

He produces pen and paper for scoring.

Joseph   What's it called?

Tim   The rules are as follows. You have to work out the rules as it goes along. All right, ready?

Colm   What?

Anna   Go on then . . .

Tim   Right. I'll go first. Now – I'm drinking Guinness.

Colm   Hold on a minute –

Tim   Wait your turn, Colm.
Your go, Ollie.

Ollie   What?

Tim   I'm drinking Guinness.
Now it's your go.

Ollie   I'm drinking Guinness too.

Tim   Correct. Sarah?

The timing of a quiz show. **Tim** *keeping score.*

Sarah   I don't understand.

Tim   Yes, I think that's OK. Now Joseph.

Joseph   What's going on?

Tim   No, I'm sorry. I'm afraid I can't accept that. Try again.

Anna   Give him a clue.

Joseph   No, no, just leave me out. Go on to Colm.

Tim   Do you not want to play?

Joseph   Well, I'd play if I could understand the rules.

Tim   You have to work out the rules as it goes along. Those *are* the rules. Go on.

Joseph   Erm . . . I'm drinking Guinness as well, I suppose.

Tim   Correct. Well done. Colm?

Pause. **Colm** *concentrating.*

I'm going to have to hurry you.

Colm   Give us a chance.

Tim   No, sorry, too late. *Nul points* for Colm there. Have to do better than that. Anna.

Anna   Not Club Orange, obviously . . . I'm drinking Guinness.

Tim   Correct. Now it's my turn again. Right.
I'm wearing black jeans. (*Gesture for* **Ollie** *to take his go.*)

Ollie   No, you're not. You're wearing red jeans; I'm wearing black jeans.

Tim   No, you're not.

Ollie (*looking down*)   I am.

Tim   No, you're not. Sorry. Sarah?

Sarah   Am I wearing jeans?

Tim   You tell me.

Sarah   Eh . . . No, I'm not wearing jeans.

Tim   Correct. Joseph.

Joseph   I'm afraid I'm completely lost.

Tim   Mmm. Yes, I think I can accept that. Now, Colm – give it your all.

Colm   Is this the jeans question?

Tim   No clues.

Pause.

Colm   I'm –

Tim   Out of time! Oh dear. Not your night, Colm. Now, Anna.

She has worked out the rules – each person speaks about whoever is sitting to the left of them.

Anna   I'm an awful mouth. (*i.e.* **Tim***'s an awful mouth.*)

Tim   Oho! Good answer. Me again. Now. I still don't know what's going on.

Ollie   Do you not?

Tim   No.

Ollie   Me neither.

Tim   Correct. Sarah.

Sarah   What?

Tim   Your go.

Sarah   Oh. Em. Pass.

Tim   You can't pass.

Sarah   This is a stupid game.

Tim   Mmm. Yes, I think that's just about acceptable.

Joseph   Well, I second that.

Tim   Do you?

Joseph   Yes. This is a stupid game.

Tim   No repetition, deviation or hesitation.

Joseph   Erm . . .

Tim   Hesitation! Now, Colm – you're playing catch-up.

Colm   I wish you'd *shut* up.

Tim   Correct! Well done! At last!

Ollie   Go on, Colm!

Tim   Now. Anna.

Anna   I think I'm God's gift.

Tim   She's on unbeatable form tonight, ladies and gentlemen! Now, let's see. My go.
I am a good Catholic. I go to Mass every Sunday.

Ollie   I'm a Catholic but I don't go to Mass.

Tim   No. Wrong.

Ollie   Aw, for fuck's sake, what was wrong with that?

Tim   You're not a Catholic.

Ollie   What am I then?

Tim   Church of Ireland, as far as I know.

Ollie   Fuck me.

Tim   Sarah?

Sarah   I'm not sure what I am.

Tim   Yes, I think I can accept that.

Sarah   Oh good.

Tim   Joseph.

Joseph   I am a collapsed Catholic.

Tim   No. Wrong. You're anything but. What about you, Colm?

Colm   What am I supposed to say?

Tim   The truth.

Colm   I'm a Catholic. I teach in a Catholic school.

Tim   Wrong.

Colm   Aw, bollocks.

Anna   I'm a liar for a living.

Tim   Interesting. Yes. Another point for Anna there.

Anna   Thank you.

Tim   Now, let's have a quick break to check the scores on the doors. Let me see now. On *one* point we have – Mr Colm Lavery. Some catching up to do there, Colm. Still, it's early days yet. On two points we have Mr Ollie Kearns and Mr Joseph Hunter – but, equal at the moment, in the lead, on three points apiece, I give you – Sarah Kidd and Anna Lavery! A round of applause, please.

Minor applause.

Sarah   What about you?

Tim   I don't count. I'm the chairman. I know the rules. Talking of which – have any of youse worked out the rules yet?

Joseph   No.

Ollie   Haven't a baldy.

Tim   I've a feeling Mrs Lavery knows the rules. Would I be right, Mrs Lavery?

Anna   Just Anna.

Tim   Oh, I do apologise. And what about Mr Lavery?

Colm   Mr Lavery needs a slash.

He rises, inches out past **Anna**, *and heads off for the Gents.*

Anna   Are you coming back?

No reply.

Tim   OK. Round Five, and things are really hotting up. Right – me again.

Calculated pause for effect.

I desperately want to shag Sarah.

Ollie   Eh?

Sarah   Fuck off and die, you dirty bastard!

Ollie   What did you say?

Tim   I *desperately* want to shag Sarah.

Shocked pause.

Tim   Your go, Ollie.

Ollie   Fucking hell. I . . . I'm on the pull tonight.

Tim   Mmmm. Possibly. I'm not sure. Half a point. What about you, Sarah?

Sarah   What? (*Very pissed off.*)

Tim   It's your go.

Sarah   I think this is sick.

Tim   Yes, I think I'll give you that. Joseph?

Joseph   I'm not playing any more.

Tim   Correct! Brilliant answer. Round of applause, please.

Tim *alone applauds.*

Well done, Joseph. You're playing a blinder. Now – Anna.

Pause.

Anna   I'd like to punch Joseph in the face.

Joseph   What?

Tim   Mmm. Interesting. Yes, I think I'll let you have that one.

Anna   Thank you.

Sarah (*sudden realisation*)   Oh, I get it!

Tim   Really?

Sarah   I think so.

Tim   OK. Don't say anything. Keep it to yourself.

Colm *returns, pauses, and moves back into his seat.*

Welcome back, Mr Lavery.

Colm   Did I miss anything exciting?

Tim   You missed your go. You can take it now. You're still on one point.

Colm   I'm going to get pissed.

Tim   Correct.

Anna   No, that's not correct.

Tim   Really? You do surprise me.

Anna   It's your turn again.

Tim   So it is. Yes, now we're moving on to the Supermatch Game. (*Sings, along with* **Ollie** *and* **Sarah**.)
   'Supermatch Game
   Supermatch Game
   Supermatch Game
   Supermatch Game!'
Now, let me see . . .
I desperately want to shag Sarah –

Colm   Eh?

Tim   – but failing that, as I most certainly will, I'm going to buy some drugs and get wasted.

Sarah   Correct. The second part.

Ollie (*to* **Tim**)   Are you having a go at me?

Tim   As if.

Sarah (*to* **Ollie**)   It's your turn.

Ollie   I think Tim's a wanker.

Sarah   Correct.

Tim   Really? That's most disappointing. I thought we were the best of friends.

Sarah   Well. There you are. You live and learn.

Tim   Ollie –

Ollie   What?

Tim   I've got a present for you.

Ollie   Have you?

Sarah   Tim's spoiling my evening.

Tim (*sarcasm*)   Care.

Sarah   No, that was my go. Tim's spoiling my evening.

Tim   Oh, I see. Yes, yes, correct. Definitely. Joseph?

Joseph (*drily*)   Enough of this madcap tomfoolery.

Tim   Chickening out, are we?

Ollie   Tim –

Tim   Shut up –

Joseph   Tim –

Tim   Joseph –

Joseph   What's the point of this game?

Tim   Well, fuck me in the mouth if I know.

Joseph   Do you still swallow?

Tim   Was that your go?

Joseph   No.

Tim   Are you playing or not?

Joseph   . . . Not.

Tim   So Joseph's the loser then, everyone. Well, you've been a lovely contestant, you really have, and nobody leaves empty handed so –

Joseph   *Tu commences vraiment à m'énerver là. Pauvre con.*

Tim   What?

Joseph   *Espèce de connard. On s'en fout de tes jeux à la con.*

Tim   Mind your language.

Joseph   If you want to play games, Tim –

Tim   Yes?

Joseph   Let's play a real game.

Tim   . . . Such as?

Joseph   It's all very well talking about the person sitting next to you –

Tim   Oh, well done. I didn't think you'd worked it out.

Joseph   But it's all a bit easy, isn't it?

Tim   Well, what would you suggest?

Joseph   Why don't we up the stakes a little.

Pause.

Anna   Truth or Dare.

Colm   Come off it.

Tim   Bingo!

Ollie   No fucking way.

Joseph   What do you think, Sarah?

Sarah   . . . It might be a laugh. True, Dare, Love, Kiss, Promise or Command!

Ollie   Some laugh.

Tim   Why, have you got something to hide, Ollie?

Ollie   (*defensive*)   No.

Tim   Of course you haven't. We can all see straight through you.

Ollie   That's what you think. Bastard.

Tim   Are we all agreed then? The truth, the whole truth and nothing but the truth?

Colm (*lightly*)   This is daft.

Anna   We played it before. In the house.

Colm   That was years ago.

Tim   And, as the man says, we've all passed a lot of water under the bridge since then.

Anna   Truth or Dare.

Joseph   But anything we say – whatever we say – stays between us. Strictly private. All right?

Anna   Right. Colm?

Colm   Go on then.

Tim   Good man, Colm. All right, Ollie?

Ollie   Aye . . . all right.

Tim   Good man, yer da! Now. Ready?

Joseph   Ready.

Tim   Let's start with an easy one. Ollie –

Ollie   What?

Tim   On a scale of one to ten – how heterosexual are you?

Ollie   Eh?

Tim   On a scale of one to ten – how heterosexual are you? Remember, the clue's in the question.

Ollie   Ten!

Groans and protests – 'Arse!' 'Bollocks!'

I am! Ten!

Joseph   The whole truth and nothing but the truth?

Ollie   Swear to God.

Anna   We'll take your word for it.

Ollie   I am!

Tim   We believe you. Sarah – same question. On a scale of one to ten, how heterosexual are you?

Sarah   It's hard to say.

Tim   Approximately.

Sarah   I don't know.

A moment, then the four men lean in intently.

Tim   Well, let's see. Have you ever actually had a lesbian affair?

Sarah   It's none of your business.

Tim   Now I could disqualify you for taking that attitude.

Sarah   Go ahead then.

Tim   Well, I'll let you off with a public warning this time.

Ollie   What? You're letting her off just like that?

Tim   What?

Ollie   You're just letting her off? We haven't finished the lesbian question.

Sarah   Yes, we have.

Ollie   Oh no. I think we should go into this in some detail.

Sarah   My lips are sealed.

Laughter and moans.

Tim   Joseph – same question. On a scale of one to ten.

Joseph   About . . . seven-ish.

Tim   Seven-ish.

Joseph   Yes. What about you?

Sarah   Yeah, come on. What about you?

Tim   Eight-ish.

Joseph   I believe that's what's known as one-upmanship.

Tim   Colm – a different question for you. Now, if you had to choose, to which member of the cast of *Dad's Army* would you give a blow-job?

Laughter.

Colm   Could you repeat the question, please?

Tim   Certainly. If you absolutely *had* to, to which member of *Dad's Army* would you give oral pleasure?

Colm   None of them.

Tim   If you absolutely had to. Which would it be? Captain Mainwaring? You look like an Arthur Lowe man to me.

Colm   They're all dead anyway.

Tim   Well, if they weren't dead. Let's take that as read. So who is it to be? John le Mesurier?

Colm   *(after some consideration)*   No.

Ollie   What did you call the Scottish one? What about him?

Sarah   How about Clive Dunn?

Colm   Pike!

Joseph   Who?

Colm   Pike.

Tim   Stupid boy ... OK. Next question – Anna –

Anna   How come you're asking all the questions?

Ollie   Yeah, give us a chance.

Tim   Be my guest. Ask away.

Ollie   Do you really want to shag Sarah?

Sarah (*mocking*)   Ugh, Ollie.

Ollie   What?

Tim   The answer is no. Next question.

Joseph   What are you thinking?

Tim   Sorry?

Joseph   What are you thinking, exactly now, this minute?

Pause.

Tim   I'm thinking about the passage of time. I'm thinking about the future passing through the tight sphincter of the present and out into the past.

Joseph   Charmingly put.

Tim   I have a way with words.

Sarah   Right. I have a question.

Tim (*sharply*)   No, it's my turn.
Colm – who's your favourite person here?

Pause.

Colm   Joe.

Tim   Really?

Colm   Yes.

Tim   Why?

Colm   Because I trust him.

Tim   But you didn't always trust him, did you?

Colm   Yes.

Tim   I don't think you're telling the truth, Colm.

Colm   I am. I never trusted you.

Tim   So who's your least favourite person here? That would be me, would it?

Colm   No. I don't have a least favourite person.

Tim   How sweet.

Colm   It's true.

Sarah (*piss-taking*)   Come off it. You don't like Ollie, do you?

Colm   Yes, I do.

Ollie   Yes, he does.

Anna   What about me?

Colm   What *about* you?

Anna   What do you think of me?

Colm   I don't think of you.

Anna   Don't you?

Colm   Och, leave me alone.

Anna   Do you want me to leave you alone, Colm? Do you?

Ollie   I thought this was supposed to be Truth or Dare.

Anna   Shut up, Ollie.

Ollie   Why aren't youse doing any dares? It's no good telling the truth if there arn't any dares.

Anna   Ollie, we're trying to talk seriously here.

Tim   No, be fair, Anna. Ollie does have a point there. If we're playing Truth or Dare there do have to be dares.

Colm   Like what?

Tim   Well, that depends.

Sarah   Either we decide on one dare and everybody has to do it if they don't tell the truth --

Ollie   -- the whole truth and nothing but the truth --

Sarah   -- or we have individual dares.

Ollie   Yes, individual dares.

Sarah   When we played this game in halls, right, the dare for everyone was to take off their clothes and stand starkers in the lift, and you had to go up and down opening the lift doors at every floor.

Joseph   Did anyone do it?

Sarah   No. Everybody told the truth.

Tim   I think individual dares is the order of the day. Don't you agree, Joseph?

Joseph   I don't know. I've never played this game before.

Sarah   Have you not?

Ollie   It was your bloody idea.

Anna   You have played it before. We used to play it all the time.

Joseph   I don't remember.

Tim   Right. Let's start all over again. Ollie – Truth or Dare?

Ollie   Dare.

Tim   I dare you to tell us the truth about you and Sarah.

Ollie   Go away and shite.

Sarah   What do you mean the truth about him and Sarah? There is no truth about him and Sarah. Go on, you give him a real dare.

Tim   That was a real dare.

Sarah   No, it wasn't. A dare's when you have to *do* something. Ollie – Truth or Dare?

Ollie   (*quite drunk now*)   Dare!

Sarah   I dare you to kiss – Colm!

Colm   No way!

Sarah   On the lips!

Ollie   No no no – truth – truth – I meant truth.

Tim   You can't change your mind.

Ollie   Ah, that's not fair. Youse are making it up as you go along.

Tim   Well, that's life, isn't it? That's what I'll have on my gravestone. 'Here lies Tim Hamill. He made it up as he went along.'

Colm   No. 'Here lies Tim Hamill, and lies and lies.'

Sarah   A big wet kiss!

Anna   That's not the way you play the game. You have to give him a choice.

Ollie   Thank you, Anna. Youse have to give me a choice.

Tim   OK. Either you tell us the truth about you and Sarah –

Sarah   Will you leave off, will you.

Tim   Tell us how you really feel about Sarah – is it true you're gagging for it?

Sarah   Fucking hell.

Tim   Or else you have to kiss Colm.

Ollie (*standing*)   Come here and give us a wee kiss, Colm.

He moves out past **Tim**.

Just a wee kiss.

Colm   Away to fuck.

Ollie   Aw come on, Colm –

Ollie *lumbers over to* **Colm**.

Anna   Sit down, you big eejit, you'll get us thrown out.

Ollie   Not till I've had a wee kiss.

Lurches forward on to **Colm**. *Giggling and struggling.* **Ollie** *manages to kiss* **Colm**.

Colm   Christ! Jesus Christ!

Ollie   Thank you, Colm.

Ollie *moves back to his seat. General hilarity.*

Sarah   How was it for you?

Ollie   He threw the tongue in.

Colm   Fuck off!

Tim (*to* **Ollie**)   I thought you were supposed to be ten-out-of-ten heterosexual?

Ollie   I have my moments.

Colm (*laughing too*)   God, that was disgusting. My whole life flashed by in front of me.

Tim   Now, Anna. I dare *you* to kiss Colm.

All the laughter silenced.

Anna   Funny man.

Tim   Not even a wee smacker for old time's sake?

Anna   Shut it.

Sarah (*to* **Joseph**)   You've gone very quiet all of a sudden.

Joseph   Have I? I'm sorry.

Sarah   Truth or Dare.

Joseph   Oh, my God. Truth.

Sarah (*great concentration*)   How exactly do you feel – just now this minute?

Joseph   I'm scared stiff.

Sarah   Stiff?

Joseph   Yeah.

Sarah   Stare you out.

Joseph   What?

Sarah   Stare you out.

Sarah *stares into* **Joseph**'s *face. Face close.* **Ollie** *increasingly uneasy.*

Tim   Right. Moving swiftly on. Anna – Truth or Dare?

Anna   What are my options?

Tim   What?

Anna   You have to give me a choice – a question, or a dare. Then I choose.

Tim   OK. Either – tell us why you're not drinking –

Anna   Yes –

Tim   Or – I dare you – to start drinking.

Anna   The former.

Tim   Which one was that?

Anna   The truth.

Tim   Why are you not drinking?

Anna   Yes.

Tim   Right – why are you not drinking?

Anna   Because I want to keep a clear head.

Tim   Simple as that?

Anna   Simple as what?

Tim   As that.

Anna   As what?

Tim   You want to keep a clear head.

Anna   Yes.

Ollie (*to* **Sarah** *and* **Joseph**)   Hey, hey, hey. Cut it out, you two.

Sarah   What?

Ollie   It's just getting good here.

Tim   Would it be fair to say, Anna, that you haven't always kept a clear head?

Anna   I suppose so.

Tim   Particularly recently?

Colm   What do you mean?

Tim   Of late.

Colm   I know what recently means.

Tim   Then why do you ask?

Colm   What the fuck are you on about?

Anna   He's saying I've been drinking too much lately.

Colm   Have you?

Anna   Yes.

Colm   Since when?

Ollie   Talking of drinking – I want something different to drink.

Sarah   You've no money left.

Ollie   I'll go to the cash till.

Joseph   No no no – these are on me. (*Standing.*) I insist. (*Inching his way out.*) What will you have, Tim?

Tim   That's very civil of you, Joseph.

Joseph   My pleasure.

Tim   Would anybody care to join me in a tequila?

Ollie (*singing and dancing*)   Tequila!

Sarah (*joining in*)   Tequila!

Tim   A round of tequilas then. Colm?

Colm   I don't know. I've never had it before.

Tim   Oh, you poor innocent child. You'll love it. Anna?

Anna   *No.*

Tim   Tequilas all round then, Joseph.

Anna   Not for me.

Joseph   No problem.

Joseph *goes off to the bar.*

Sarah (*getting up*)   I'll go and give him a hand.

Ollie   Eh?

Sarah   He can't carry them all on his own. I'll go and give him a hand.

Ollie (*standing*)   No no. (*Mock American accent.*) You just sit your pretty little ass down there and I'll help him. (*To the others.*) I'll be back-ack-ack-ack.

He follows **Joseph** *off.* **Sarah** *slumps back into her place.*

Tim   Wouldn't it be great if it was like this all the time?

Colm   No, it would be shit.

Tim   Joseph's looking well.

Colm   You really are a right shit-stirrer, aren't you, Tim?

Tim   I am, yes.

Sarah (*to* **Tim**)   What have you got against him?

Tim   Are we still playing Truth or Dare?

Sarah   Yes.

Tim   Then I'll take a dare.

Sarah   I dare you to tell us the truth.

Tim   No, that's my line. And you say, 'A dare's when you do something.'

Sarah   No really, tell us.

Tim   . . . Ask them. (**Anna** *and* **Colm**.)

Sarah   What's going on with you lot?

Colm   Never you mind.

Sarah   I think he's nice.

Anna   He is nice.

Colm   What do you mean?

Anna   What do you mean what do I mean? I mean he's nice.

Tim   Anna's always had a soft spot for Joseph, haven't you, Anna?

Sarah   Why did he go away?

Anna   He had to.

Sarah   Why did he have to?

Anna   They made him go away.

Colm   What are you on about? We made him go away?

Tim   I think your memory's playing tricks on you, Mrs Lavery. Must be the demon drink.

Anna   It's the truth. Youse made him go away.

Colm   That's bollocks and you know it. He left because he wanted to.

Tim   He ran away.

Sarah   But why?

Joseph and **Ollie** *return with the drinks, plus lemon and salt.*

Joseph   Here we are.

Tim   Good man, Ollie. Fire them down there.

They distribute drinks and sit in.

Sarah (*to* **Joseph**)   We were just talking about you.

Joseph   Oh, dear.

Sarah   Yeah, we were talking about why you left.

Joseph   Why I left?

Sarah   Why you went away.

Joseph   I see.

Colm   Still, that's all over and done with now, isn't it. Now you're back.

Ollie   From outer space. Here, have a lemon. (*Distributes them.*)

Joseph   It was a long time ago. I'm sure we've all changed a lot since those days. I'm not the same person at all.

Anna   Really?

Tim   Are we ready?

Sarah   Salt? (*Distributes it.*)

Tim   Come on, Colm. Wake up.

Colm   What do you do? Do you put the salt around the rim?

Ollie   Sounds painful.

All laugh, except **Anna**.

Tim   You put the salt on your hand. So it's salt, tequila, lemon. (*Brief mimed demonstration.*)

Anna   Do you remember the night before you went away, Joe?

Joseph   The last night. Yes.

Anna   You and I went back to the house. And Colm was there.

Colm   I don't remember.

Anna (*to* **Colm**)   You were in the kitchen. You were cooking. You don't remember that?

Colm   No.

Anna   You were cooking as we came in. An omelette. You were mixing the eggs in a metal bowl. And you were kind of giggling. And when you saw us, you started – spitting, into the bowl. You went on mixing the eggs, and spitting into them. You don't remember that?

Silence.

Joseph   I was just saying that I have changed. I have changed completely. I mean, let's not forget Heraclitus –

Ollie   How could we forget Heraclitus.

Joseph   'You can't step into the same river twice.' The principle of flux.

Tim   For flux sake give over.

Ollie   Yeah, come on. Shut up and drink up. Down in one, all right? Ready?

Tim   Are you sure you don't want one, Anna? Go on, you can have mine.

Anna   No.

Tim   Go on. I dare you.

A moment, then **Anna** *takes the drink.*

Music: 'Le Bruit du Frigo' by Mano Negro.

Ollie   One – two – three –

They drink.

Music loud: 'Letter to the Censors' by Mano Negro.

Blackout immediately.

Interval.

Scene Five

Everyone in the same positions as before, still in the pub snug. So, from left to right again – **Tim**, **Ollie**, **Sarah**, **Joseph**, **Colm** *and* **Anna**.

Tim (*to* **Anna**)   Go on, I dare you.

A moment, then **Anna** *takes the drink.*

Music (again): 'Le Bruit du Frigo' by Mano Negro.

Ollie   One – two – three –

The drinks downed in one, followed by salt and lemon and the usual spluttering.

Then, as they recover, the music draws down.

Tim   So, Colm – give us your considered opinion. What do you think of tequila?

Colm   Not bad now. Not bad.

Ollie   Not bad? It's, like, excellent.

Joseph   It's *like* excellent?

Ollie   What?

Joseph   You said it's *like* excellent.

Ollie   Yeah.

Joseph   So it's not *actually* excellent. It's just *like* excellent. In your view.

Tim (*to* **Ollie**)   It's just *similar* to excellent. Is that it?

Ollie   Are youse taking the piss?

Tim   Like, yeah.

Joseph   *Like* yeah?

Tim   Yeah.

Anna   Now, now, boys, don't be picking on wee Ollie.

Sarah   What about the game?

Colm   What *about* the game?

Sarah   Where were we?

Ollie   It was your turn.

Sarah   Was it bollocks.

Ollie   It was. (*To the others.*) Wasn't it?

Tim   No, no, Ollie. It's you next. I went last. Now it's your go.

Ollie   Go on, then.

Tim   OK. Ollie, in your view, which is the king of ice lollies – the Joker or the Frostie?

Ollie   Tricky one.

Sarah   That's a stupid question.

Tim   Well, I'm not asking you.

Ollie   I'd have to say the Joker, Tim.

Tim   Why's that?

Ollie   Because of the orangey bit. The Joker has all the advantages of the Frostie, plus an orangey bit.

Tim   Good point.

General murmurs of agreement.

Anna   Now it's Sarah. Ready?

Sarah   Yeah. Ask me a sensible question. I'm getting into this.

Anna   Who would you say is the most selfish person here?

Sarah   The most *selfish*?

Anna   The most selfish person around the table.

Sarah   I don't know . . .

Anna   Take your time.

Sarah   Ollie's very selfish sometimes.

Ollie   What? I bought you all those drinks. I bought youse all drinks.

Sarah   That's not the same thing.

Ollie   Well, what is it then?

Joseph   I think Ollie's been very generous.

Ollie   Thank you, Joseph.

Sarah   Generous with his money, aye.

Ollie   What's that supposed to mean?

Sarah   It's not supposed to mean anything.

Anna   What about Joseph? Do you think he's selfish?

Sarah   . . . I don't know. I'm only after meeting him, like. I don't *think* he's selfish. And Colm's definitely not selfish. He's always cool about me hanging about the house and all.

Ollie   Not the night, he wasn't. He was going to kick us out. And I bloody well live there.

Colm (*ominously*)   Not for much longer.

Ollie   What?

Colm   Your days are numbered, mate.

Ollie (*worried*)   Aw, Colm . . .

Pause. **Colm** *glares at* **Ollie**, *who pales.*

Tim (*shouts*)   Fished in!

Colm *erupts in laughter and a chorus of 'wanker's.* **Ollie**, *relieved, giggles into his drink.*

Ollie   Bastard.

Tim   What about Anna, then, Sarah? Do you think she's selfish?

Sarah   . . . Well . . .

Anna   Well what?

Ollie   I think she is.

Tim   Why?

Ollie   She was selfish to leave Colm.

Anna   What?

Sarah   I can speak for myself, Ollie. I do have a tongue in my head.

Ollie (*to* **Anna**)   You should've seen him after you left.

Tim   Here we see Ollie's unexpected caring side.

Ollie   Well it's true, though. He was in a right state. (*To* **Sarah**.) And then I moved in.

Tim   That must have cheered him up no end.

Colm   Look, will youse shut up about that. It doesn't matter.

Ollie   She never even called him or anything.

Tim   Luckily he had good friends like you to see him through.

Anna (*to* **Ollie** *and* **Sarah**)   Youse don't know what you're on about.

Sarah   I only know what I heard.

Anna   And what did you hear?

Sarah   Look, it's none of my business, is it?

Anna   No.

Sarah   Then sort it out among yourselves. You don't need us here.

Colm   Exactly. We're not going to talk about this here in public.

Tim   Yes, you bloody are. We're all going to talk about it here – in public. In the public arena. In the public house. Best place for it. Don't you think so, Joseph?

Joseph   Whatever you say, Tim.

Tim   I mean, let's face it, we're not going to go to confession, are we? Well, apart from Colm. And maybe Ollie.

Ollie   Wise up. Confession.

Tim   So let's have it out here and now.

Colm   Have what out?

Tim   *It*! Have *it* out!

Anna   Tim, I warned you.

Tim   Well, that's why you came here, isn't it? To talk things out? It was your idea. So go on – say what you have to say.

Anna   I don't *have* to say anything.

Tim   Yes, you do. You know you do.

Anna   I'll say what I choose to say.

Tim   Well, go on then.

Ollie *raises his hand.*

Tim   What?

Ollie   It's not her turn.

Tim   What?

Ollie   It's not her turn. It's Joe's turn – after Sarah. Is yours finished, Sarah?

Sarah   Yes, thank you.

Ollie   You're welcome.

Tim   Jesus fuck.

Anna (*smiling*)   You have to play by the rules, Timothy.

Ollie   Right, so it's Joe's turn now. Anybody got a question for Joe?

Sarah   I have a question.

Ollie   Go on then.

Sarah (*to* **Joseph**)   Why did you go away?

Joseph   . . . I was anxious to leave.

Tim   I bet you were fucking anxious about coming back.

Joseph   Yes, I was.

Anna   Then why did you come back?

Joseph   I was – driven.

Ollie   Did you not take the plane?

Joseph   I came back to see my friends. To talk to my friends.

Tim   So have you found any of them yet?

Colm   We were all good friends.

Tim   Aren't you forgetting something, Colm?

Joseph   Tim – do you remember the time we hired a car and we all drove down south?

Tim   No.

Joseph   We went to Galway. You don't remember that?

Tim   No.

Anna   Come on, Tim.

Colm (*to* **Tim** *and* **Joseph**)   Mind the night youse two sang 'Hong Kong Phooey' in the pub and the people started giving youse money?

Joseph   We were so drunk! Don't you remember? (*Sings.*)
  'Hong Kong Phooey –
  Number one super guy – '

Tim (*coldly*)   You've lost me.

Colm (*sings*)
  'Hong Kong Phooey – '

Anna (*sings*)
  'Quicker than the human eye – '

Ollie (*sings*)
   'He's got style
   a movie smile
   and a car that just don't stop
   when the going gets rough
   he's super tough
   with a Hong Kong Phooey chop!'

With the last time, he playfully aims a karate chop at **Tim**. **Tim**
responds with a quick hard punch; no joke.

Tim   Fuck off.

Ollie   That hurt!

Tim (*standing*)   I need a drink.

He moves out towards the bar.

Sarah   Get us one, Tim.

Ollie   I was only messing, Tim.

Tim   Aye, right.

He goes off.

Ollie   He's a touchy bastard.

Sarah (*to* **Joseph**)   You still haven't answered my question.

Joseph   What question was that, exactly?

Sarah   Why you went away.

Joseph   Oh, who cares.

Colm   Tim and Joe had a bit of a run-in. Years ago.

Anna   Just Tim and Joe?

Colm (*edgy at this*)   No – we all did. It was stupid.

Anna   It was stupid? Jesus, Colm –

Joseph   It was my fault.

Sarah (*to* **Joseph**)   Why?

Joseph   I let the side down, I'm afraid.

Colm (*lightly, laughing it off*)   What are you on about? Let the side down.

Tim *returns, with some drinks. Tequila again, and lemonade. Ready for slammers.*

Tim   Here. (*Drinks for* **Colm** *and* **Anna**.)

Colm   Cheers.

Tim (*to* **Joseph**)   Yours is coming.

Joseph   Oh, thank you.

Tim *heads back to the bar.*

Colm   Are you still into your music, Joe?

Joseph   Yes, very much so.

Colm   Indie. Jingly jangly guitar pop.

Joseph   Not necessarily.

Colm   That's what you used to listen to.

Anna   Constantly. You used to torture us with it.

Joseph   I thought you liked it.

Colm   You were taken in by the Soup Dragons.

Joseph   I was not!

Colm   You were. You thought they were class.

Joseph   Let ye who doesn't have a dodgy record in your collection cast the first stone.

Anna   Do I really have to mention the word 'Falco'?

Joseph   Oh Jesus! Falco!

Ollie   Jesus Falco? Didn't he play for Brazil?

Joseph   'Rock Me Amadeus'!

Colm   No, no, it wasn't me!

Anna   You bought it.

Colm   No, it wasn't me. It was my evil twin.

Joseph   I like all sorts of stuff.

Anna   You don't still like Morrissey, do you?

Joseph   No. He's gone to the dogs now.

Anna   Yeah. He's shit.

Ollie   He was always shit.

Sarah   Quit changing the subject. If youse were all such big mates –

Anna   We were.

Ollie   I bet youse were.

Colm   What?

Ollie   I bet youse were all good friends.

Joseph   What do you mean by that?

Ollie   I'm just sayin'.

Anna   What the fuck's it got to do with you?

Ollie   Fucking bike.

Colm   What did you say?

Ollie   Fucking bike.

Joseph   Meaning?

Anna   Meaning me?

Sarah   Ollie –

Colm   Ollie, that's out of order. That's fucking out of order.

Ollie   No, it isn't. It's Truth or Dare.

Tim *comes back on, carrying the rest of the drinks.*

And honesty's the best policy. Isn't it, Tim?

Tim *ignores this, and sets to preparing the drinks for slamming.*
Suddenly **Anna** *rises and throws her drink over* **Ollie**. *She takes*

Tim's *lighter, flicks it on and holds it close to* **Ollie**.

Anna   I think you owe me an apology.

Ollie   Jesus Christ!

Anna   Are you going to apologise?

Colm   Anna, for God's sake –

Anna   Are you going to apologise?

Ollie   Sorry! I'm sorry!

Suddenly, violently, **Tim** *slams his drink and downs it. Everyone silenced.*

Tim   Shut up and drink up.

Pause. Then **Anna** *flicks off the lighter.*

Anna   Come on then. Drink up.

Anna *slams her drink and downs it.* **Joseph** *follows, then* **Colm** *and* **Sarah**. **Ollie** *last of all. Coughing and spluttering.* **Anna** *has to sit down.*

Tim (*to* **Anna**)   That was a shocking waste of alcohol.

Anna   I quite agree. Get me another one.

Tim (*to* **Ollie**)   Go on, you.

Ollie   What?

Tim   Get the drinks in.

Ollie   I'm broke.

Tim   For fuck's sake. (*Stands up to get money from his pocket.*) Move your hole.

Ollie *stands.* **Tim** *gives him a couple of notes.*

Ollie   What do youse want?

Tim   Ask for flaming Sambucas.

Ollie   What?

Tim   Six flaming Sambucas.

Joseph Jesus.

Colm Anna's had enough, Tim.

Anna No, I bloody haven't. Get me six flaming Sambucas.

Tim Fair dos. (*Privately, to* **Ollie**.) And here – (*He takes a box from his pocket and gives* **Ollie** *a pill.*) That's for you.

Ollie What is it?

Tim It's great. Take it with your drink.

Ollie How much?

Tim It's a present. Go on.

Ollie Aw, cheers, Tim. (*Heads for the bar. Stops.*) No hard feelings there, Anna. (*Off.*)

Anna Fucker. The fucker.

Sarah Leave him alone.

Anna Leave him alone?

Tim (*firmly*) Look, let's all settle down now.

Joseph Ah, the calming tones of Tim Hamill.

Tim That's right.

Pause.

Colm (*brightly*) Let's get back to the game.

Anna Sod the game.

Colm Come on now.

Sarah Yeah, go on, Colm.

Colm It's Tim's turn.

Joseph Right. Tim. Which is the very finest Elvis film?

Tim (*a smile as he agrees to keep playing*) Fun in Acapulco.

Joseph Is the correct answer! Well done.

Tim I thank you. Particularly notable for its fine flashback sequences, I think you'll find.

Joseph   Very fine flashbacks. Agreed.

Tim   Jesus, I haven't played the Elvis Movie Drinking Game in ages.

Joseph   God, it's been years!

Sarah   What do you do?

Joseph   The Elvis Movie Drinking Game is very simple –

Tim   Right. You drink when Elvis sings a song.

Joseph   And you drink when Ann Margaret sings a song.

Tim   And you drink at any major cleavage moment.

Joseph   And you drink any time there's a fake backdrop.

Tim   You can get very pissed during *No Room to Rhumba in a Sports Car.*

Joseph   You can get absolutely wasted during *Fun in Acapulco.*

Ollie *comes back, with a tray of Sambucas, as yet unlit.*

Sarah   Ollie, you're just in time for your go.

Ollie   Oh, goody.

The drinks are distributed. **Anna** *stands up to go.*

Colm   Anna . . .

Anna   Piss.

She goes off. Pause. **Tim** *stands and glares at* **Ollie**.

Tim   Right, Ollie.

Ollie *(weakly)*   Wha'?

Tim   Name the best sweet of the seventies.

Ollie   The what?

Tim *grabs* **Ollie** *by the nipple and twists.* **Ollie** *shrieks.*

Tim   Name the best sweet of the seventies.

Ollie   Spangles! Spangles!

Tim (*letting go*)   No, sorry, it was Pacers.

Colm   God aye, whatever happened to Pacers. You never see them any more.

Sarah   We must have eaten them all.

Tim   No, in fact it's to do with the peace process.

Sarah   Eh?

Tim   Pacers, if you remember, had green and white horizontal stripes. Green and white horizontal stripes. In other words, they were wearing the Celtic strip.

Ollie   Right.

Tim   Now, in the current sensitive political situation, if there is to be a sweet wearing the Celtic strip, there would have to be a corresponding sweet wearing the Rangers strip. Agreed?

Joseph   Agreed.

Tim   However, as you know, no one wants to eat blue sweets. Therefore no one produces blue sweets.

Ollie   That's a well-known fact.

Tim   And if you can't have Rangers sweets, then the powers that be have decreed that you can't have Celtic sweets either. So, for the sake of public order, the humble Pacer was effectively banned.

Ollie   No, they were not banned. They were in fact interned. It was an outrage. (*Sings.*)
    'Armoured cars and tanks and guns
    Came to take away our Pacers.'

Colm   Are you on drugs?

Ollie   Not yet.

Ollie *takes the pill and beams at* **Colm**.

Sarah   There used to be blue Smarties.

Tim   What?

Sarah   There used to be blue Smarties. You said nobody produces blue sweets, but there used to be blue Smarties.

Tim   Yeah, but they got rid of them, didn't they? My point exactly.

Sarah   I used to love Pacers.

Tim   I wouldn't have thought someone of your background would have been encouraged to eat Celtic sweets.

Sarah   I wasn't encouraged to eat them. I just said I liked them. They were *minty*.

Tim   Yeah, but still. Fenian sweets. But then you've always hung around with Ollie and his lot, haven't you?

Sarah   So what about it?

Tim (*to the others*)   You know the way women who hang around with gay men are called fag hags? I suppose you could call Sarah a Fenian hag, couldn't you?

Sarah (*to* **Tim**)   You're fucking weird, mate.

Anna *returns and sits in.*

Colm   Whose turn is it now?

Joseph (*lifting his drink*)   'Ah daddy, I wanna stay drunk many days.' (*To* **Tim**.) Do you remember that?

Tim   Frank O'Hara.

Anna   Your memory's coming back, then.

Joseph   And Tim, really, do you not remember Galway?

Tim   Of course I do. I remember everything.

Joseph   What about *Godot*?

Tim   We were brilliant! You were good.

Joseph   Under the able direction of Anna, of course.

Anna   You're too kind.

Colm   I was there, too. Don't forget about me.

Tim   Yes, of course. (*To* **Ollie** *and* **Sarah**.) He played Godot.

Colm   Ha bloody ha.

Ollie   Hands up who knows what we're on about.

Sarah   Behave yourself, Ollie. Who are you to cast nasturtiums?

Ollie   You're right. I have no nasturtiums to cast.

Tim   Are we right?

Joseph   We're right.

Tim *lights the drinks. Music – 'Disco Inferno' by the Tramps, very loud, continuing until* **Ollie** *goes down.*

Tim   Burn baby burn!

Ollie   Burn that mother-fucker down!

All the drinks downed in one. The usual spluttering from everyone – but **Ollie** *continues coughing after the others. Presently he collapses, his head smacking down on to the table.*

Sarah   Ollie! (*Shaking him.*) Ollie? Jesus!

She stands, tries to rouse him.

Tim   Man down!

Sarah   What's the matter with him?

Tim   He's fucking pissed. That's what's the matter with him.

Sarah   Ollie? Ollie?

Anna   Is he all right?

Sarah   Of course he's not fucking all right.

She struggles to move him.

I think he's dead.

Tim (*standing*)   Of course he's not dead. Ollie? (*Taking him by* *the face.*) Ollie?

He hoists him up, helped by **Sarah**. *The others standing in concern.*

He just needs a breath of fresh air.

Joseph   Maybe coffee or something?

Colm   Get him some water.

Tim   Sit down. Sit down. Don't worry.

Tim *and* **Sarah** *manoeuvre* **Ollie** *out of the snug.*

We have the technology. We can rebuild him.

They start to move off, holding **Ollie** *between them.*

Colm   I'll come with youse.

Tim   Stay where you are, Colm. Keep us our seats or we'll lose them. He'll be fine. Incoming wounded! Incoming wounded!

They go off.

Colm   Jesus.

Joseph   I've never seen anyone in that state.

Anna   Listen, I've been in that state often enough myself.

Colm   That's nothing to brag about.

Anna   I'm not bragging about it. I'm just saying he'll be all right.

Colm   I hope so. God.

Anna   Go on, say a wee prayer for him.

Colm   Don't you start.

Joseph   Yes, say a wee prayer for him, Colm. Say a wee prayer to the baby Jesus.

Colm   What?

Joseph   You're still friends with the baby Jesus, aren't you?

Anna (*to* **Joseph**)   What's wrong with you?

Joseph   There's nothing wrong with *me*. I don't know why I fucking bothered coming back. It's pointless.

Anna   Well, we never invited you. Why *did* you bother?

Joseph (*angrily*)   I don't know.

Anna   Why didn't you just stay in France or Germany or wherever you were? Why?

Joseph   Because –

Anna   Why? We don't want you here.

Joseph (*seriously, pleadingly*)   Because I'd learned those languages, Anna. I've finished with them. I had to come back here and talk to you.

Colm   To her?

Joseph   To all of you. In my own words. In my own language.

Anna   Bullshit. Pretentious bullshit.

Joseph   It's the truth. I shouldn't have bothered. I might've known you'd be like this.

Colm   Like what?

Joseph   It's pathetic.

Colm   What's pathetic?

Joseph   You are. You are fucking pathetic, Colm. With your baby Jesus and your sausages triangles –

Colm   Well, if it's pathetic to teach kids to read –

Joseph   It's not about your job. I don't care about your job.

Colm   Just because I believe in something.

Joseph   But you'll believe in anything. You even believe in me! For fuck's sake, why can't you stand up for once and –

Anna   What? Punch you in the face?

Colm (*to* **Joseph**)   What are you having a go at me for?

Joseph   How can you let me come into your house and sit there and make conversation and talk about school? At least Tim has the balls –

Colm   Tim's an animal.

Joseph   Well, what are you, then? A man?

Anna   That's what this is about, isn't it? Big hard men, the three of you.

Colm   You shut up.

Anna   No, fuck you, I won't shut up. You won't shut me up.

Colm   You're just bloody heartless.

Anna   Oh, am I?

Colm   You always have been.

Anna   You'd know.

Colm   Yeah, I'd know. And look where it's got me.

Anna   Look where it's got *you*?

Colm   Yeah, you never think of that, do you?

Anna   Jesus Christ, Colm, if you could hear yourself.

Joseph (*to* **Colm**)   I ran away. But at least I came back. You stayed here all this time and you still can't face it.

Anna   He's right.

Colm   Thanks very much.

Anna (*moving close to* **Colm**)   We have to talk this out.

Colm   Talking's what fucked things up in the first place.

Anna   You won't face things, Colm. And you have to. We have to get a divorce.

Colm   Look, I don't want to talk about this.

Anna   I know you don't but we have to. We have to get a divorce, Colm.

Colm (*shouts*)   We *can't*, Anna . . . I would lose my job, for God's sake. You can't have a divorced teacher in a Catholic school.

Anna   Fuck the school. We're talking about our lives here.

Colm   My job is my life.

Anna   So you holding on to your job is more important than the both of us getting on with our lives?

Colm   What are you in such a hurry for? Do you have somebody else lined up?

Anna   For fuck's sake! This is mental, this is fucking mental!

Joseph   Listen, both of you –

Colm   This is none of your business, right?

Joseph   I'm just saying –

Colm   I don't care what you're just saying. I have nothing to say to you. (*He gets up.*)

Anna   Come on, Colm –

Colm   I have nothing to say to either of you. I'm going home.

Anna   Don't be stupid, Colm.

Colm   Stupid and pathetic.

Colm *is leaving. As he goes off he almost collides with* **Tim**, *who is entering with a tray of drinks and nuts.*

Tim   Where's he away to?

Pause.

Oh, I see. Well, maybe you two lovebirds want to be alone.

Pause.

No?
May I join you then?
Thank you.

Tim *sits in.*

Drinky?

Anna *takes a drink.*

Anna   You just missed Joseph singing your praises. He thinks you're a real man.

Tim   Really? Well, yes, I suppose I am. I'm sorry I missed that. But if I may return the compliment, I must say I think Joe's quite the real man himself.

Joseph   Thank you.

Tim   Nothing wrong with your sperm count, eh Joe?

Anna   OK. That'll do, Tim.

Tim   You mean, 'Leave Joseph's sperm out of this'?

Anna   Yes.

Tim   Say no more.

They drink.

Well, that's us down to the hard core now.

Joseph   Where are the others?

Tim   Who?

Joseph   Sarah and ... eh ... Ollie...?

Tim   They've gone.

Joseph   They've gone?

Tim   Yes.

Joseph   Just like that?

Tim   Just, as you say, like that.

Joseph   They went without saying goodbye.

Tim   How very rude.

Anna   How is he?

Tim Who?

Anna Ollie.

Tim Oh, you're concerned about him? I seem to recall you trying to set his head on fire earlier on.

Anna Forget it.

Tim So are you having a good time, Joe? Catching up on old friends.

Joseph *stays silent.*

Anna (*to* **Joseph**) How long have you been back?

Joseph A while.

Anna What's a while?

Joseph Three months.

Anna Three months?

Joseph Approximately.

Anna Why didn't you call me?

Joseph What?

Anna I mean, this little get-together – I wasn't even invited. Why?

Joseph I didn't think you'd want to come.

Anna Big lad's night out, was it?

Joseph No –

Anna You haven't even asked me how I am.

Joseph Well, how are you?

Anna Peachy creamy. Thanks for asking.

Pause.

Joseph What are you up to?

Anna I'm writing for the *Tele*.

Joseph For the telly?

Anna No, the *Belfast Telegraph*.

Joseph But –

Anna But what?

Joseph Isn't that a bastion of . . .

Tim Bastards?

Anna Well, yes, it is a bastion of bastards, but what do you want from me. I have to pay the rent. I have to eat.

Tim And drink.

Anna Yes. Talking of which –

She stands and downs her drink.

(*To* **Joseph**.) Do you want anything from the bar?

Joseph I've had enough.

Anna I haven't.

Anna *heads off.*

Tim (*after her*) I'm fine.

He shifts over, close to **Joseph**.

I think you're in there, mate.

Joseph Wise up.

Pause.

God, I haven't said that for years. 'Wise up'.

Pause.

I better go.

Tim Where to?

Joseph I don't know.

They laugh a little together.

Tim It's good to see you back, Joseph.

Joseph   Really?

Tim   Yeah, of course. It's good to be able to reminisce. I'd almost forgotten about Galway. And *Godot.* All of that shite. Here – (*He stands and turns.*) Do you remember the house?

Joseph   Of course I do.

Tim   We decorated the bog wall with pictures of minor celebs.

Joseph   Yes.

Tim   W. D. Flackes off *Scene Around Six.* Jon Pertwee.

Joseph   Yes.

Tim   Michael Rodd off *Screen Test.*

Joseph   Yes.

Tim   And do you remember –

Joseph   Yes?

Tim   The night you stood there . . .

Joseph   Yes?

Tim   You stood there and watched as three or four big bastards kicked my shite in.

Pause.

Yes?
It was a drugs thing, of course. Drugs. But then you knew that already, didn't you?

Joseph   Yes.

Tim   Or of course it could have been some rogue paramilitary gang of theatre critics. Objecting to some performance or other.

Joseph   Tim . . .

Tim   Do you know what I did after that, Joe? I got myself a gun. I got a gun to protect myself. A real one, not a prop.

Joseph   Tim, I just froze. I want to explain . . . It hurt me –

Tim   More than it hurt me? Fuck, that must have been terrible for you.

Joseph   I want to tell you, Tim. I think about it. I replay it.

Tim   Forget it.

Joseph   I can't forget it.

Tim   Well, of course you did have a better view of it than I did.

Joseph   Tim . . .

Tim   I don't really remember it very well myself but I have some groovy scars to remind me so I haven't forgotten altogether.

Joseph   God, Tim . . . I'm so sorry . . .

Tim *looks closely, enquiringly at* **Joseph**. *A moment, then he speaks with seeming sincerity.*

Tim   Forget it. It doesn't matter. It doesn't matter any more.

Joseph   But . . .

Tim   It's good to see you back, Joseph. You are my friend, Joe. We were best mates.

Joseph   I don't know what to say.

Tim   You're pissed. You won't even remember this in the morning.

Joseph   Yes, I will.

Tim *produces the little pillbox from his pocket.*

Tim (*singing*)   I've got a little something for ya . . .

Joseph   What?

Tim   Here. Take this.

Puts a pill in **Joseph**'s *hand. Also takes out one for himself.*

Joseph   What is it?

Tim   Go on. Take it. It'll give you a kick up the arse poetica.

Joseph (*laughs a little*)   OK.

Tim   Here.

Tim *gives* **Joseph** *a beer, and manoeuvres their arms so that they lock, in a drunk-bloke sort of way.*

Right – you take the pill – then you take a slug of your drink. OK?

Joseph   OK.

Tim   Ready?

Joseph   Ready.

They swallow the pills and knock back the beer.

Tim   Yeah!

Joseph (*coughing*)   What was that?

Tim   Black Fucking Bush.

They take a moment to recover.

Joseph, do you remember the poems you used to write?

Joseph   Yes.

Tim   You used to slave over them for hours.

Joseph   Yes.

Tim   Do you still write poems?

Joseph   No.

Tim   Thanks be to fuck for that.

Joseph (*coughing*)   I feel sick.

He slumps, holding his head. **Anna** *returns with her drink.*

Tim   Well, hello there.

Anna   What's the matter with him?

Tim He's fine. He's had a little too much to drink.

Anna He was all right a minute ago.

Music – 'B-Boys Makin' with the Freak Freak' by The Beastie Boys.

Tim Right. Let's get him out of here.

Light change. Darkness with swirling lights.

Music very loud.

Scene Six

Darkness with swirling lights.

Tim *and* **Anna** *hold* **Joseph** *between them. He thrashes and struggles. Breaks away from them when the lights come up.*

They are back in **Colm**'s *flat.* **Tim, Anna, Colm** *and* **Joseph**. *Music drawing down.*

Joseph's *game of Language Roulette.*

Joseph Get out of it you ... I know you ... I know all about you ... you stupid ... fuck ... mother-fucker ... oh, you stupid ... ugly ... little shitty ... mother-fucker ... (*Shouts.*) Mother-fucker! ... Cock-sucker! ... you stinking, arsing, cunting, fucking, cunting ... fucking ... bastard! ... you're for it now, pal ... you're fucking for it now, pal ... you ... cunt! (*Shouts.*) Cunt! (*Giggle.*) ... *Connard! Putain! Bordel de merde!* ... excuse my French ... you said it, pal ... and a pint of your blood, you bastard ... you fucking asked for it, you're fucking well gonna get it ... (*Shouts.*) Right? ... you've had it ... stupid bloody bastard lying bastard ... just you wait, you cunt ...

Pause. **Joseph** *now on his knees.* **Colm** *tries to help him.*

Colm Joe, come on now –

Joseph Leave me alone, you cunt ... (*Shouts.*) Arsehole! Fucking arsehole!

Colm For God's sake, Joe.

Pause.

Joseph (*quiet now*)   Oh, God ... (*Giggly.*) Jesus ... Colm?

Colm (*crouching down beside him*)   Yes, Joe.

Joseph   Colm –

Colm   Yes, Joe.

Joseph   Give us a hand up there, Colm.

Colm   Come on, Joe.

He tries to lift him up. **Joseph** *sprawling and falling all over the place.*

Joseph   Colm ... (*His arms around him.*) help me up ... (*Still giggling, with pepperings of 'fucks' and 'Gods'.*)

Colm   Good man, Joe. (*Struggling to lift him.*) There we are, Joe.

Joseph   Colm ... do you remember –

Colm   Yes, Joe.

Joseph   Do you remember the day at school –

Colm   Come on, Joe, that's it.

Joseph   Do you remember the day at school –

Colm   I do, Joe.

Joseph   Do you remember the day at school when you and I had a fight?

And with sudden strength, **Joseph** *bowls* **Colm** *full over, jumps and lands on him, pinioning him to the ground.*

Joseph   Do you remember, Colm?

Colm   Joe, for fuck's sake –

Joseph   And I was holding you down on the ground, kneeling on you, do you remember?

Colm   Joe!

Joseph   And you were screaming –

Colm   Joe!

Joseph   Do you remember? Do you? (*Still giggly, not vicious or malicious.*)

Colm   For God's sake, Joe!

Joseph   And I – (*Giggle.*) and I –

He is about to spit, but before he can, **Tim** *comes up behind him. He grabs* **Joseph** *from behind, clamps his hand over his mouth, and drags him off* **Colm**.

Tim   Right, that's enough, Joe.

Colm   He's gone mad.

Anna   Don't hurt him.

Tim *takes his hand off* **Joseph**'*s mouth.*

Joseph   Please . . . listen to me . . . please . . .

Anna   Lie him down on the sofa.

Colm   No, you shouldn't lie him down. He could choke on his own vomit.

A moment.

Like Jimi Hendrix.

Tim   I don't know who's more delirious, Joe or Colm.

They manhandle **Joseph** *into a spread-eagled sitting position on the floor, up against the sofa.*

Joseph   Please . . . please . . .

Anna   What do you want, Joe?

Joseph   We could remember it between us.

Colm   Shush, Joe. Don't try to talk.

Anna   Joe. It's me, Joe.

Joseph   Anna . . .

Tim   Any chance of a coff, Col? Have you any Jammy Dodgers?

Colm   Fuck off and get it yourself.

Tim   Charming. Well, I'll fuck off and get it myself then, shall I?

Colm   What?

Tim   Coffee.

Colm   Will you shut up about coffee.

Anna   Joe?

No reply. **Joseph** *unconscious.*

Joe?

Colm   Is he all right?

Anna   Jesus, he's out cold.

Anna *stands and turns on* **Tim**.

Anna   What did you give him?

Tim   Eh?

Anna   You got him like this.

Tim   Did I fuck. He's just a bit pissed.

Anna   Pissed my arse. *I'm* a bit pissed. He's fucking catatonic.

Tim (*all smiles, all innocence, sings*)
    'I'm feelin' catatonic
    gimme gin and tonic' –

Colm   We're gonna have to call an ambulance.

Tim   No. Leave him alone. He's all right.

Colm   Of course he's not all right. Look at him. We're gonna have to call an ambulance.

Tim   You can't.

Colm   Why not?

Pause.

Tim   Look, he'll be fine.

Anna (to **Tim**, *in anger*)   What did you fucking give him?

Tim   He can handle it.

Anna   Like Ollie could handle it?

Tim *approaches* **Joseph** *and takes him by the face.* **Joseph** *seems to come round slightly.* **Tim** *gives him the fingers, close up to his face.*

Tim   How many fingers am I holding up, Joe?

Anna *hits out at* **Tim**.

Anna   Leave him alone.

Tim (*brushing her off angrily*)   That's what I'm saying. Leave him alone. He'll be all right.

Colm   He's gone again.

Tim *heads for the kitchen.*

Anna   Where do you think you're going?

Tim (*angrily*)   I'm getting him some coffee. He needs fucking black coffee. Is that all right by you? Do I have your permission?

Anna (*chastened*)   All right.

Tim   Thank you.

Tim *to kitchen.*

Tim (*off*)   There's no clean cups.

Colm   In the sink.

Tim (*in doorway, with washing-up gloves*)   Fuck, this place is disgusting. No wonder she left you.

Colm   Fuck off.

Tim   Oh, sorry. Don't be rude, Tim, you bad man. (*Slaps his*

hand, and dons the gloves.) Here's Colm *(Sings.)*:
   'Now hands that do dishes
   can feel soft as your arse – '
And this is me *(Sings, raucously.)*:
   'Fuckin' catatonic
   gimme gin and tonic
   wanna ride with you
   in your BMW – '

Anna   Will you shut up.

Tim *(drained)*   Tell you what, I'll shut up now, shall I?

Joseph *(eyes open)*   Anna . . .

Anna   Yes, Joe?

Joseph   Anna . . .

Anna   What is it?

Joseph   You could give him my name.

Pause.

If he is a him.

Pause.

You could call him after me.

Colm   Don't try and talk, Joe.

Joseph   Joseph Lavery!

Colm   Joe, don't –

Joseph   Imagine that!

Colm *(to **Anna**, to **Tim**, in general)*   Shut him up!

Tim   Right, Joe –

Joseph   I'm joking, of course.

Tim   He's joking, of course.

Joseph   You couldn't call him Joseph.

Tim   Course you couldn't.

Joseph   People would talk.

Tim   Don't they always.

Joseph   Tim –

Tim   Joseph –

Joseph   Can I tell you something?

Tim   You know you can rely on me.

Colm   Stop it.

Tim   Stop what?

Colm   Stop playing games.

Tim   You preferred him unconscious, did you?

Joseph   Can you keep a secret, Tim?

Tim   Cross my heart and hope to die.

Joseph   Really?

Tim (*raises his hand*)   Hand to God.

Colm   Anna.
He's fucking sick, Tim, leave him alone.
Anna, say something.

Anna *says nothing.*

Joseph   I've got room-spin.

He waves his arms in the air to represent the room spinning.

They say if you close your eyes –

He does so, and reels sickly. Opens them again.

– it gets worse.

Silence. **Joseph** *slumped on the floor.*

My mother sent me a letter. It was on blue paper. She couldn't have known what she was telling me. She just said, 'Isn't that awful sad? Isn't that awful sad and them only married a year.'

Anna   Six months.

Joseph   I was in Paris. I read the letter in a café. I carried it there in my pocket. And the thing is, I didn't think it was awful sad. I just thought it was an awful fucking relief and that something was over and full stop and an end to it. For Anna and Colm and Tim and me. And was it a relief for Colm too?' And I'm sure it was.

Pause.

Tim   Truth or Dare, Colm. I dare you.

Pause.

I fucking dare you.

Colm   Yes, it was. Yes, it was because of him, and because of you (**Tim**.) and your lies.

Tim   Did I lie, then? Ask them if I lied. Truth or Dare.

Colm   Forget all your bloody games.

Tim   It isn't a game.

Joseph   You can't believe what Tim says. He's out to get me. You can't believe what he says.

Colm   I know.

Tim   Oh right, fucking blame it on me again. That's easy. Tim the shit-stirrer, stirring it up, telling lies.

Colm   You're a liar, Tim. A liar for a living. You admitted it yourself.

Tim   No way. I'm the fucking truth-teller. (*To* **Anna**.) I lied for you and Joe back then. (*To* **Colm**.) I lied to keep you in the dark. I lied to protect them. Mummy and daddy here. But when I saw what it was to have your best friends stand by you, when I saw what it was to have your best friend stand by while you get beaten to shit, I changed my mind. I became the fucking truth-teller. I told the truth about all of us and that put an end to our incestuous little happy family, didn't it? And now you want to start it up again, with the prodigal son coming back and welcome home and everything's left unsaid and all is forgiven. Well, bollocks to that.

Colm   All I wanted was for us to see each other and for it to be like before and for us to forget about all that shit.

Anna   Forget about all that shit? Is that what it was? Shit?

Colm   I wanted it to be like before.

Anna   Before what? Before me? Before me and you? Before me and you and . . . ?

Tim (*to* **Anna**)   You and – ? You and *it*?

Anna   And it was a *relief* for you? God, Colm, it was a *relief* for you?

Sarah *lets herself in with* **Ollie**'s *key. The others are silenced. A pause.*

Tim (*to* **Sarah**)   What do you want?

Sarah (*angry and afraid*)   They took Ollie to the hospital. I thought you'd want to know.

Tim   What?

Sarah   He was hitting his head on the wall. He smashed his teeth up. I think he swallowed the half of them.

Colm   Jesus.

Sarah   He was cold. His lips went blue. They've called his parents. And the police.

Tim   Oh, for fuck's sake.

Sarah   I left before they arrived or they would've kept me there all night.

Tim   Your loyalty is touching.

Colm   What did you give him, Tim? Did you give Joe the same thing?

Sarah (*seeing* **Joseph**)   Joseph? Jesus, Joseph! Fucking hell. What's going on with you people? What the fuck's wrong with youse?

Tim You want to know what's going on? Do you? (*He stalks up to her. She backs off. He follows.*) All right, then. Joseph here, the man you've been trying to get off with all night, our dear home-coming friend, is a liar and a traitor and a coward who ran away because he couldn't face –

Colm Shut up, Tim.

Tim He couldn't face any one of us, and now he comes back all guilty and wanting forgiveness. He was fucking scum from day one. He was fucking scum. Well, he was fucking her (**Anna**.), which is more or less the same thing.

Silence.

Anna Fucking scum?

Tim Sorry, out of time. Joe's turn.

Colm More fucking games.

Tim It isn't a game, Colm. It's Truth or Dare. Do you want an answer?

Colm What?

Tim Do you want an answer?

Colm I don't know what you're on about.

Tim Truth or Dare, Joe!

*He drags **Joseph** off the ground and up on to the sofa.*

Joseph Truth.

Pause.

Tim (*to **Colm***) Ask him. Go on, ask him. He'll tell you.

Tim *takes out his gun, holds it at his side.*

Fucking ask him.

Colm *stays silent.*

You can't even ask the question. How can you have an

answer if you can't even ask the fucking question?

Colm   I don't want an answer.

Tim   Don't give me that shit.

He raises his gun and levels it at **Colm**'s *head.*

Ask him.

Pause. **Anna** *steps between* **Colm** *and* **Tim**.

Anna (*to* **Tim**)   Fuck you.

Tim *slowly lowers the gun.* **Anna** *turns to face* **Colm**.

Ask me.

Pause.

Colm   Anna . . .

Anna   What?

Colm   Was it . . .

Anna   Was it what?

Colm   Was it ours?

Anna   It was *mine.*

Tim   Oh, I see. An immaculate conception, was it?

Anna   It was *mine.* And *I* lost it.

Silence.

Joseph   We could remember it together.

Anna   No, Joseph. We can't remember it together. You wouldn't be able to remember it with me. None of you.

She gathers up her handbag, and takes a moment to tidy herself.

Youse can kill one another for all I care.

She leaves.

Sarah   Youse are all fucked up. (*To* **Tim**.) See, if anything happens to Ollie –

Sarah *leaves.*

Colm *and* **Tim** *left standing,* **Joseph** *slumped.* **Tim***'s gun hangs by his side. A long pause. Blackout.*

Lights up again. The final reprise. **Colm** *and* **Tim** *standing,* **Joseph** *slumped.* **Tim***'s gun hangs by his side. A long pause.*

Blackout.

Closing music – 'Lo-boob Oscillator' by Stereolab.

Daragh Carville was born in Armagh in 1969. He studied Drama and Film at the University of Kent and after graduating lived and worked in Paris before returning to Ireland to complete an MA in Irish Writing at Queen's University, Belfast. His first play, *Language Roulette* was premiered by Tinderbox Theatre Company at the Old Museum Arts Centre, Belfast in May, 1996, before touring Northern Ireland. The play, winner of a 1996 Stewart Parker Award, was then revived in 1997 with two sell-out weeks at OMAC, a tour of Ireland and performances at the Bush Theatre, London and the Traverse Theatre, Edinburgh. In 1997, *Language Roulette* was nominated as Best New Play in the Barclays TMA Awards and as Best Drama Production in the Belfast City Council Arts Award. His second play, *Dumped*, was also premiered by Tinderbox Theatre Company at the Reid Hall, Armagh in September 1997 before touring venues in Northern Ireland, including the Old Museum Arts Centre, Belfast.

Disco Pigs

by Enda Walsh

Disco Pigs was first staged in September 1996 at the Triskel Arts Centre, Cork, by the Corcadorca Theatre Company and subsequently at the 1996 Dublin Theatre Festival. It was given its UK premiere at the Traverse Theatre, Edinburgh on 7 August, 1997.

The cast was as follows:

Pig   Cillian Murphy
Runt   Eileen Walsh

Directed by Pat Kiernan
Designed by Aedin Cosgrove
Sound Design by Cormac O'Connor

Disco Pigs was workshopped for a week prior to rehearsals.

Lights flick on. **Pig** *(male) and* **Runt** *(female). They mimic the sound of an ambulance like a child would: 'bee baa bee baa bee baa!!' They also mimic the sound a pregnant woman in labour makes. They say things like 'is all righ, miss', 'ya doin fine, luv', 'dis da furs is it?', 'is a very fast bee baa, all righ. Have a class a wator!' Sound of door slamming. Sound of heartbeats throughout.*

Runt   Out of the way!! Jesus, out of the way!

Pig   Scream da fat nurse wid da gloopy face!

Runt   Da 2 mams squealin on da trollies dat go speedin down da ward. Oud da fookin way!

Pig   My mam she own a liddle ting, look, an dis da furs liddle baba! She heave an rip all insie!! Hol on, Mam!!

Runt   My mam she hol in da pain! She noel her pain too well! She been ta hell an bac, my mam!

Pig   Day trips an all!

Runt   Da stupid cow!!

Pig   Holy Jesus, help me!!

Runt   Scream da Pig, Mam! Her face like a Christmas pud all sweaty an steamy! Da 2 trollies like a big choo choo it clear all infron! Oudda da fookin way, cant jaaaaa!!

Pig   Da 2 das dey run the fast race speedin behine!

Runt   Holy Jesus keep her safe. Holy Jesus keep her safe!

Pig   Mamble my dad wid a liddle mammy tear in da eye! I'm da liddle baba cummin oud, Dada, I'm yer liddle baba racer!!!

Runt   Da trollie dey go on

Pig   an on

Runt   an on

Pig   an on

Runt   an on

Pig   an on

Runt   an on

Pig   an on!

Runt   My mam she suck in da pain, grobble it up an sweat it oud til da liddle skimpy nighty it go

Pig   . . . black wet black.

Runt   2 gold fishys oudda da bowl!!!

Pig   A gasp gaspin! I'm ja liddle baba commin out! Open up ja big fanny!

Runt   Trollie stop!

Pig   An leg open!

Runt   Da fatty nurse schlap on with the rubbery glubs! Stop! An leg open! Da 2 fat sous pooshhh an poooshh ta spit da babas oud!!

Pig   Push girls push!

Runt   Scream da das oudsize!

Pig   Scream da das oudsize!

Runt   My da he wan fur his din dins real fas, yeah!

Pig   Take your time, love!

Runt   He say, stopwadch in han! Da fannys dey look like donna kebabs!

Pig   Bud looka da liddle baba heads!

Runt   Pooosh da baba poosh da head!!

Pig   Pooshh, Mam, poosh!! Poosh da Pig!

Runt   An Poosh da Runt! She wan oud, Mama!

Pig   An he wan oud, ta Dada!

Runt   Pooosh, sous, pooosh!!

Pig   We da liddle born babas!

Pig *and* **Runt**   Pooosshhhhhh!

Silence. We then hear the sounds of babies crying. Music.

Runt   An it wuz.

Pig   19 . . .

Runt   . . . 79.

Pig   An da liddle baby beebas a Pork sity take da furs bread inta da whirl.

Runt   Da hop-i-da-hill all Bambi an Thumper!

Pig   Hey looka da liddle bunny, baby!

Runt   An looka da nursey face, is sall rosey like a buuk full a roses!

Pig   An da 2 liddle babas all wrappt in pooder, ka nice smell pooder!

Runt   My mam's nighty pink!

Pig   An my mam's nighty pink!!

Runt   An my mam she pain no more! Sorta happy wid wat she fart out.

Pig   Bud my mam she cry all blubbery wid dad sittin on da bed flickin thru da Echo!

Runt   Yeah, Pork sity was luvly amay bak den.

Runt   Da peeplah dey really nice. Dey say:

Pig   She's a lovely little thing!

Runt   Goo ga goo!

Pig   Look the little button nose!

Runt   Ahhh gaga ga!

Pig   And the fingernails, ahhh look!

Runt   Goo gee gee!

Pig   She's happy in that pram.

Runt   Gaa gee goo goo!

Pig   She looks just like her mam.

Runt   Fuck off ja!

Pig   Nell may bak den an me an she weez take a furs bread inta da whirl. A bobbly baby-boots girl she . . .

Runt   Runt! An a fat fatty fatso fart by da name a . . .

Pig   Pig! But fatty no more! As ja can say, Slimfast fans!

Runt   Oud we bounce inta a whirl of grey happiness!

Pig   We wa beautiful amay bak den!

Runt   *Jar* beautiful! *Jar* beautiful, Pig!

Pig   Beg yer pardon, pal! *Jar* beautiful! Jar beautiful! Da liddle baby babbies a Pork sity!

Runt   Sa tell em who was furs sa!

Pig   Runt a cause!

Runt   Tell em who was secon sa, saucey!

Pig   The Pig!

Runt   Owney one sec tween da girl an da boy! An us no brudder or sis or anyth!

Pig   Fuckin amaz-zing, man! (*Beat.*) Les go Marbyke, yeah!

Runt   Righ so!

Pig   Race ya!

Pig *and* **Runt** *run racing each other. Sounds of heavy breathing.* **Runt** *stops and looks at* **Pig** *continue.*

Runt   So off we go! Zoomin as always! Pig's a real fass! Down da Marbyke Bark we go war dem mens an womens do da race an all. I wadch da Pig race an he run really really fass aboud da trak, yeah. Sonia O'Sullivan tinks Pig migh be da superstar star!

Pig   Ya noel ol Sonja . . . dem light weighty running vests aand panties mean noting when ya got the finish line in sites! Ya gotta believe, girl ... without that yer fuck all! (*To* **Runt**.) Les go my place.

Runt Me da runnin don matter dat much! But see whadda Pig wear? I choose dem! Splendid! I one step ahead in dat race, race fans! Fashion my life. Was goin down downtown, righ in da bum hole a Pork sity, sall import ta me, yeah! I noel betta den mos fox down French Crotch Street! Pig, he nee da big big elp, dat fella. Withoud Runt poor Pig look like da sausies withoud da skin. Crap!

Pig Is a hippyidy happidy birrday for my pal Runt n' me!

Runt Happy birrday, to you.

Pig Happy birrday to you, pal too! 17, hah?

Runt 17 yeah! Pig?

Pig Yes oh ligh a my life, my liddle choccy dip!

Runt Wa colour's love, Pig?

Pig Love? Don no! Wa sorra love, love?

Runt Don no!

Pig Hoy, Mam! Way da din dins! Way da sausies an da saucey, hey, Mam! Schlap it there la!!

Pig *and* **Runt** *eat. We hear the sounds of them eating mixed with them oinking. They stop.*

Runt Las get righly gone, ya on! Cider back a da bed, yeah?

Pig Up up up up up up up up up up!

Runt Down da gob an grab da lot! Up for it are ya?

Pig A hippidy happidy in it?

Runt Les go!

Pig Race ya so!

Runt Ah fook yes!!

Pig *and* **Runt** *drink. It is a race.* **Pig** *breaks off and goes to the toilet. Sound of pissing.*

Pig   Good, in't she? Gallon by gallon deep we go! A buddel a rider's an awful ting, yeah, but hey, an wad da fuck! Da ting it works! Inta da skull like ka lawn mower it mix me an Runt all aboud! 2 fishys a swillin it back a swillin it back a swillin it back . . . down da belly an oud da spout! Ders me dad a decoraten per use-jew-al. Give it up, will ya! Get a job, ja langer!

Runt   Hey, Pig man!

Pig   Hey, luvvy! Dis roam is it all! Da ress a da house is par shitheads an wankers! Dis roam is my kingdom! Pig da king! My bed da trone . . . da clodes dat Runt did make . . . sacred! Me an Runt . . . brudder and sis bud much maw, drama fans! We jar it! We fuckin jar, ya know! Excuse me but odders are weak, yeah . . . like spa childen ja drown in da river, I drown my mam an dad *now*! If dad no so busy wid da wallpaper, a cause! Da faggot, scone head!

Runt   Ta da, bum hole, shall we go?

Pig   Shall we cause!

Runt   Quids?

Pig   Pock-full a tens!

Runt   Regal!

Pig   Les go so!

Runt   Les go so disco!!

Loud disco/techno music follows. **Pig** *and* **Runt** *scream and chant '17'. Music eventually stops. Sound of bus stopping.* **Pig** *and* **Runt** *get on the bus.*

Pig   Las time Pig an Runt eva give mona to da bus . . . mus a bin a baba, a lease! Why nee ta pass wid any kish? Bus boss he well loaded, yeah! Jacussi in sall da bedroams, I bed. So me an Runt jus barrel on!

Runt   Come here to me!!!!

Pig   . . . scream da ugly wase fat cunt of a diver!

Runt   Fook off!

Pig   . . . say Runt. Problem solve, yeah! Easy. He noel his place. Sits. Drive da bus on. Slow. I sees him liddle eyes in da mirror! He scare in da eyes! Pig raise da han . . . Buss fass now. Good.

Runt   Bus-stop . . . stop bus!

Pig (*recognises someone*)   Oh yes. Yes.

Runt *laughs.*

Foxy locksy, in it?

Runt   Is Pig.

Pig (*stands*)   A birrday giff! Cova me, girl!

Runt   Will, Pig.

Pig   Righ so! Hi dee hi!

Pig *mimes kicking Foxy around the place.* **Runt** *narrates.*

Runt   Pig an Foxy go all da way! Pig hate Foxy! One nigh, yeah, Pig he gasp for da glug glug glug glug! Down ta Blackcruel we drool. Off licence war Foxy work. Did work, mo like.

Pig   Free drink, pretty please.

Runt   No ney panic button Foxy he panic. He say, 'I can't Darren.' Pig he get da buzz in da ead he wanna fisty!

Pig   I ass ya nice, nice man! Han fuckin ova!

Runt   'You know I can't.'

Pig   I fuckin kill ya!

Runt   'Darren!'

Pig   I get ja mam fuckin burn her, boy!

Runt   'The boss will kill me, Darr. . . !'

Pig   A shut yer gob, shut yer gob, shut yer gob ya fuckidy-fuck!

Pig *mouths* **Runt***'s lines below.*

Runt   Took Pig ten mins smash all buddels in dat drink
shap. All but one, yeah. Pig take da buddel Bacardi slinky . . .
he kiss da buddel . . . an off. 'Pig! Jar pock-full a tens!' He
stamp na Foxy face. Da nose like tomato itgo squish n' drip
drop. Foxy cried, cried like his mam jus bin smack in da ead
by da golf club . . . which she war . . . nex day.

Pig   Shmackkk!!!

Runt   Pig hate da Foxy. He hate em.

Pig   Schmack schmack schmack schmack schmack schmack
schmack schmack schmack schmack schmack!! An let dat be a
less on ya Foxy! Dis bus is no purr you!!!

Sounds of a quiet bar. Television can be heard. **Runt** *and* **Pig** *look
around.* **Runt** *whistles 'God Save the Queen'.* **Pig** *laughs.*

Pig   Pig n' Runt stop tear furs. Is a sleepy ol' Provo pub ta
Pork purr years, yeah! Runt always do dat. Funny ho hey?!
(*He laughs.*) No soul drink ere! No one gis a fuck aboud dem
nordy bas-turds. Way bodder? News a da week is let dem do
each odder in!

Runt   Use-jew-al?

Pig   Oh yes darling. (**Runt** *gets drinks in.*) I park a top a da
seat by da pool an jus calm an wadch! Good like! Don cost
no-ting eeder! I tink bout Foxy an my boot ta jaw face. I let
da buzz go bye bye an down my ead it go . . . Pig breed it
oud. Calm, brudder, calm down. I wadch in real calm now.
(*Beat.*) Is a sad ol place dis! De ol town, yeah! 9 peeplah inall,
cludin dat bar keep. Big dime steamer him. Marky. Marky.
'Hoy, Marky! Dat a Tang Top?!' (*He laughs.* **Runt** *returns.*) Ta
ta, girl. Some old man, alco mos likely, he sit at da bar lashin
inta da spirit. He talk bouts Jack Charleton an a liddle tear
come to his eye when he says . . . Dinny Irwin . . . Roy
Keane! A fling a beer mat dat go Schmack! Roy Keane, I
know dat fella . . . oh yeah . . . madge him cry an cry . . . an
him ol-ler an all!

Runt   Rea, Pig?

Pig   Oh yes. Roy a da Pullovers I used call him!

Runt   Nancy was he?

Pig   Was ta me, girl!

Runt   Wow!

Pig   To you, pal.

They toast.

Runt   To you, Pig. (*Beat.*) Got a gawk at dat postur, Pig! En-
ter-tain-ment!

Pig   Tom Borrow evey, ol pal!

Runt   Sad sad story! Boo hoo whoo!!!

They laugh. Big silence.

Pig   Da delly playin a show wid Terry Wogan. He watch
dees tings dat go all da wonky, yeah. He's Irish, Terry
Wogan. Really funny! Real good show, delly fans! Top show!

Pig *looks at the telly and goes into fits of laughter.* **Runt** *laughs too.*

Pig   Les go disco! Les go wild one!!!!

Pig *and* **Runt** *in a night-club. They dance. They are well gone. The
music is loud.*

Pig   Jus me jus me jus me jus me jus me!! Oh yes!! Dis da
one!! Real soun set. Pig swimmin an swimmin in da on-off
off-beat dat is dance! Beat beat beat beat beat thru da veins
full a drink! An pig he wee wee full a drink! Dis is sex -in-
step to dat beautifull soun dat deep deep down thru me pump
da danceflower. On-an-off da off-beat dat is dance, on an-off
the off beat dat is dance Pig move alone bud ta da crawd too
he belong a family-a-sorts is wad he make wid deez
happysoun fox. Pump pump pump pump oh fuck my head ja
luvly beat deep inta me an take me home ta beddy byes an
pump me more to sleep soft an loss lost . . . an still yeah I
feel da finish of dis real music. I let da music leave da
soul . . .

Sound of a poxy dance tune is faded up.

Pig Fookchaa!! Stoodent, in a?

Runt Lookalike.

Pig All dat chit-chat, chit-chat, chit-chat ... SHAT!! Pork's brightest oud der an whod a guessed, Runt? I men, look dat yoke!

Runt Pig poin ta a lanky skin-an-bone dress in da height a ration!

Pig Jesus da hairy an Joseph!

Runt He nee Runt style help! His tapioca skin globby eyes an bum hole moud all sittin lax need a mooppy hair style long since gone!

Pig Das pugly, hey Runt!

Runt Dem stoodent type got no soul! Style in't in it!

Pig Das righ, girl!

Runt De men dey act like ol dolls, da ol dolls do up like men! No tuck an seamed, no press liedly wid da iron.

Pig Like yurs truly, yeah!

Runt Like dancin bags a Oxfam, dey no shame! Shame!

Pig All dis chat give me a fuck a da throat!

Runt Pine, Pig?

Pig Ta ta, yeah! We rob all in sied! Every nigh purrmotion nied! A liddle Smurph all alone it sit! Poor liddle lonely ting! War da mammy war da mammy?

Runt I'm ja mammy!

Pig (*shouts*) Wat you lookin at?

Runt Tanks, pal!

They drink.

Runt I look a deez students yeah, I tink a all da learnin das

goin in ta dem, I tink a da books dey do read all stack tall
inside dem oblong heads, I tink a da exam an all, all dat
A B C plus an minus F an all . . . an Pig . . .

Pig Wad now, ol girl?

Runt Wa do dey wanna be?

Pig Dey wanna be der mams an dads a course!

Runt Wadda we wanna be, Pig?

Pig Leff alone. Righ pal!

Runt Righ, Pig. Mu zack up!

Music begins. **Pig** *dances with a woman.* **Runt** *plays the woman.*

Pig Ja wanna dance?? Make no odds! I take her up
anyhowways! I wine my charm aboud da waste! She say
sometin . . . I don no dat squeak too well. She food inta me
though an soon she in dance heaven! Kiss da face, will ya!
On da lips, want ya! Don pull amay, hah! Owney baba cry!
A full mast in da kax Pig he ready to set sail! She cry all
elploss. I like ta lick da neck, yeah! Jus like a big lolly! She
pinn close! Ohhhhhhh now look a da liddle titsies! Who da
baba cry? Was jar name, lover?

Runt Liddle baby tiny tears?!

Pig She's a terrible tease, hey Runt?

Runt 2 hail marys an an our father, hey sister! War da fook
is my man so!!

Pig Ah pik da fucker Runt!

Runt So Runt move in on misty mothball! Da tapioca king
is who we'll take! Up reel close! Da boy he dead ugly okay!
He got stoopid all ova him. Da liddle chalky face an tacky
eyes. So on-an-off da off-beat dat is dance we move . . . me
an dineasaur Barney, dat is. Da boy dance like a baba who
nee ta piss o jus done a piss an nee ta leave! He stick a
sweety han onta my neck an mamble a squeak I don
understan! He sway-in an ova, da moud come-in like a gian
manhole. An den he . . .

Pig   Den he kiss Runt! An dat my cue! Ova I move! Move real fass, yeah! Scream ou loud I scream an grab da liddle fuck an Runt she say:

Runt   He kiss me, Pig! He gay me tongue an all, ya dirty-doggy!!

Pig   An Runt she nee an Oscar for dat, yeah, I almos give a liddle applause an all but da boy he say:

Runt   Sorry, boss! Hands off, look!

Pig   But da damage it is *done, ya bad boy!* Oud a da door a dis poxy disco an oud onta Stoodent Straight I trow dis streaky stretch a bad bacon! See I pay da par a da boyfriend, soap opera fans! Is jealous all ovur, in it! Smash! Ya fillty bollix! Smash smash smash smash smash smash smash smash!!!

Pig *beats him up.* **Runt** *cheers him on for a bit.*

Pig   Goo fun, hey! Nice trick, cat woman!

Runt   Birrday present in it?

Pig   Jar my bird day giff in life, Runt!!

Runt   Pig the Chrissy cracker! Bang bang bang bang!!

Pig   You're the one sweet ting!

Runt   Better be better be!!

Pig   Jarr my bes pal in da whole whirl.

Runt   Jarr my life, Pig.

Pig *grabs at* **Runt** *and kisses her. She struggles and pulls away. A moment.*

Pig   Way da buzz go hun?

Runt   Dis place pox. Les go eat yeah?

Pig   *Burger baps-a-go-go*!!

Runt   Lead da way fas-boy!!

Pig *and* **Runt** *in a burger place.*

Pig   Mister Kung Fu! 2 battur burgurs! 2 sauce! 2 chips! 2 peas! 2 tanora! (*Beat.*) An 2 fawks, Gringo!

Runt   Our 2 mams all sweety an stinkin a new born babas n' blood! I member open an look my eyes an ja see a liddle baba in the nex bed. An dat liddle baba he look righ inta me, yeah. Our mams all da full of happy but da new babys say an do no-ting. We look cross da liddle-big space tween da beds . . . I see own him an he own see me. Deez liddle babies need no-ting else. So off home we go all packed! An da baby houses side by side la! . . . an birrday in birrday out . . . us togedder. An peeplah call me Sinéad an call Pig Darren but one day we war playin in da playroom be-an animols on da farm an Darren play da Pig an I play da Runt! An dat wuz it! An every beddy time our mams pull us away from da odder one. 'Say night to Sinéad, Darren.' But Pig jus look ta me an ans (*Snorts an oink.*) An I noel what he mean. So we grow up a bit at a dime an all dat dime we silen when odders roun. No word or no-ting. An wen ten arrive we squeak a diffren way den odders. An da hole a da estate dey talk at us. Look nasty yeah. But me an Pig look stray at dem. An we looka was happenin an we make a whirl where Pig an Runt jar king an queen! Way we goin down in dis clown-town is run by me an Pig fun fun. An Pig look cross at me jus like he look when we were babas an he alla say, 'Les kill da town, ya on?' An I alla say, 'Corse I'm on – I'm ja pal, amn't I?' An liddle tings we do like robbin an stealin is a good old feelin, yes indeedy. An we read dem buuks on howta figh da peeplah ya hate. An Pig own has me . . . an Runt own have him. But we make a whirl dat no one can live sept us 2. Bonny an Clyde, ya seen da movie! Fannytastic, yeah! (*Laughs.*) But ya know, we liddle babas no mo. Is all differen. All of a puddin, ders a real big differ-ence.

Pig   I'd grobble all da battur burgurs in China cept I'm stuck in dis grubby tub, hey Runt!

Runt   Say again?

Pig   I'd grobble all da battur burgurs in China cept I'm stuck in dis grubby tub!

Runt   Yeah! Course!

Pig   Wa do dey call Chinese takeaways in China, Runt?

Runt   Don no!

The 2 sit in silence for some time. Eating.

Pig   Up up up up up up up up!!

Runt   Off homes, yeah?

Pig   Not off, no! Not off but out, Runt!! Not off but more more more much more!! Sa out da door an da liddle ones step out onta Patsy Street! (*Calling out.*) PORK!! Cheerio ol pal!!

Runt   Pig!

Pig   TAXI!!

Runt   Purr us Pig!?

Pig   We're da reel ting, ol girl! Les split dis party, yeah!

Pig *and* **Runt** *in taxi.*

Pig   Crossheaven! Drive on, Mister cabman!!

Sound of a car.

Runt   An off we do!

Pig   Now das reel class!

Runt   Look how da scummy wet grey a Pork Sity spindown da plughole . . .

Pig   . . . as da 2 speed on, an on we speed! Sa so long to dat sad song, hey Runt!!

Runt   Up an out ova da valley, Pig!! An da black a da cuntry like a big snuggly doovey it cuddle us up reel good yeah!!

Pig   Snuggle down outta town!!

Runt   Hey da fresh air, pal!!

Pig   Wine down da windy an drink it all in, Runt!

Runt   Da taxi so fas dat da fresh air fill me up like a big happy ba-loon!!

Pig   Not like da stenchy piss dat we all know!

Runt   Look a da moo moo, look!!

Pig   Was me ol mam doin der, Runt!!

Runt   Is way pass yer beddy times, ya silly cow!!

Pig   So fook off home, why dan jaa!! On an on, Mister cabman!!

Runt   On an on, an let da fas fresh air kiss an clean dis liddle girl up!!

Pig   Yer bird-day gif, Runt!

Runt   Where, Pig?

Pig   Taxi stop!

Car sounds stop.

Pig   Crossheaven, da colour a love, dis where it is hun!!

Sounds of the sea have been faded up over the above. The 2 look out.

Runt   Nice.

Pig   Der ye are, pal. Das da big blue der. All dat wator, hah. Is all yers, Runt.

Runt   Mine, Pig?

Pig   I got big bag in my plopet I can lash it inta. (*Laughs.*)

Runt   Big open space an jus we standin here, Pig.

Pig   Like 2 specs a dust on da telly, hey girl.

Runt   S'all calm dat move. Da sea dance up slow and down to up slow again. Is beautiful hey, Pig?

Pig   Top a da whirl, in it!

Runt   Jesus, wad a smell!!

Pig   Salt. Salt sea smell.

Runt   An da soun a da sea too . . .

Pig   Yeah, Rover at his doggy bowl, hey Runt?! Lap lap lap!

Runt   I wanna walk inta da sea an neva come back. I wan ta tide to take me outa me an give me someone differen . . . maybe jus fur a halfhour or so! Dat be good, wouldn't it, Pig?

Pig   Jesus, Runt! Dat be impossible! A half hour, fuck! (*Beat.*) I wanna a huge space ship rocket la, take it up to da cosmos shiny stars all twinkle twinkle an I shit in my saucer an have a good look down on da big big blue. Derd be a button named Lazer dat blast all da shitty bits dat ya'd see, yeah. I press dat button an Lazer would fireball all below an den back down I fly to Crossheaven happy dat all das left a Pork Sity is my roam your roam an da Palace Disco cause das all dat matters, Runt . . . ress is jus weekday stuff.

Runt   Da Palace Disco. Is a dream, Pig.

Pig   Pig know way da Palace is, Honest!

Runt   Sure, Pig.

Pig (*beat*)   Les go home, yeah. Beddy byes, hun! Yer place furs stop, yeah!

Runt   No race. Les stay.

Pig   Handsome.

Long silence as the 2 listen to the sea.

Pig   Happy birrday taday, Runt!

Runt   Da bes', Pig! Til nex year, hah.

Pig *nods. Beat.*

Pig?

Pig   Yes ol, pal?

Runt   Tanks! Is real nice dis.

Pig *and* **Runt** *remain standing looking out at the sea. The sound of a car horn is heard.* **Pig** *looks over his shoulder.*

Pig   Fuck an wait, ja langer!!

Runt *smiles at* **Pig**. *They look out. Lights fade to a new state.* **Pig** *and* **Runt** *returning home. Music.*

Runt   Say night to Sinéad, Darren!!

Pig *oinks.*

Runt   Tomborrow evey ol pal!!

Pig   Night, Runt!!

New state. **Pig** *and* **Runt** *watching an episode of* Baywatch *which we hear under music. It's the next day.*

Runt   Jees Pig, top a da delly dis!

Pig   God it all, pal!

Runt   *Baywatch* da true winner, yeah!

Pig   Soun, sea an san!

Runt   An sex too, pal!

Pig   Da 4 's'is, hey Runt! (*He laughs.*)

Runt   Oh yeah! (*She laughs.*) Look a dat boy! Bronze, he a blue eye boy wid da real big beach balls, pal!

Pig   Imagine dat chunk doin da breast strokey on ol Runt, hey!

Runt   Fook off, you!

Pig   Imagine me gainst dat bloke in da race, hun! Who da winner den, pal?

Runt   Pig, a corse!

Pig   Easy peasey, bronze boy! Takey ye all on, ya Caliphoney babies!!

Runt   Oh pal, look at dat der!

Pig   Nice gaff, yeah!

Runt   Jiff clean, Pig! Da toilea bowl all a sparkly like is Jesus Christ's very own bog. Is beautiful.

Pig Imagine havin a wazz in dat bowl!

Runt Oh yeah, pal! A pock-full a tens ta wipe da bum hole an all! (*She laughs.*)

Pig Now das class girl! (*He laughs.*)

Runt Imagine me born der?

Pig An me too yeah! 2 *Baywatch* babes, Pig an Runt!

Runt Hoy, Mam! Wat time ya call dis, daff girl!! Dat da dins?! Runt she starve but who da you care, hey?!

Pig Tateys an gravy, yummy yummy! Shlap it der look!

Runt Da fookin telly, Mam! Outta da fookin way, fatty!

Pig Move it, maestro!

Runt Get da fook out so!

Pig Don give up da day job, hey mammy!

Runt Nice woon!

Pig Ta ta girl! (*Beat.*) Hey! Look a dat girlly there!

Runt Oh yeah!

Pig Pamela Anderson!

Runt Beautiful. Beautiful girl!

Pig But dat dress she wear, pal! It move like . . . like . . .

Runt Pig?

Pig Like some liddle fedder ya can see fall in da sky oudda a birdy dat fly by.

Runt Ohhh yeah!! (*Beat.*) Eat up, yeah!

Music. **Pig** *stands out.*

Pig Why I kiss da honey lips a Runt? An now all dat I put my gob to is Runt I take an tase. I close da eyes an see da inhide a Runt legs. Da silk a da tighs an da liddle heaven a panties dat sit above. Dat liddle furry tuff dat wid ma paws I cup an knead. Runt she get all sof an moise an she gendle

press inta my han which seem to call her in . . . she come in.
An we on da floor an lick da stiff tips a tits an all da time
she on my fingur an da tongues dey disco dance an we move
da wet spit aboud our face. I feel dis da time. Pig nee to be a
man. I all caught up in da pants an zip zip Runt fold her
han aboud me. She take me oud an me all shiny an hard I
open her real sof. Open. She wet an moan. Liddle moan. I
poosh an touch da way in. And now Pig an Runt are da one.
We move an all is warm an sof wet, an da 2 well lost in da
sex we move slow an gendle, yeah, an Runt she give one mo
moan an Pig he pour inta da Runt. We man an woman now.
We kiss wid tongues. Pig go nice sof inside. My liddle baby
seal wants oud. I kiss Runt eyes. She all shiny an glow as I
pull-ou.

Music stops.

Pig En ter tain ment! Ya on?!!

Runt Wat?

Pig *and* **Runt** En-ter-tain-ment!

Runt Now, Pig?

Pig Off out, yeah!?

Runt Wer da bobs, so!?

Pig A few bobs, Runt! Wat ya say?!

Runt Tonigh, Pig! Now?

Pig 17, yeah!

Runt Yeah!

Pig Well les make up to flip out, yeah?!

Runt *and* **Pig** Up up up up up up up up up up up!

Pig Raceyaso!!!

Runt Fook yes!!

Sounds of the quiet bar are faded up slightly louder.

Pig Hoy, Marky!

Runt   So back in da Provo pub purr a secon nigh surprise yeah, an we in nee a da drink. Solids come in da shape of a scampi fries which Pig do hate but I do adore. So in da drinky fish mush my belly bubble an lisson as Pig wine up Marky an play da liddle bad boy! When all of a puddin . . .

Pig   Get a gawk at that yoke! Is a fookin karaoke! Hoy Markie, was dis, boy? Charity funk or wat?!!!

Runt   It's a Cork Sinn Féin do!

Pig   Say Markie, under another of his mam's *tang tops!!*

Runt   Wid dat da doors a da pub flap op an close as da Sinn Féin army pile-in an gadder bout da stout taps! Five hundred a da bas-turds all in nees of a good shave an da girlfrens like cocker spaniels come in oudda da rain! Da place go crazy!!

Sounds of extremely busy pub an somebody singing 'Danny Boy'.

Pig   Ere, shouldn't ya be out plantin bombs an beaten up ol ladies, ya fookin weirdos!!

Runt   Fair dues, boy.

Pig   Pine, girl?

Runt   Bag a scamp too, yeah!

Pig   So at da bar I mee da karaoke-man himself of which I fine his name is Trevor. So Trevor, I say to dis small speccy spec-a-fuck, how match a go, hey man!? Trevor say, it's free. Dat righ Trev? Trouble is, says Trevor, only Provo songs tonigh, ol pal! Really, Trev? A fiver saw Trevor all righ for a surprise for my girl, yeah das her wid da packet a scampi, a course she's nice, Trev-boy, she beautiful her!

Runt   Oh get da fook off da stage, ape man!

Pig   Real lady, Trev!

Runt   A crease ball wanders over. Da girlfren a Danny Boy it seem! 'I'll fuckin claim ya if ya don shift yer hole righ now!' says she. I stan up. Smell da cheap fume frum way under da Martini. Her chip paper skin wid drawn on eyes an lips dat lookalike well dangerous skidmarks. I face dis ugly puss an holdin a fist full a scampi fry I mash it inta her gob! When SHLAP!! (**Runt** *reacts to punch in the face.*) She pack a punch dis doll! SSMACKKK!! (*Reacts the same.*) Opens up da nose an blood all drip drip drop from da Runt! She hold hold a my hair an spit da scampi mush back inta my face an onta da fancy top I do wear. Dat stain won' shift too easy, I tink! FUCKKKKK!!! (*Reacts.*) Where Pig? Where ya now, Mister Kissy!? Mister Kissy! Mister Kissy! Mister Kissy! Mister Kissy!!

'Be my Baby' by the Ronettes comes on. **Pig** *performs it karaoke style miming to the original. Meanwhile* **Runt** *is seen to be reacting to some violent punches to her face.* **Pig** *finishes mid-song.*

Pig   Runt

Runt   Outside, pal!

Runt *turns to* **Pig**. *Blood pours from her face.*

Pig   Wat mess! Look dat beat up face!

Runt   Les ship out, yeah!

Pig   I fuckin burn da fuck who did dis! Who did, poin da way! Won't take long o no-ting! Justice see der face smash in! Who, Runt, who hey?

Runt   No figh no more!

Pig   Lie back an die is dat da chant, Runt!

Runt   Off home, yeah!

Pig   Is dis not Pig an Runt side by side, remembers? A silen deal is wad we may way back in sain fridgets ward, we join, remembers, an in dat look we set out Runt, you an me pal, to make us king an queen a Pork sity!

Runt   Leave!

Pig (*beat*)   Yeah ol pal, leave! Les leave all dat scum to dat scum!! An nows breed it in, pal! Breed in Pork's own poxy air. Elp sued da cut an bruise ya da have, Runt. Jees, Runt, wadda fook dat, hey! Sorry pal! Jus stay in real calm an Pig he put tings righ, hey! Smar boy!! So no tears liddle one! . . .

please! (*Puts his hand over her eyes and covers his eyes with his other hand.*) Calm mother, calm! An sleep an res, ol sweet ting! Calm liddle pretty skin. (*Lowers his hands from her eyes.*)

Runt   Oh my gian fuck of a beautiful white marbly mosque! Is da Palace. Is da Palace Disco.

Pig   Oh my guardy angel ya come up trumps dis time fella!!!

Runt   How did dis big white house dat mus be da size a da Pork ferry ta poxy England, how did dis gaff play hide-an-seek purr dis long, pal? Is Pork dat big?

Pig   Not big, no, but manky. Not big, Runt, bud a big black barrel a black dat only do pause purr da pissy grey rain. Bud ya know, ol girl, even a great big poo poo has its diamonds an dis great big great marbly monstrosity which you did righly call da size of da Pork ferry, dis is Pork's own liddle gem!

Runt   It take a Captain Cook like my very own bes pal ta sniff it out, hey! Wat a tresure you bot are! Dis is really it, Pig!

Pig   Oh no pal, dis is much more dan it! Ya know where da top stops, well dis stop . . .

Runt   . . . is one step on top of dat top! Dis is like da cream cept beighy creamyer!

Pig   One hundred per cent don tell da true facs here, Runt!

Runt   Dis is bettur den gold . . .

Pig   Da pick a da bunch!

Runt   Champain . . .

Pig   Ta everyone elses Fanta! Man United . . .

Runt   Ta everyone elses West ham!

Pig   Ya noel wen Sonia finally become champion da wonder horse an gallop her way to suckycess bak in old Godden-burg, yeah? An Sonia stan on da winny po-dium wid da whirl medal all a dangle from da pretty liddle neck as da nationalist rant-hymn blast da fuck oudda da sky an da green white an porridge all a flutter in da breeze. An all da Irish aroun da track an in da whirl, an anybod who even fuck an Irish dey all have a liddle tear a boy in der eye when dey say, 'Dis is a great day for Our-land!' Well Runt, dis is a bettur day!

Runt   Fuck, yes!!

Pig *and* **Runt** *go to enter the Palace.*

Runt   Stop!

Pig *stops.*

Pig   Ah bollix!

Runt   A gian cyclops a bricks wid bouncer tatooes on his toilea face.

Pig   Jus my luck, hey! So wers Hans gone, ol Chew-back-a?!

Runt   Regular are ya?

Pig   Once in da moring an again in da evening, doctur!

Runt   Pig too smart fur dis tic toc! Da man he screw up da face an lookalike a playt a mash an mushy pea sept a bit more starchey. He look down na Pig an he say, 'I think you know my little brother.'

Pig   Who he, fat man?

Runt   He worked down in the off licence in Blackpool! But now he's on the dole.

Pig   Das a sad an sorry story.

Runt   I watch Pig as da past tap em on da shold wid a hi-dee-hi. Off licence. Blackcruel. Fuck me.

Pig   Yeah I noel Foxy, good bloke yeah!

Runt   Bud da big man no who Pig is.

Pig   He place his shovel han onta ma head an den he say:

Runt   ˙I hate the little bollix, myself!

Pig *(laughs)*   Tank fuck! *(Both laugh.)*

Runt   Excuse me, so what's the password, then?

Pig   Sorry boss? Password? Is that wat you say, ol boy? Was da password, yeah?

Runt   You know, what's the colour of love?

Pig (*beat*)   Wad sorra love?

Runt   The sort of love that you feel. The sort of love that only one colour can tell you about. The sort of love that can pick you up with a stupid grin cut ear to ear and can then cut your throat just as easily. (*Beat.*) An I look a Pig. An Pig he loss jus like da Runt is. Wad we know, hey? We all alone on da Palace Disco step wid Foxy's big pox of a brud. Seems like hours tic-by an Pig he jus look an stare straight ahead. (*Beat.*) An den, Pig, frum somewers he say:

Pig   Blue. Blue da colour a love. Is blue, yeah?

Runt   An da big double decker in da pink dicky bow wave his kingsize han an say, 'Cloakroom on the left.'

Music up. They're in. **Pig** *goes for the drinks.*

Pig   Pine, pal?

Runt   G and T, yeah yeah!!

Pig   Ohhhhhhhhhh righhhhhh, hasta be, hasta be, Jo-Hannah Lum-mel-lee!!

Runt   An a pak a scampi fries, Pig!

Pig   Three paks in dis side a heaven, girl!

Runt   *Three*, Pig!??

Pig   Dis a free cuntry, ol girl! Is yer want ta suck on dose liddle poxy fishy tings dat remind me a Nero's balls or sum schlop ya put out fur a liddle hungry kitty kat, yeah!! Runt ol pal, yer wish is my demand!

Runt   My hero!

Pig   I fuck off so!

Pig *gets the drinks in.* **Runt** *alone. Looks about.*

Runt   So Runt she touchdown on all da chrome an da sky
blue draylon! Who'd a guesst? Pig wid da righ ans fur Foxy's
big brud an open sess me an Pig in a Cinderella ball, yeah,
cept no sad old Billa or anythin panto, tank fuckin Jesus!
Surprise surprise! Fur a sec I tink, hey mayb all dat drink
drink play sum sorta shake it all abou insize my beautiful
liddle head so I do da pinch an den da eyes all close den
peep-op again an . . . an is true. Me in da Palace Disco!! 17!!!
All grow up! True story no fict!

Pig   Das three packs, yeah! Three! Fur da ol doll!

Runt   All da beautys in here! All dancin good da on an off
beat dat in real real dance! I spy sumthin begins wid Princess!
She in black chambray dress fit an flare mid-calf, seamed. She
know da fash! Real nice job! An I tink me as her dancin wid
all da frens, yeah! All laughin, all dancin da same as one!
Maybe we dress before in my room! Maybe we chit chat an I
say, I don fancy, Frankie, no, ohhh does it really show? An
we all laugh an gozzel back another boddle a Ritz! No gozzel,
no, sip! An we at da Palace Disco fun fun fun an jus maybe
dis bloke dream cum true who look like Phil Babb or sum
odder hunk mayb he say, 'Nice dress,' an I say, 'Tank you, I
made it myself,' an he kiss my han an not try to tickle my
insize wid his Tayto tongue! Mayb dat be good! Mayb dat be
good fun jus ta try, ya know!

Pig   Remarkable in it! I mean look at dat daycor, Runt, few
bob der I'd say! Real class, all righ! Imagine dis yer gaff! Cept
da prices mayb – a cheepur a course!

Runt   Cheers, pal!

Pig   To you, hun!

Runt   Who'd a guesst, hey?

Pig   All fur one!

Runt   Yeah das righ. (*Sees something in front of her.*) Ders a
mirror, look!

Pig   Who dat beautiful pair?

Runt   Us a course!

Pig   Like a misty an misses, Runt!

Runt   Zact same. (*Beat.*) An Pig an Runt sit in da big bubble dat is my life! 17 years an fuck all chane. Pig still look ta me an dat look keep me in Pig-step! Runt da real runt in dis liddle carriage. Well, up up up up up up up up up up up up up up up up, get up girl! Is yer choice, party girl!!

Pig   Was dis!?

Runt (*beat*)   Toilea.

Pig   Ja wan more a da scampi ta soak it all up?

Runt   Tanks bud no tanks.

Pig   Maybe up latur an show off da piggy dance, ya on?!

Runt   Maybe, yeah!

Pig   Handsome!! (*Beat.*) An Runt off, leave da Pig in wat be a well ol feelin, yah yah! See I wan da buzz, yeah! Look les stop all dis chitty chat shat an les sees whos da number plum aroun here! Dey all look an laugh a me! Hear dem?!! I can see it, yeah! Dey loads a cash an look a Pig an, who he, dey say! Who'd da liddle boy in da a confirmation suity?? Well, fuck anuff! I all calm fur *she* know who, but no more! Dis no me, no!! Pig he wan ta balance it righ an da Palace Disco need a less an Pig he da real teach tonigh, all righ! So who da furs hey?

Runt   Tank you, I made it myself!

Pig   Was dis! Oh yes! Jus like before, yea! Good ol Runt! She play da girlfren an misty pig he play da boyfren! But dis time I read da message purr real! She wan *us* purr real! Me an her! We jar it! We fucking jar ya know!

Runt *holds out her hand which we imagine is being kissed.*

Pig   An thru da pump pump pump a da disco dance I see it all! Pig on his marks an all set as misty hansome move in on Runt an . . .

Runt   Kiss my hand.

Pig   An das my cue!!! Ova I move! Move real fass, yeah!
Scream ou loud I scream an grab da liddle fuck an Runt she
say:

Runt   Jesus Pig no! No!!!

Pig   Oud oud oud oud oud oud OUD OUD OUD!!!!!! Take
oud! Move oudda da fuckin way! Door open shut! Throw!
You dirty liddle fuck she my girlfren bollix! Smash! Kassshhh!
Open da nose da eye! Blood blood blood! An Smashhh
smasshhhh smash! I am da king, ya fuckidy fuck! Ashtray!
Smash kaasshhhh head smasshhh! Head crack op! She mine,
luvver boy! She my girl! Me an her, king an queen ya bad
boy! Scream baby liddle baby scream an SMASH SMASH
SMASH . . . SMASHHH!!!!!

Runt   Oh, fuck.

Pig   Dead hun, just like an action flic! Big mess dis!

Runt   Cheerio. So-long pal.

Pig   Wat? Stay! (*Overlapping.*) STAY STAY STAY STAY
STAY STAY STAY!!!!

Runt (*overlapping*)   GO GO GO GO GO GO GO GO GO!!
An Runt race good dis time! Mus ged away! No mo all dis
play an pain! So so-long to all dat pox! Go girl! Leave! An it
well ovur, drama fans! Runt race her ways up da piss-grey
straight wid da Palace Disco an poor ol Pig on her back! Jus
me! Jus da liddle girl all aloneys! An still I see Pig like he
besie me, yeah. He my one an only, he da bes an da worse
pal in dis bad ol whirl. An I wan Pig an I wan for all da
buzz an all da disco we do dance but hey ho an wadda ya
know I wan fur sumthin else! Sumthin differen! Sumthin
differen! Fuckin freedom!! Jus me!! Jus da Runt!! So mayb ta
Crossheaven, mab das where a girl can sleep sleep sleep an be
alone. Jus me an da big big colour blue. Dat colour blue!
(*Beat.*) An Runt take a breeder on Christy's Ring . . . an I look
a da sun creep up on my pal Pork . . . *Cork.* An da sun it
really is a beautiful big thing. (*Beat.*) An Runt she alone now.

But is OK now, is all righ. (*Beat.*) Runt, she calm, calm
down . . .
an I watch . . .
da liddle quack quacks . . . I look . . . at the ducks . . . as they
swim in the morning sun . . .   in the great big . . .
            watery-shite . . .

                        that is the river Lee.

Where to?

Light slowly fades down on **Pig** *until out.*

Then light slowly fades down on **Runt**.

Blackout.

Enda Walsh has been the Artistic Director of the Cork-based theatre company, Corcadorca, since January 1996. He has written three plays for the company: a radical adaptation of *A Christmas Carol* in the winter of 1994, *The Ginger Ale Boy* in the spring and autumn of 1995, and *Disco Pigs*, which played in autumn 1996. *Sucking Dublin*, for the Abbey Theatre's Outreach Department, was seen in Dublin in autumn 1997. He is currently writing a one-man show, *Love Underneath*, and developing *Disco Pigs* as a feature-length screenplay for Temple Films.

Enda Walsh won a 1996 Stewart Parker Award for *Disco Pigs* and the 1997 George Devine Award for *Disco Pigs* and *Sucking Dublin*.

Bat the Father Rabbit the Son

by Donal O'Kelly

Acknowledgements

Donal O'Kelly wishes to record his gratitude and appreciation to Rough Magic for producing the play; to Declan Hughes for his invaluable contribution both to the first draft and to subsequent rewriting; to Siobhán Bourke, manager of Rough Magic, for sending the show out on such successful tours; and to Marie Tierney who stage-managed every production of *Bat the Father Rabbit the Son* – over one hundred performances in all.

Bat the Father Rabbit the Son was first performed by the Rough
Magic theatre company on 27 September, 1988 in the Mansion
House, Dublin, as part of the Dublin Theatre Festival:

Performed by Donal O'Kelly

Directed by Declan Hughes
Designed by Robert Ballagh
Lighting by Paul O'Neill

Characters
Rabbit is an Irish, middle-aged, self-made haulage magnate. In
the course of the play, he becomes so obsessed with the memory
of his father Bat, a 1916 Citizen Army veteran and pawnshop
assistant, that his mind and body are taken over by Bat from time
to time.

Setting
The set consists of an aluminium table and chair on a steel-blue
carpet.

Lights up on pinstripe-suited **Rabbit** *in his office, crouched, sniffing, on his desk. He is interrupted by the arrival of his subordinate Keogh (needless to say, invisible to the audience).*

Scene One
Rabbit Cuts a Deal

Listen, Keogh! I know you and you know me so we won't fuck around. Right!? I built this company out of nothing. Right!? Don't fuck around. Out of nothing. Right!? Do you know what I had when I started? A bicycle! A ladies' bicycle with a fucking big basket on the front! And I went out to Howth every morning and knocked off a basketful of cod and beat it back to Moore Street and flogged it to the oul wans before it got bright. In hail, rain, sleet and snow! So don't tell me about haulage. I made this company, Keogh. I gave you your job.

Swings around and presents his legs to Keogh.

You see these legs? Feel them! Go on! Squeeze! Have a real feel! Like Butlin's Rock. Only hairy. That's muscle, Keogh. And that's what I've got. Don't fuck around. (*Brushes Keogh's hands away.*) That muscle hardened, Keogh, galvanised, concretised, on every hard wet ride to Howth and back. And that same muscle is the muscle I hold in haulage, Keogh. So don't fuck around! Don't give me your expertise in nitty-gritty ponce Trinity College administration larkabout. I was in haulage before you were born. On a fucking ladies' bicycle! And you walked into my glass office with an umbrella. You never got wet because I built this glass office for you to walk into, out of my sweat, and rheumatism, and punctures and cobblestones, and lumbago, and baskets, and out of my muscle, Keogh. And don't you ever, ever forget that! Don't fuck around, Keogh, don't fuck around! I'm getting to that. I'm getting to your fucking report.

Pause.

I don't want you to get the feeling, Keogh, that I don't like

you. Or that I think you're an overspoilt privileged brat with
a silver spoon stuck in your cake-hole from the day you were
born. Because, Keogh, I think you have got something to
credit you. Now you could never do anything on your own or
anything like that, but with a lot of – structure behind you
I've noticed you can sometimes get things done. I'd say you're
bordering, Keogh, I'd say you're bordering, on brains. Don't
protest! Take it like a man! It's not everyone can get things
done and it's good to see the beginnings of it, especially in a
young fella.

Now, Keogh, about your report! Your report stinks, Keogh. It
stinks because it lets Mick Smurfit in. It stinks because my
name goes off the trucks. And it stinks because you're trying
to promote me out.

(*Roars.*) Don't fuck around, Keogh!

Gathers himself.

Letting Mick Smurfit in, Keogh, is like blowing a million out
the window. If I got an electric fan, Keogh, and aimed it at
the window, and put a million notes in front of it, and
switched on the fan, Mick Smurfit would get rid of it quicker.
As well as that I can't abide the fucker. But about the trucks:
two hundred trucks built by my muscle will carry my name,
Keogh. End of story, right!? You're a back-stabbing bollocks
to try and promote me out, and I have done some terrible
things to back-stabbers in the past. So my answer, Keogh, my
answer is . . . yes. On three conditions: One. That I never
hear Smurfit's name within these glass walls. Two. If the
trucks change, my name changes with them! And three. You,
Keogh, will be my personal assistant for the next twelve
months.

(*Sticks out hand.*) Shake! It's a deal. Come on! Shake fucking
hands!

Pause. Keogh's not that easy to take.

Look, Keogh, look. . . ! Look at these glass walls, Keogh, open
your chicken eyes and look! Look at my desk, look at my
chair, real kid leather doesn't sweat no sticky arse, sit in it,

you gobshite! Look at Rabbit Haulage all around you, look at
the shelves, look at the bit of treated pine, look at the lovely
Louis Le Brocquy, isn't it nice, now, nice, and there's Night
Nurse the famous racehorse, and the Bobby Ballagh job on
yours truly, not too sure about it myself but just the same. . . !
And come over here, oh Keogh, come over here and look at
the yard, and look at all the trucks, the red and yellow trucks
with the big black letters on the side, look at the spacious
new car park and soon it will be tarmacadamed, yes,
tarmacadamed, oh Keogh, look, quick, look at once over
there at the gate, a truck coming in full to bursting with some
exotic produce, pâté perhaps, from a far-away place across the
sea, Dusseldorf or Stuttgart please God, and a big fat driver
hopping from the cab – look at his chubby happy cheeks, and
he's only driven one, Keogh, one, think of the two hundred
others trundling down the autobahns of the empire, sailing
smoothly on the ferries of fortune, bringing the luscious foods,
hazlett, Keogh, and picnic roll, maple-cured bacon, butter-
basted viandes, fowl from Flanders, grouse and moorhen from
the divil knows where, ho-ho, listen to me now with your eyes
growing wide . . .

Silver-skinned onions from the plains of Provence, blood-red
carrots from loess of the Loire, apples grown from the battle-
richened soils of Philippi, beer from Bavaria, currant-cakes
from holy Jaysus Cracow, sardines from Sardinia, and fish,
from the Baltic and Barents, the Ionian and Aegean wherever
the fuck the Bay of bleeding Biscaya, all hurtling towards our
feet, Keogh, wrapped in yellow and red containers. (**Rabbit**
the tempter.) All this can be yours, Keogh. All this and more.
All this and a slice of Smurfit's too. All this and your paddy-
waddy bum on a stern leather seat sitting fair and square at
the polished oak board of easy-eye ballcock Smurfit
International. Wouldn't that be nice, oh Keogh? Won't that
be lovely! Oh so . . . comfortable, yes Keogh, that's what you
want, yes, and that's what you're going to get . . . yes . . .
(*Bangs fist on table.*)

If you do what you're told to do!
Snaps, Keogh, snaps!

Get me some snaps!
Snaps of me, and snaps of my father, and snaps of me and
my father together! No questions! Ah-ah! Ah-ah! Go! Do it!
Or the deal is off! (*Keogh indicates compliance.*)

That's better. Now you're learning. And get them blown up,
Keogh! Big, boy, big! Snaps, Keogh, snaps!

Rabbit *hugs himself in anticipation, spinning on his tabletop, legs in
the air. He jumps into action at Keogh's entrance.*

Scene Two
The Snaps

Rabbit *pulls his chair down stage, and sits leaning his elbow on the
back of it looking at the slide screen (out in the audience).*

Rabbit   Jesus, Keogh, terrific! What have you got? Slides!!
Well now, Keogh, you have excelled yourself! Sony is it, good
man! You can't beat the Japanese. That's what I like to see.
A self-starter! Energy and enterprise! Good man, Keogh! All
right, I'm ready, steady, go!

Flash of white light as if slide projector is flicking on to the first slide.

It's me looking out through the bars of my cot. Where did I
get those curls? Sampson. Grr. Pulling down my bars. Grrr.
Next!

Flash.

There's my father out with his old battalion, would you lookit
he's as thin as the Mauser he's carrying, but sure he was
happy I suppose to be out and about in the thick of it all
God bless him. Next!

Flash.

There's the two of them cutting the cake for better or worse.
Great definition, Keogh! I wonder were they thinking then of
little Terence to come . . . a twinkle in the eye, eh? They look
very shy. Next!

Flash.

Jesus! I'd forgotten! Me in my Stella Maris togs and my Uncle Mattie's boots he sent from Birmingham with a special tin of polish to preserve them, with the roundy ankle pad for the bowsies in the Fifteen Acres and the biting cold, like a team of bloody snowmen with the soggy old leather getting heavier and harder . . . Next!

Flash.

Now what is that – it looks familiar. A whole lot of men lined up before a building with a banner, let me see . . . 'We Serve Neither King Nor Kaiser But' . . . aw yeah, yeah, yeah. There they are in lines. With a hole fifth from the left in the second row. A hole. Jesus! There's shy and there's shy but he really took the biscuit! Next!

Flash.

Me and my father down the corner of Cathal Brugha with the horse and cart . . . The horse and cart, Keogh! I loved that horse with his soft warm nose, and I fed him leaves of cabbage when the meeting had dispersed and the half of the crowd started back off up towards Dalymount and Frank what was he called, the big hero of the gathering, Frank what the blazes was it, oh, a great big straight man who got the biggest cheer, and I fed the leaves of cabbage to the lovely lazy horse and he munched them in a funny sideways kind of way but he wouldn't eat the stalk, no, not for all the tea in Kingdom come damn the bit of cabbage-stalk would pass his leather lips, oh no now thank you very much, and Frank what the blazes was it well anyway he upped and offed to Spain to turn the Spaniards communist, throwing nuns to the crocodiles ah no not at all no crocodiles in Spain must have got them in from somewhere else or was it alligators anyway Frank, he laughed a big loud laugh and said, 'Rabbit, you're your father's son,' for why I don't know, for if I'm not my father's son who the fuck's son could I possibly be, between the wall and you and me!?

Rabbit, *agitated, sits on the table and motions Keogh to sit in the chair* *down stage facing him. He has a confessional manner.*

Scene Three
The Secret of the Missing Snap

Rabbit   Oh Keogh Keogh Keogh ... Let me tell you a
secret. A secret is a lovely thing. A wonderful gift to give. Do
you know the funny thing about a secret? A secret has a very
direct self-destructive instinct. Your ordinary secret? A regular
kamikaze! A secret isn't happy till it's down done destroyed.
There, you have a secret safe inside your head. Safe. And
what does it do? It hammers hammers hammers until the
doors begin to strain, then a particular moment when you
least expect it – whoosh, there it is sitting on the bar after
falling out your mouth, folding its arms and laughing at you.
Then it drops dead. That's a secret for you.

Pause.

So here's a secret, Keogh, that I'm going to kill in order to
give it to you. Ah don't be so alarmed, Keogh, you're such a
nervous freak! The secret I'm sacrificing to you, Keogh, is
this: *you can't go forward unless you look back.*

Pause.

That's a secret I found, Keogh, and now it's a secret no
more.

Keogh is obviously not picking up the threads.

You see, when you stop and put the periscope up, all you'll
likely see is pure blue sea, and sure what the hell use is that?
Do you follow? But, what if you see the track behind, the
wash coming out from the back of your ship – well! That's a
different story! Gives you a clue as to where you are! Do you
know what you call that? A vector! Direction without the
magnitude. Honest to Jaysus! There you are! So! Direction we
seek. Magnitude we'll add. So first to look back at the track.

Pause.

Keogh, one of the snaps is missing. It's not your fault I'm
sure, sure I'm getting soft on you again. No. Maybe it's lost.
Or maybe it's drowned. Or floating adrift on a distant bay-
wave . . . But it's not on that Sony, Keogh! Not on your
ninny-nanny Sony sonny – no!

Rabbit *closes right up on Keogh, hoist between pleading and*
threatening. He sweeps the chair away back upstage.

Scene Four
The Old Square Wooden Box Camera

Rabbit   Keogh. This terrible thing. So sad . . .

(*Snaps.*) Get me a camera, Keogh! No! Not an Instamatic! An
old square wooden box camera. An old, square, wooden . . .
box.

Pause.

Camera!

Rabbit *is suffering some kind of panic attack.*

No, Keogh! Don't! Don't get it!

The reason for **Rabbit**'s *panic attack becomes apparent. His father*
Bat *bubbles up from inside him irrepressibly, taking over* **Rabbit**'s
tight squat body with his roly-poly loose-limbed wide-eyed persona.

Bat   You get . . . don't get . . . little get! Stand still little get!

Rabbit *manages to regain control for a second.*

Rabbit (*desperately*)   Don't go, Keogh!

Bat *bubbles up again, taking a snap of little* **Rabbit** *in the long grass*
with the old square wooden box camera. He stands up on the chair for a
better view.

Bat   The sun behind my shoulder. Standing on a boulder.
Hold it to my tummy-tum-tum. Tummy tum tummy tum
tummy tum tum. Twiddley-diddley smell of the leathery
yummy yum yum. Stand still, little get! Fidgetin gibbet! Come

on now, Big Chief Zulu sittin' on a drum. Come on now Big
Chief watch the cockatoocanary-oh . . . ! Stick your head up
high in the air! Stretch! Stretch up on your tippy-toes so's I
can see your smiling little mug . . . ! Hoe-de-oh-doh that's a
grumpy countenance, my fairy philosopher man!

Bat *submerges again leaving* **Rabbit** *shaken by the ordeal.*

Rabbit   High grass, Keogh! All around me! Higher than my
head! My father standing on a rock. Jigging up and jigging
down staring into a box he's holding at his navel. Try to
brush the dry stalks out of my way, give me a clear view. But
move one away and another falls across. Long stiff ribbony
blades of tindery grass like tiger's camouflage. Obscuring my
vision of my father standing on the rock with his old square
wooden box . . . Camera. Damn these lanky weeds! They're
getting in my way! Cluttering the picture about to be
snapped! Wait! Until I clear! Make nice! The! Hold! Just a – !
One goes west and another sways in – two! Three! Ouch!
Fucking nettles now as well! As if not enough to be – ! Some
day soon, maybe longers, then no fear of nettles. Has he took
it yet? Shove the shiny silver lever and – tsssk! Lovely liquidy
click.

Rabbit *emerges from his involuntary flashback.*

Here in my pocket, Keogh, is the stiff remains . . . The stiff
remains! The snap, dimwit, the snap! God help me, do you
not speak poetry? The stiff remains? Do you understand, my
poor boy wonder? Do you understand, Keogh?

Rabbit *sits at his desk.*

Scene Five
The Wood and the Trees

Rabbit   Do you understand? Anything? On the level –
anything? Because I sometimes think I – I . . . ! Must keep a
grip! But oh God, Keogh, it's so sad. This – understanding
thing . . . Or lack of – ! Awful sad. Awful.

Pause.

Something to do with the wood and the trees. Can't see the grass for grass. Can't see the stalks for blades. The wood and the trees! Wood: A wood? Or just wood?

'I can't see the wood for the trees.' It's very good, Keogh, isn't it? The best old saying I know. Top of the list! But Keogh? Does he mean *a* wood or woody wood? A forest of trees or timber *in* the trees?

If I say I can't see the wood for the trees is it because there are too many trees in my way and I can't see the *wood* that I'm in? Or is it because I can only see the trees and not the *wood* within? Aw, Keogh, I get all sweaty when I think about it. Feverish and nausea.

When I was a baby, Keogh, lying in my cot with the woody bars, saying my prayers for ever and ever, Keogh, at the end of every prayer except the Our Father and the Hail Mary, all the others, Keogh – for ever and ever. World without end . . . Everlasting peace . . .

Lying behind the bars of your cot in the dark contemplating all eternity is a terrible fucking thing for a four-year-old! But the same awful feeling Keogh . . .

Sucks his thumb.

My Mother? Yes, my mother put a stop to that. Don't think about it says she and I didn't and never bawled since.

But this business of the wood and the trees has me sickened since I first touched. The trees *are* wood and the wood *is* trees . . . Like the snap my father took! There's me in the long grass but – they're a part of it too! The stalks!

The perfect sight of me and my father staring airily eye to eye will never be! Do you see? If it's not the dry stalks in between, it's maybe a sea mist, or the jiggy of a see-saw, or sun in my eyes or the shadow of a grey wall, or the whip of the east wind, or the cracka-chugga of an elephant JCB, or an infinity for ever and ever of other things between! And that's what the real thing is! The whole Jaysusin' muddle!

Pause.

I think.

Rabbit *has to lean against the table to recover from such heroic self-absorption.*

Scene Six
A Terrible Man

Rabbit   Keogh, my father, oh Keogh my father, me da, Keogh my father was – a terrible man. I don't mean any disrespect, but Jesus! I've a question, Keogh, can you tell me – no, you probably can't – where oh where do people lose the bit of – thing that they've got? How does it happen or maybe they never had it in the first place but just looked like they had and sure that's half the battle won in any case –

Bat *erupts suddenly.*

Bat   – whack fol de diddle diddle durum di ay. Ah sonny my boy, my funny little mank, you've more to learn than I can ever teach. What did I tell you, you little Mickey Drippin', standing close to the puddles like that? Come here to me – come here to me, black puddin' on a Monday! Look at the cut of you! Your socks are soppin'! We'll have to bring you home-ee-oh to the little red house. Home-ee-oh we'll go-ee-oh, soppy-bum!

Rabbit *regains himself but only for a mo –*

Rabbit   Ah Keogh! Puddle water dripping down my leg. It makes you want to wee-wee . . .

Bat *bubbles up again –*

Bat   Here we are! Hold on just a jiffy till I open out my big brown coat! (*Turns back to audience.*) Up again the wall now! Safe as Mountjoy! Not a sinner to see you! Widdley-whiddley there we go, run, river, run . . . (**Bat** *follows the stream with his eyes.*) Hello Mrs Tully grand day thank God ah-ha . . . oh please God! (*Back to the matter at hand.*) Finishy-uppedy shake

the dribblies ups-a-daisy diddley-aiddley off we go, up the airy
mountains and down the Russian glen, we daren't go a
hunting for fear of little manks just like you de diddley
doodley ooh!

Rabbit *recovers himself. He stands behind the desk.*

Rabbit   Keogh, my daddy worked in a pawn. Curbishley
Antiques they called it, but I had my Rabbit nose even then
and I knew it was a pawn. My father laid out all the items,
big and small, without breaking anything, ever. Every damn
thing you could think of found its way into his sausagey hands
and on to the clean white sheets of butcher paper. China
plates, cut-glass bowls, trinkets, cruets, goblets and cups,
stuffed ducks, marbley eyes, ornamental frogs, delph from the
Oriental, crockery from Persia, Venetian glass, Louis
Quatorze . . .

Scene Seven
Mr Curbishley's Fishing Trip
One: The Invitation

Rabbit   One day, Keogh, Mr Curbishley said to my father:

– Bat, I'm going out for an afternoon's fishing in my boat on
Sunday, you're more than welcome to join me.

– Right you be Mr Curbishley, said my father, that would be
most enjoyable.

And off he skedaddled all excited to a fella from his old
battalion for the loan of a rod and some tackle. But tackle
was one thing, fine as it was, and bait was another.

Mr Curbishley's Fishing Trip
Two: The Bait Shop

Rabbit *(cont.)*   So on Sunday morning after Mass, with me
still smelling from my bath of the night before, my father and
me walked down the quays to the Ha'penny Bridge, and he

was diddley-eiddling like he always did when he was happy,
happy with his rod and a little bag of sinkers and hooks, and
I was hoppiting up and down to see over the wall and catch
a glimpse of the green ploppy swell, and then we went into a
shop.

Plonks chair on to table top to make the bait shop counter-hatch.

Well, I got this smell, Keogh, and I swear at that moment
Keogh, I knew Keogh, I knew it was important. The stench
of salt sea and stiff sand ... And a feeling came over me –
yeah go on laugh! – and the salty sand smell came from the
rows of wet wooden boxes with bits of seaweed sticking out
from under the lids, and when the man put his hand out and
opened them – Jesus, they were full of worms and maggots,
each box had a different kind, ragworms, lugworms,
roundworms and maggots, all squirming and wriggling in their
beds of seaweed and sand. When I saw those worms Keogh,
rolling around with their pinchers snapping, I knew I'd like
the sea. And the man dug in a little shovel like a sweets jar
shovel, and put a shovelful of live lugworms on a bit of
Herald, threw on a scatter of seaweed, wrapped it up in a
handy-packed parcel like a lunch, and gave it to my father for
tuppence.

Up on to the chair.

Mr Curbishley's Fishing Trip
Three: The Tram to Howth

Rabbit (*cont.*)   Next thing there we were sitting on top of the
tram to Howth with the wind blowing brightly the way it only
blows on Sundays. Out through Ballybough and Fairview,
Clontarf and Killester, Baldoyle and Sutton Cross, hardly
stopping at all because it was early. And my father was ready
to burst, with the kind of joy you only feel on Sundays,
digging in his tackle bag and counting what he'd got.

Bat   Three lead sinkers, plumbum! – plug-your-bum, two
German sprats ho-ho it takes the Germans – My Li-hili

Marle-hene, My li-hili Marlene . . . a couple of colourdy
tracers! You're a spinner! You're a topper! You're a rig-stig-
stopper! Catch a cod! Catch a plaice! Catch a baldy man's
face – Whoa! Feathers up your nose! Fly away Pet-er, fly
away Paul, feathers-on-a-hook! Come back all! Oh-hoh we
caught a dazzler!

Rabbit   Then we played fish.

Bat *and* **Rabbit** *play their fish game on top of the tram to Howth.*

Bat   Pollock.

Rabbit   Pinkeen.

Bat   Mackerel.

Rabbit   Shark.

Bat   Salmon bass.

Rabbit   Hammerhead shark.

Bat   Skate.

Rabbit   Octopus.

Bat   Dogfish.

Rabbit   Blue whale.

Bat   Flatfish.

Rabbit   Flying fish.

Bat   Herring.

Rabbit   Dace.

Bat   Plaice.

Rabbit   Cat fish.

Bat   Fishy-fish.

Rabbit   Tuna.

Bat   Fatty-fish.

Rabbit   Scuba.

Bat   Bummy-fish.

Rabbit   Tortoise.

Bat   Eaty-beaty-fish.

Rabbit   Sneaky-deaky-fish.

Bat   Birdy-wurdy-fish.

Rabbit   Cuckoo-clock-fish.

Bat   Broken-potty-fish.

Rabbit   Stand-on-your-head-fish.

Bat   Nelson's-Pillar-fish.

Rabbit   The Biggest Fish in the Whole World!

Rabbit *hops off the tram at Howth.*

Mr Curbishley's Fishing Trip
Four: Your Daddy Never Told Me

Rabbit *sits himself down in the chair on top of the table like any fireside storyteller.*

Rabbit   Mr Curbishley took off his hat and coat, and laid them folded on the leather of the car seat.

– Bat, like a good man, said Mr Curbishley.

– What is it, Mr Curbishley, said my father.

– Would you ever go and fetch Sweeney the boatman, said Mr Curbishley.

– Certainly, said my father, but where should I go?

– To the boozer of course, laughed Mr Curbishley. And my father laughed too.

– Which one, laughed my father.

– How should I know, laughed Mr Curbishley.

– What does Sweeney look like, laughed my father.

– Oh just shout and see if he's there, laughed Mr Curbishley.

– Right you be, said my father.

Mr Curbishley looked at me. I looked at Mr Curbishley.

– Well, little Rabbit, do you like fishing?

– My name is Terence. Yes I do like fishing.

– Well, you can't come with us today. Your daddy never told me you were coming, and I didn't bring a lifebelt.

A big yellow yacht sailed by the lighthouse . . . daytime now! No need to waste the batteries!

Your daddy never told me! And here's the fucking eejit now, walking and talking to Sweeney. And Sweeney staggers down the steps and into a half-sunk punt. And Mr Curbishley dances down the steps carrying his tackle and rods. And my father shuffles his feet in great excitement, he spiders down clutching his stuff, he stands in the punt and turns around.

– Come on, he says, don't keep us waiting!

– Hold your horses, Bat, said Mr Curbishley. Without a lifebelt it's out of the question.

– What? said my father. Are you planning to leave the chiseller here?

– It's my boat, Bat, and I won't take the risk. Can he swim?

– You needn't worry, Mr Curbishley. I'll keep an eye on him.

– Now, now, Bat! That's not the point.

– He can take mine and I'll take the chance.

– Sorry, Bat! It can't be done and that's that!

– Ah fuck it, why!?

– That's the why!

– You can't leave the chiseller here.

– Well, now . . .

The yellow yacht changed its sail from starboard to port. A raindrop wet the back of my neck. My father looked up at me on the granite step. He looked at Mr Curbishley sitting pretty in the prow of his punt feeling his reel. My father never said one word more. He stepped carefully out of the punt and on to the slippy stone step. He took my hand gently in his, and started to walk back down the pier.

– Don't worry, it suits me just as well, Bat, cried Mr Curbishley. She's in need of a little maintenance which Sweeney can help me do.

**Mr Curbishley's Fishing Trip
Five: The Long, Long Walk**

Rabbit (*cont.*)   My father kept walking, lugging his rod and bag, and holding my cold fist in his big warm hammy hand like he did with the antiques, and the raindrops grew thicker, and all in a surge my eyes got hot and filled up so sudden and overflowed and poured and poured down with the raindrops for why I couldn't tell and my father didn't sing like he always did, or didn't doodle-de-ay but just kept walking looking at the blotching granite flags and making a strange foreign noise in his nostrils. We walked down the long pier, and along the prom past the bandstand, a long, long walk with little legs, Keogh, and up the short pier where the trawlers were, and I was still bawling without a sound Keogh, buckets of tears, sweet Jesus tears in fucking buckets, and at the end of the pier my father climbed up the five steep steps.

**Mr Curbishley's Fishing Trip
Six: A Funny Incident**

Rabbit (*cont.*)   – Stand clear now till I make my cast, he said.

And I stood and watched. The cast dangled. Two feathers, three big silver hooks, and a German sprat on the end. He

stretched it out on the top step. Out with the paper parcel.
He tore it, picked up the slithery lugworm. He pushed it on
to the hook, easing it up the silver steel. The hook went in
the back of his neck, so he could still move his head and look
around, trying to bite, I suppose. My father still wasn't
singing. Not even a hum. He hooked another lug, a big long
one, only half of him could fit on the hook, even squashed
up, his tail just hanging off the end. He went for another a
rag this time, a sloppy-looking maggot with big pinchers.

– Ouch, you fucking bollocks you, said my father without the
hint of a lilt, stuffing the hook in the ragworm's head then out
the other side then into his tail and out and back in up
through his middle until he was just brown wriggly mush on
the hook.

– Now, you fucker, said my father in a whisper.

He swung his cast forward and back, and forward and back,
he pushed the bow of the reel across, he held the line in the
crook of his fatty finger, forward and back, forward and back,
he wet his lips, forward and back, he puffed his cheeks, pulled
back further than before, danced a gentle quickstep and –

Three bits of worm scattered in the sky and a German sprat
was dug in my father's bum and the more he pulled like a
bull on the bending rod the more the sprat got stuck in the
seat of his sagging pants. Then he stopped and stood.
Fiddling. No use. Because he couldn't see. Making it worse.

Isn't that a funny story, Keogh? Like a comic. Dennis the
Menace. Or Desperate Dan. Nobody was laughing. Except
Mr Curbishley. He was in a good mood. He swept around in
a bow bend with Sweeney on his fancy Evinrude:

– Everything all right, Bat?

My father didn't hear him.

– Everything all right, Bat?

He said it louder.

– Come here son, said my father in a low voice, come here

and pick this funny fish out of my bottom.

– Yes Dad, I said, climbing up the steps.

– Don't bear a grudge, Bat, it's for your own good, shouted Mr Curbishley.

I had to push it back into his trousers to get it out again, and I think his bottom was bleeding.

– See you tomorrow, Bat.

Brrrrrmmmm,

Then my father whispered very long and very low, so low I hardly heard it.

– Blueshirt bastard.

Pause.

– Thanks, you're a buddy, he said, kneeling down to unravel the troublesome knot in the line.

Mr Curbishley's Fishing Trip
Seven: The Swing

Rabbit *gets down. He struggles to grasp a memory hovering just beyond his reach.*

Rabbit   Keogh, do you remember, no you wouldn't, well maybe – the open shed at the end of the trawler pier? A trawler was unloading. Boxes of fish. Big square wooden boxes piled high. Full of wet dead fish. They dragged them into the open shed with such a smell of fish as you never knew before. I stood watching the boxes pile higher. I went into the middle of them. The men didn't mind. I always had an honest face, even then. And still the towers of boxes got higher. And there in the middle, Keogh, was a fish box hanging like a swing on ropes from the rafters, some other kids must have made. I sat on the fish box, creakedy-creak, nice and comfy . . . I pushed off nice and easy.

Rabbit *sits on the table reliving sitting on the swing. He sways back* *and forth making swing noises.*

Did you like swings, Keogh? I loved swings. The hairs on
your legs get blown. Breezy feeling. I had a dream once. Do
you remember your dreams? Good man yourself! I never
remember mine. Or maybe just a snatch. Not much use.
Makes no fucking sense. But I had this one dream once,
Keogh, and God it was a beautiful dream. You see I had
these second cousins once removed who lived in the
Strawberry Beds. Well I was on the swing in their vegetable
garden, all on my own-i-o. Swinging away to my heart's
content on a very smooth swing. The hairs on my legs. The
sun in the sky. The Liffey between my knees. A well-oiled
swing. No squeaks – aah. Tops of the trees. Bend my knees
and straighten. Look at the ground. It moving not meee. Tops
of the trees again – and an angel was sitting there. She was
smiling at me, picking berries off the tree. She fluttered her
wings, big billowy wings of cloud. She had a white dress on
and red sandals with white soles spotlessly clean, because she
could fly, you see, and didn't need to walk on earth. And she
had red hair in ringlets and her face was full of freckles. And
her arms all freckles too. Then she upped and flew and
landed on the crossbar of my swing and sat there on her
hunkers looking at me swinging. And underneath I'd go and
up the other side and underneath again and up behind, and
underneath again and laughing at her upside down, and she
was laughing too and back down under and that was even
funnier and she laughed too and good and loud and then she
took a Granny Smith and polished it on her ribbon and went
to take a bite but no she thought her manners and offered it
to me, and under I went and up again and out she leaned
the shiny fruit and shook her wings once more, and mouth
agape I tried to take a mid-swing bite and – yes, surprising it
worked, I munched and then we laughed much more and I
swung higher to be nearer up above the treetops and then I
nearly fell down backwards off the swing but the red-haired
angel took to flight and stood on the swing behind me so no
matter what I could not fall, there leaning against her legs
and down, her wing-tip brushed my cheek and down and she
was solid as a rock with wings as soft as mist and freckles on

her fun-filled face and no matter how high we swung the next time swung we higher and higher and the swing went faster and she pulled us up behind up stop . . . and we hurtled towards the ground and out up in front up up higher and higher and over we went in a loopy-the-loop the holy living Jaysus by the fucking Lord Harry in a topsy turvy defiance of the God-almighty force of all-pervading gravity-ee-ee-ee . . . and swung a little more we did but gently now and lo and behold I felt her wing-tips kiss my cheeks and off she flew to the secret place from whence she came and where she waits for fun on the swing in the happiest hereafter . . .

Where haulage is fucking well unknown!

And trucks are never used!

And silent swings are dangling from every apple tree in sight . . .

Scene Eight
The Quest for the Green Glassy Buoy

Rabbit *dangles in the wistful afterglow of his swing dream. His gaze falls on the table. An idea dawns. He grabs the table. He lifts it up and sits down on the chair, the table resting on his lap and leaning on his – clunk – head. He thinks, fingers drumming the tabletop. He slides the table down, looks at the bottom side. He shunts it upside down along the carpet. He steps 'into' it. He sits down on his hunkers in it. He grabs the chair, overturns it, drags it adjacent to the upturned table. He grins. He sways as if on a sea-swell. Schlucky water noises. His grin widens. He looks up at Keogh.*

Rabbit   Get in, Keogh! Come on! Get in!

After some hesitation, Keogh gets in.

Now Keogh! It's time to tell you a story. I'll tell you a story. Long ago, Keogh, before you were born – ah Jesus no not that long ago at all – before . . . before they built the pleasure marina axe-me-arse here in Howth, for as long as the years I've lived the harbour would be full to choking with all manner of boats.

Over at the short pier, there were the dirty scaly fishing
trawlers caked with pitch and gizzard. Over beside the
lighthouse pier was the yachts, big ones and small, but all in
shiny mint condition. And in the middle Keogh, bobbing up
and down, were the little fishing boats, the twenty-footers,
hundreds of them, all waiting for the weekend, and all tied
nice and firmly to their different-coloured buoys, and the
different-coloured buoys tied just as firmly to the rocky seabed
down below.

Over the years, during some storm I suppose, when there was
nobody watching, or when Sweeney the boatman was
watching the end of an empty, my guy-rope upped and
snapped, or wore away, or got rotten, or got nibbled by a
bloody swordfish, or no matter what the blazes, Keogh, the
next thing I looked and here I was out near fucking Ireland's
Eye bobbing up and bobbing down on the backs of the mad
white horses, no earthly sign of my green glassy buoy
anywhere to be seen, and that's what fucking well happened,
Keogh, my moorings were gone! My moorings were gone,
and my trusty twenty-footer was taking a trashing in the
fucking choppy waters in the sound.

Pause.

Now do you see? Keogh, we're going to find my green glassy
buoy, we're going to find it and I'm going to grip that green
glassy buoy in the palm of my hand once more, and I'll tie it,
Keogh, I'll chain it, I'll fucking weld it to my leg of Butlin's
rock and never let it go. God help me, I rue the day I lost
the green glassy buoy of my past.

But now, Keogh! That's enough of looking at the wash! What
am I saying – the wash!? Here we are stuck without a
direction again with not even the wash to guide us! Stoke it
up there Keogh! Wind up the tug-rope on our trusty old
Seagull outboard engine! Pull it good and hard: chugga-
chugga-chugga.

Try it again, Keogh! Don't lose heart! Try, try and try again!

Wind it up again, Keogh! Grip the toggle! Hold your breath! Pull it, fuck it, pull it! That's the stuff it's caught! Push the throttle over! Open her up, Keogh: Brrrngggmmm . . .

We're away! Green glassy buoy here I come, ready or not, keep your place or you'll be caught!

Rabbit *leans out in the prow of his craft, pounding into the waves powered by the trusty Seagull outboard chair.*

Scene Nine
Out into the Bay

Rabbit *shouts back over his shoulder to Keogh in the stern, manning the engine.*

Rabbit   Oh-ho it's a lovely day, Keogh. We'll head out north of the Eye. Out by Lambay north of the Eye. It's a lovely bay. (*Repeats.*) Bay, Keogh, bay! It's a lovely *bay*. A beautiful curve of bay. We're on the wrong side though. Only getting the back of her hand out here. There's her nice white knuckles on the summit. And the tips of her graceful fingers splashing in the sea. The fingernails of white rock growing around the bend to pretty picture Red Rock, and waving over there to Blackrock – in a cloud, we can't see – away on the side beyond . . .

The lovely lady, resting her arms on the sides, as she slips down into her deep brown bath . . .

What about her feet? Oh, away out there . . . the Kish, and the Rockabill, winking in the waves . . .

Rabbit *scours the horizon.*

Gulls feeding! Oh dirty birds! Dirty filthy fucking birds. They'd eat anything! Letting the gullet rule! Fill my gull-gullet! That's their one and only rule. Look at the dirt of them! Brown-flecked underbellies from sitting in it and not a smidge of shame!

Looks over the side.

There it is! The everyday legacy of the populace of the Pale.
Floating and turning in glory! Food for brown-bottomed
beady-eyed gulls! From one set of gullets to another I suppose,
Keogh, think for a minute! Just for a minute – of all the love,
and all the care, and all the affection, the formula feeds, the
tins of alpha spaghetti, the tender livers of lamb, the juicy
favourite cutlets, the slices of cherry madeira . . . Jesus, Keogh,
more than a whole cityful of carefully chosen food given with
deep and genuine love but all, Keogh, all to finish up here,
turning over slowly, smelly . . .

Can you smell your own, Keogh? Ah no! Not out here! Too
many by far! You couldn't possibly. You're not Superman! I
mean in normal life? You know – would you recognise? Your
own – ? I know my own and no mistake! Like a nice tobacco
pouch.

Mine is in there. So is yours. Turning slowly and going grey
. . . An enormous amount of effluence! Sweet Jesus to think of
it all! And that's not just today's! Yesterday's is in there too!
And the day before's! And before that! And Sunday's! All the
way back! Months! Years! Decades! Until it breaks apart and
some cod comes along . . . and swallows it, and a loved one
gives you fillet of cod on a plate with mash, and down it
goes, and out, and back it comes out here again floating and
turning over slowly and going grey again and again and
again . . . !

And then you see another thing: There's them that came and
went before, generations Keogh, right back to Laurence
O'Toole, well – back as far as the bowl and chain in any
case. Twyford's and Victoria and a pipe coming out to the
sea! Every second of every day! Somebody making their feelies
felt! Victoria! A daily flow of articulation coursing through the
pipes of generations! Victoria! Until it all goes gradually grey,
turning over slowly out here in harmony with everybody
else's! Victoria! Victoria! Victoria!

Pause.

Well, that's history for you! All gone grey . . . ! Chemical
interaction!

Scene Ten
Entering the Maiden's Clutches

Rabbit   Keogh, move it! Out of here! We've taken enough of the back of her hand. Wheel around to the starboard bow! We'll enter the maiden's clutches in the quest for my green glassy buoy. Open the throttle and give her full whack! We'll enter the maiden's clutches. Enter the maiden's clutches!

Rabbit *leans into wind and wave, bending to starboard, as if rounding Howth Head to enter Dublin Bay proper. Then he sits back in the stern letting Keogh plot course and worry.*

Mackerel. Shoals of mackerel underneath. (*Pause.*) Oh a filthy fish the mackerel. The corner boy of the deep. (*Looks up.*) Bad company the gulls. And always found in vulgar shoals hanging around a pipe. That's the tasty flavour of the flesh. Sure they'd eat anything! Bottle tops and butts when you scrape out their gizz! Still – they give the meat a good strong taste. I suppose – the fish has *lived*. Runs in the bloodstream – the minerals or whatever seep through the stomach walls and taint the flesh with the distinctive mackerel flavour. Ah . . . not a filthy fish! No! A . . . gamey fish, a bit of a rascal, sly grin on his greasy face. Can't help himself when temptation is put in his way! I *love* mackerel. My favourite fish of all. Scrumptious! Mmmm . . .

Pause.

Ah fuck it, Keogh, I'm sick of talking. I'm sick of the sound of my own fucking voice. No smart remarks from you! You're still hanging from an unfulfilled contract. 'All this can be yours' – yeah yeah oh no need to remind I know I know!

Pause.

(*Quietly.*) Silence is golden.

Pause.

(*Sings/roars.*) Silence is golden golden golden.

Pause.

Silence is golden.

Keeps silence for a while. Scans the horizon. Gloom.

I wish there was something to look at. No ships out. No mail-boat. You'd think there'd be a . . . a − a passing ship somewhere in the bay. Then I could say . . . there goes the mail-boat. Or . . . there's B&I still hanging on. Lucky for them, Holyhead is only over the way, not like the other poor crowd the *Irish Cedar* − merchant ship − was it stuck in Lourenço Marques or was it somewhere else that neck of the woods in any case poor fucking gobshites . . . !

Pause. **Rabbit** *is feeling dangerously idle.*

Scene Eleven
In Between her Concrete Thighs

Rabbit *(cont.)*   It's a grey old day now.

Pause.

Can't see Dun Laoghaire any more. Or the Sugarloaf . . .

(Conspiratorially.) There's − a mist coming down . . .

Rabbit *kneels low in the boat, peeping over the prow.*

Clouding our progress. Cloaking our actions in fog . . .
The steam from her bath. Steaming us up to − full steam ahead, Keogh! Stoke her up to full steam ahead for the Pigeon House pointing in its own peculiar way to Chapelizod where we're bound. In between her concrete thighs, Bejasus! Chapelizod here we come! Chapelizod here we come! Head for the Pigeon House Keogh! *(Looks right.)* Dollier over that side! The Virgin on the Rocks watching us as we pass!

− Bold boys, she says. I'm watching youse.

− Watching what? says us.

− Oh now, says she, I know everything.

− We're doing nothing wrong, says us.

– Don't tell lies, says she.

– We're only two fellas out in a boat, says us. We're clean.

– Oh now, says she. And there I'll leave youse.

– God bless now, says us.

Full steam ahead, Keogh! There's the Pigeon House, one finger in the air not good enough and quite right too had to build two, yeah two! And then the gasometer fading into fog and Liberty Hall over there in the distance (*Disparagingly.*) Liberty Hall – how are yeh!

Bat *bubbles up at the mention of Liberty Hall.*

Bat   Liberty Hall how are you! Steps to the door back in them days you know and no skyscraper lark of course, Keogh, oh no. The only cut I got was off the glass when I poked my Mauser through to fire a shot – ripped my fucking thumb.

Rabbit *reasserts himself for a moment.*

Rabbit   Seventeen storeys of trade-union bloody troublemakers!

Bat   Wasn't too bad – all very well in fact until the *Helga* bloody big gunboat in the entrance to the river started shelling – Boom-boom! – it'd deafen you.

Rabbit *reassumes command but he is greatly shaken. He babbles a bit.*

Rabbit   Liberty Hall my arse! Get her up the fucking Liffey, Keogh! Amn't I a great fella all the same thinking up a plan like this? We won't get complacent though. There's no call for that. Stick to the task at hand! That's the trick of success. Now, Keogh, these are the things you should be watching. A young fella starting off like you should be watching me like a . . . ? Like a hawk! Now concentrate on what I'm telling you. Do you know what they call this? This is a . . . ? A learning experience. This is inspiration, Keogh! Corporate inspiration! 'Mens sana in corpore sano'! Did the Brothers teach you that . . . ? Oh Belvedere – the Jesuits, I see, I see, well that explains a lot, Keogh. Still, maybe you can learn. You see, the likes of Smurfit and O'Reilly wouldn't be caught dead doing this. And it's their loss, Keogh! The loss is definitely theirs! You listen to me now. 'Mens sana in corpore sano': A successful corporation needs a brainy man at the top! And that's where these fuckers lose out. They're limited Keogh, sadly, extremely, lim– . . . No Keogh, I mean limited in mind Keogh, yes I know limited – PLC – (*Loses temper.*) Who are you trying to tell, you thick spalpeen!? (*Regains what passes for composure.*) But they, would never dream, of going, on a voyage, Keogh . . .

Rabbit *voyages forward to the prow of his upside-down desk, arms embracing the upturned legs, head low.*

To Chapelizod, Keogh, all the way up, up, up to Chapelizod, and then scurry up the bank through the little green gate and up, up and around-around the magazine Fort and into the furry funny fuzzy Furry Glen and there, Keogh, there I think I'll find . . . something. Do you follow? Can you take that – on board?

Scene Twelve
In the Mist

Rabbit *tries to find his bearings. He surveys each side.*

Rabbit (*cont.*) Keogh! The river's very narrow here. We should be near the East Link by now. Unless they have the drawbridge back. But the river's very narrow just the same! (*Looks left.*) I can see a wall on that side. (*Looks right.*) And there's – ah Jesus, Keogh – there's seaweed over this side! No! Reeds! Bunches of reeds over this side! Jesus God almighty I swear I saw a duck! Sure a duck couldn't live on the Liffey!

Rabbit *pitches forward, Stasis! A problem with propulsion!*

What was that!? Have you broken my Seagull outboard engine!? Holy God have pity on me I'm surrounded by fools and imbeciles. Keogh. . . ? Have you any idea. . . ? Where we are!?

Bat *resurfaces.*

Bat Where are we now!? Well you may ask! I hate mist.

Pause as **Bat** *takes in what he can see of the scene. Not much.*

Saturates you more than rain droppedy-droppedy-drops. At
least you know where you stand with rain. But you can't see
mist. Well of course you can see mist. But you can't see what
you're looking for with mist. That's it. So you know it's there
but you can't see it. You can feel it. Well no you can't feel it
but you know it's there so you *think* you can feel it. There
now I think that's it. I think you can smell it. Slightly. A
damp kind of smell. So taken altogether even a blind man
knows there's a mist. Maybe knows even better than us that
can see. Ah sure what's all the fuss? No need to make a song
and dance all right all right –

Rabbit *grits his teeth in a valiant attempt to regain control but no:*
Bat *holds on, affronted.*

Bat (*cont.*) – oh now I see my son the wicked brow is
creasing, ah yes go on and tell me that I'm rambling like you
always used to with your – paddy-whack a great pair of
chords and no doubt about it there was damn the bit of what
you choose to call my rambling that I ever got away with
since the day I took you fishing out beyond in Howth the day
before I lost my job in Curbishley's pawn for slamming
Curbishley square on the bonce with the lid of a Byzantine
pot.

That's the day that the funny little half-grin washed from your
face! That's the day that you closed your little cast-iron door
of your kisses and tears! That's the day that your nose began
to twitch from always sucking in and never venting out!

Rabbit *savages his way back to power.*

Rabbit Ah that's enough of that! Home-truth bullshit since
the age of twelve. Don't mind the geezer, Keogh! He's always
been a loser since the day that he was born. Not that he
knows! The day he was born! Found in a basket! Outside
Beggars' Bush Barracks! By the squaddies coming in from . . .
looking after the populace.

Bat *bursts in just as* **Rabbit** *is getting into a flow.*

Bat   There's North Strand.

Rabbit   What are you raving about?

Bat   There's North Strand coming up. And there's Wiggins Teape you know that makes the sellotape and envelopes.

Rabbit   How can you see in the mist? Wait a sec! Jesus that's – ! I think I saw – ! Keogh there's Roadstone on the East Wall Road! (*Pause.*) We're in the fucking Tolka!

Bat   Ah yes, of course we are! Mind your heads now, ho-ho Keogh, most of all 'cause we're heading for the bridge . . . oh here we go with the gentle ebb and flow . . .

Rabbit   Stop the boat Keogh! (*To* **Bat**.) Out! You're out here! You can get a taxi credited to me.

Bat   I can't.

Rabbit   Keogh, remove this man from my boat!

Bat   He can't.

Rabbit   Keogh! Do what you're told at once!

Bat   Sure he can't throw me out without throwing you. (*To audience.*) Isn't that right? Common sense – it's fucking obvious. (*To* **Rabbit** *and Keogh.*) Mind your heads now, oh, nice and easy . . . (*Going under bridge.*) That's it now. Wet walls. Ballybough next. Luke Kelly Bridge! Now there's a change I like. I'm enjoying myself now, I have to admit. Better than the last time I needn't tell you . . . !

Scene Thirteen
Bat: The Boats/Rabbit: The Bots

Bat (*cont.*)   That makes four now. Four times in a boat! No, I tell a lie I'm going too fast can't keep up with the Connemara ponies! Must be five, now, five! Let me see – (*Counting.*) Over

to Frongoch. And back from Frongoch. And standing for a
minute in Sweeney's punt the day beyond in Howth. And
here now, here now. And then there was once to Garnish
Island, very nice by all accounts. Fancy forgetting that! On
my honey-mum-bumps-a-daisy-diddley-eiddley, but feeling very
queasy from the honey-nunny night before . . . Didn't get to
the island at all! Had to ask the man to turn back to give me
a chance to settle – terrible agitated stomach! Not to mention
a problem with the foreskin! Sorted out after yes thank God!
Not that anything happened! Not the full thing! Not the first
time! But sooner or later, everything fine – sure there he is
now, solid as rock . . .

Rabbit *manages to claw his way back into embodiment.*

Rabbit   Right Keogh – I know you're watching! Now! How
to handle a crisis! You've got to adapt! Turn things round!
Look at every side! Find new angles! A rabbit knows how to
keep his head when all around are . . . Keogh! You get out
and push! No, no, no we can't do that sure the Tolka doesn't
go to Chapelizod sure that's the fucking problem! Adapt
Keogh, adapt! Remember to adapt – the Bots will do instead.
The Bots! The Bots! The Botanical Gardens! We'll pull up at
the Rose Garden and see what we'll find. Fertile plain . . . !
Fiddle with the sundial . . . ! Green glassy buoy buried in the
dung . . . ?

Out you get now! Only a mile or so! That's it. Lift your leg!
Good man! Mark my words Keogh – you'll go far!

Keogh is wading and pushing now. **Bat** *pops up.*

Scene Fourteen
The Bath

Bat   Careful now Keogh. Well, what an unexpected
pleasure . . . ! In a boat, no less . . . ! (*Looks up into mid-distance.*)
How rose-mantic Mamie . . . (*Pause.*) Not like down in
Garnish. The tummy let me down. Pity that it's not the real
thing. 'Cause it's not.

Bat *stands up and steps out of the 'boat' on to the carpet.*

It's not the real thing. Not like the time . . .

Bat *turns the table on its side —*

— our new enamel bath . . . !

Bat *slides the chair into position — the sink next to the bath —*

— that your brother plumbed in. I thought he'd never leave.
Barmbrack it was, slice after slice, determined to get his
pound of flesh after doing the workies. Fair enough I suppose,
but still, I thought he'd stay all night. And then he went with
his little bag of tricks.

— *Slán abhaile*, say I.

— *Go n'eirí an bóthar*, says you.

— Give over that gaw, says he.

And we smiled a small complicity as he swung his leg over
the saddle and pushed on up the hill ahead. I remember you
ran, a little skippy-jumpsy-bumps-a-daisy, you were so
delighted when you ran the water in and the kitchen filled
with steam . . .

And you said:

— Jesus, it's a scream, and you pulling the top up over your
head:

— the water's roaring red!

— You can thank the little geezer with his mouth on fire, says
I trying to joke.

You lunged and gripped me under the oxters.

— Woh-hoh-hoh-hoh, my little revolutionary.

Sure that always got me going how well you knew, and we
danced a hoppy-skippy polka to my little revolution as our
bath filled up we were kissing in the steamy, dancy
pantaloony ball in the kitchen, not a good idea rationally
speaking 'cause I bit my lip — or was it you? — hard to tell

the details but this I *do* recall –

Rabbit *struggles up.*

Rabbit Jesus! Do you mind! That's my *mother* you're alluding to!

Bat Ah now no harm, we're all men here.

Rabbit What about Keogh? Do you want him to hear? What about me!? I don't want to hear. That's my fucking mother!

Bat Stop interrupting now! I'm dying to tell the story. Anyway, I'm not talking to you! I'm talking to Mamie! So go and fuck yourself you broke her heart!

Rabbit I broke her heart?

Bat Yes you broke her heart. Oh no, Kimmage not far enough, Kilmanagh further, Bawnogues better, Jobstown, I can't believe the gall to call it Jobstown! Jobstown!

Rabbit You're ranting and raving now. Fit to get committed!

Bat Ah you make me sad to think I – I . . . well, Mamie, you know, bore you. Where was I? And the bath had a good ten eleven inches and the water still hot, and the steam made the kitchen hot we were both in our pelt – goose-pimples, yeah, but not from the weather – and no jokey-joking now, dance a little slower, my hands were lifting up your breasts just a little, oh Mamie what a lovely – weight, and you with your hands front and back and up and down and rubbing me all over and your lips on the side of my necky-neck 'cause you didn't like the blood around my lip – understandable enough – and your hands were back and front and up and down and back and up again and then, then you dipped your toe in –

– Just another bit of cold, I think, you said and then – And sure then we started giggling again watching the ripples and splashing our hands and then we tumbled in thank God (*Down in behind the side of the bath.*) taking care not to bump your head on the big brass taps.

– Oh Jesus it's great, you said, and squeezed me to you.

– Are you all right, I said.

– Am I all right you *amadán*!? Do you think I'm sick or what!? And you rubbed the Sunlight soap on my shoulders that you always called my ballcocks.

– Are you sure, says I.

– Oh yes, says you.

– I hope you don't drown, says I, only joking half.

– Oh, it's lovely, says you, sure what a way to go don't you think in our new enamel bath.

– Oh-ho Mamie my love and so smooth, smooth, smooth oh buttery, but Mamie, the water might go in ahead and harm, you know, the insides –

– Ah blather me shite, do you think it's a bloody bung-hole down there lovey lovey dovey God above that's the way my darling revolutionary –

Sure then I didn't care a damn, thrashing in the water – lovely feeling mind you – and the four pigs' trotters underneath holding up the bath no bother, and we both came together like a fairy tale finish with a roar and then a shshshsh 'cause the people next door and a rake of plates came sliding off the draining-board and landed on the backs of my legs . . . But none of them broke! Thanks be to Jaysus! Oh Mamie, Mamie . . .

Bat, *pleased and exhausted, slams the table back down flat.*

Scene Fifteen
The Sewers

Bat (*cont.*)   Good man Keogh! Ballybough – hello.

Rabbit *manages to struggle up again.*

Rabbit   Only Ballybough!? There's a long way to go. (*Roars.*)
Green glassy buoy can you hear-me-oh!? Push, Keogh! Push!
Think of Michael Smurfit! All right then! Think of someone
else! Think of Cement Roadstone! A quarter of a billion in a
year! The pebble-shittin' bastards! That'll make you push!
Push, Keogh! Push!

Bat *resurfaces, with little effort, on a wave of good feeling.*

Bat   And you were laughing Mamie fit to burst at the lion's
roar noise that the bung-hole made and the tickly little
whirlpool sucking at your bum sucky-bum sucky-bum sucky-
sucky-bum. (**Bat** *moves forward to the 'prow'.*) The flood poured
out the little bung-hole and down the pipe outside, splashing
on the grating in the yard. Bubbles of Sunlight soap and some
of my seed sticking to the bars – sticky mickey snot! Djoysch
went the bath water down to the sewer, brloosh it turned a
corner with Mr Darcy's potty shite yellow God help him from
the pills very burny I believe, glush glush glush glush
underneath the city far below going down dark to the sea,
joining forces with everybody's waste, the pot-washing water
from the Gresham, Guinness's slops, golliers and phlegm long
drawn out from straggling in the urinals caught around a butt,
and lung-blood too strealing through the pale yellow piss, still
carrying the echo of the ga-ga-gah and retch that brought it
up-ay-ah, splat, yeh fuckin' hoor yeh, and more blood too,
from the floor tiles down in the Rotunda, the hospital I mean,
not the Roto no, ho many's the night that you and me oh yes
now, yes, but no, Mamie no the hospital I mean, ah Jesus
when I saw the sheets and your poor new white cotton nightie
Mamie Jesus and your pale white forehead all lines and they
all scurrying around as if it's normal NORMAL!? The curse
of Jesus on them and a doctor fucking well winking at me –
good man he says, as if I was a five-year-old come back to
say thanks, God the blood you must have lost went flowing
down the gully to the drain gate, to be followed on the very
next day by the first little black–brown puddle in a tissue from
his bowels, and what else now, what else, ah yes a hundred
thousand jugs-full from all over Dublin of the knee-washing
water after tea on Saturdays wash the Fifteen Acres off – look

at the bruises and scrapes – and ready nice and clean for the
grace to come tomorrow from the tabernacle – early morning
Mass, and of course there's vomit too, adds a bit of colour
tossed in from the totty rinsed with the wash from the flush,
and caked vomit too, stout-smelly vomit, from off the sheets
and shirt-fronts rumbled in the countless kitchen sinks by the
red-raw knuckles on the rivets of the humming washboards
djum djum djum djum glucka-wugga gluaaashshshsh, all
mixed together in the torrent through the pipes to bigger
pipes and down a hole to a lower pipe and gulley gulley wash
wash ging gang goo ging gang goo, gulley gulley wash wash
ging gang goo ging gang goo, underneath the city in the dark,
gulley gulley wash wash gulley wash gulley wash wash, under
bay water now, pipe pipe piping gulley all the stuff gulley
gulley wash wash staying down low low low beneath the bay
bed granite, gravel, silt, and sand, gulley gulley got to keep it
moving to its resting place at sea, resting place at sea, well not
really resting place, more slowly moving place out beyond the
bay . . .

Pause. **Bat** *looks around, is surprised to find himself at sea.*

Out beyond the bay . . .

Scene Sixteen
The Tryst at Sea

Bat (*cont.*) (*shouts triumphantly*)   Out beyond the bay!

Pause.

Isn't that a funny thing now? I thought I felt a chill.

Pause.

Always cold at sea. Ask any sailor!

Pause.

Carried in the salt, I think they say. Keeps the temperature
down some way.

Pause.

Wish I had a cup of tea.

After a long pause, **Rabbit** *reasserts himself. He is in a desperate state. He looks around to find himself back out at sea again. He is flabbergasted and furious.*

Rabbit   You contrary old bollocks, you!

Bat   Any chance of a cup of tea? Ah no sure you never knew how to make it – piss-water God help us, never had the patience to give it time to draw.

Rabbit   I give you an inch and look what you've done!

Bat   Go and fuck yourself you never gave anyone the steam off your piss. Ho Keogh you're the one who's going to get a land!

Rabbit   You've ruined my quest. Green glassy buoy a million miles away. You've fucked us out to sea again however the Jaysus you did it!

Bat   I'd give my eye teeth now for a nice cup of tea.

Rabbit   Don't talk to me about tea! My green glassy buoy is lost and you've scuppered any chance I ever had of finding it again with your long-drawn-out claptrap – put us back to square one again!

Bat   Sure you could be sitting on your green glassy buoy and you wouldn't have the wits to know! 'Big hard boil on my bum today. . .'!

Rabbit   Don't you talk to me like that! You stupid fucking pauper you're a failure, you're a reject, you're nothing but a character of my imagination! And anyway you're dead!

Bat   You could be sitting *inside* your green glassy buoy and you wouldn't think beyond remarking on the overcast nature of the weather for the past few days.

Rabbit   I can put the calipers on you to stop the stream of putrid-smelling shite you're putting out! I have the strength, I have the will, and by Jaysus but I think I've stumbled on the way!

Bat   You could be squinting with your nose squashed up
against your green glassy buoy diddley-oy-doy and your haw
spreading out on either side haw-haw, and you'd still shout at
Keogh to move the mossy-coloured obstacle so that you can
see!

Rabbit   That's enough, now enough! There's only one
bloody medicine will cure your colic and I'll show you that
I'm man enough a rabbit to give it!

Bat   They should give you a long white stick ah no they
shouldn't 'cause you'd use it as a bloody weapon so you
would – blind all the rest with a well-directed poke here and
there and then we're all evens thanks be to God oh yes that's
the way you work and I should know that reared you!

Rabbit   Save your breath you rambling old cock! I'll put a
stop to your gallop. The way you're talking so superior it's
such a fucking joke you couldn't even hold down a job as a
pawnshop assistant! A bloody malcontent then and by Jaysus
but you haven't changed your tune one iota!

Bat   Oh the sharp bitter tongue and the evil beady eye!
Such a pity that I didn't slap the manners on you when I
should've! Chance gone now there's no going back with you
oh no you're too far gone.

Rabbit   Too fucking right I'm too far gone thanks be to the
merciful no going back to the every day a mixy-up
conundrum in your bloody book nothing but confusion! I'm
clear! And sharp! With two hundred and nineteen trucks!
Twenty-eight refrigerated!

Bat   Tap tap. Tap tapa tap. There you go with your white
stick now! Tapa tapa tapa tap. Sitting in a boat with the
engine broke out beyond the bay, talking to yourself out loud,
looking for a green glassy buoy that you're never going to see
never mind going to find, but you still blow your trumpet! I
don't know where you got it, where you picked it up not from
your mother either God rest maybe off the floor whatever you
were licking!

Rabbit   I don't have to listen to your half-baked rant. I control the body so you're fucked!

Scene Seventeen
Rabbit's Final Solution

Rabbit *steps forcefully out of the boat. He whips the table and chair back to their original state in his office. Between each bulleted phrase, he clamps his mouth shut tight to prevent* **Bat** *from bubbling up.*

Rabbit (*cont.*)   I've got clout! Rabbit clout! No fucking joke! I'm living in the present! A realist! A pragmatist! A down-to-earth common-sense economist! A pacifist!

Rabbit *stands behind his desk, teeth clenched.*

Until I'm pushed – too – far!
I know the price of success!
The price!? I know the *smell* of success!

Rabbit *stands on the table, arms outstretched, fists in the air.*

I know the value of cash! Converted!
And land! Re-zoned!
And dwellings! De-slated!
And assets! Stripped!
And friends! Well-placed!
And favours! Returned!
And art! On – My – Wall!!
Value! Valuation! Punts! Dollars! Fucking yens!
International banking centres!

Pause.

Now I'm feeling better.

Squats, then leans back into his chair, feet on the table, mouth firmly shut.

Much improved.

Pause.

Bat *makes an effort to burst forth, but after a grapple,* **Rabbit** *swallows him down again.*

Pause.

Bat *tries again.* **Rabbit** *is determined. He keeps his lips zipped, teeth clenched, and* **Bat** *subsides again.*

Pause.

Rabbit *starts to get bored. His eye is caught by a butterfly. He watches it fluttering over the audience, then on to the stage and up behind him. He's bursting to talk, to give vent to some observation. Eventually, he yields to the pressure.*

Rabbit   I wish I could fly.

The open mouth gives **Bat** *his chance. He bursts in immediately.*

Bat   All I want is a nice cup of tea. I'd love a cup of tea. That's all. Just a cup of tea and I'd be game ball, game ba–

Rabbit *clamps his mouth shut again. He looks at his hands. Gradually, they rise up and reach for his throat. They squeeze, forcing his head over the back of the chair.* **Bat** *struggles desperately to rise back up again, but the hands squeeze tighter. The fingers continue to squeeze until* **Bat**'s *resistance is dead.* **Rabbit** *is also dead.*

Rabbit the Show-stopper

Hold in fading red light until a thin ethereal voice rises from **Rabbit**'s *throat, singing angelically.*

Rabbit
  You always hurt the one you love,
  The one you shouldn't hurt at all.
  You always pluck the sweetest rose,
  And crush it till the petals fall.
  You always hurt the kindest heart,
  With a single word you can't recall.
  So if I broke your heart last night,
  It's because I love you most of all.

Rabbit's *fingers click – one-two-three – then bright lights and* **Rabbit** *explodes into a pumping thumping Las Vegas rendition of that great romantic number:*

You always hurt – the one you love!
The one! You shouldn't hurt – at a-all!
You-ou a-a-a-always pluck! The sweetest rose . . .
And CRUSH it . . . till the petals fa-all!
You-ou-ou a-a-a-always hurt! The . . . kindest heart
With a sing-le WORD! You can't – recall . . .
So! If! I broke! Your hea-a-a-art last night
It's be – cause! I! Lo-o-ove! You-ou-ou! Mo-o-ost! Of!
A-a-a-all!!!

Snap blackout.

Donal O'Kelly is an actor and playwright. His first solo play *Rabbit* was followed by the highly successful *Bat The Father Rabbit The Son* which he performed in New York, Australia and New Zealand as well as on tour in Ireland and Britain. His third solo play *Catalpa* won a Fringe First award at Edinburgh 1996 and played the Gate Theatre, Dublin and the Melbourne Festival, 1997. Other plays he has written include *Asylum, Asylum!*, *The Dogs, Mamie Sighs, Hughie On the Wires* (also broadcast on RTE Radio) *Trickledown Town* and *The Business Of Blood* (with Kenny Glenaan) and *Mulletman and Gullier* (with Charlie O'Neill). As an actor he is best known for his performance as Bimbo in the film of Roddy Doyle's *The Van*, while recent roles on stage include Joxer in the Abbey Theatre production of *Juno And The Paycock*, and Beckett's solo play *Act Without Words I* in the Gate Theatre's Beckett Festival at the Lincoln Centre, New York. He is a founder-director of Calypso Productions, Dublin, and is director of the justice and peace organisation AfrI – Action from Ireland.

Frank Pig Says Hello

by Patrick McCabe

Frank Pig Says Hello was first performed at the Dublin Festival in 1992. The cast was as follows:

Frank Pig   David Gorry
All other characters   Sean Rocks

Directed by Joe O'Byrne

Scene One

Frank   Hello.

Snort, snort as **Piglet** *appears with a birthday cake.* **Frank** *plays two lines of a song on his trumpet.*

Piglet (*sings*)   I am a little baby pig and I'll have you all to know
With my little curly tail and my nose that's turned up so.

Frank   This is me when I was young. (*Sings two lines of song.*) As you can see I was a happy young piglet (*Plays on trumpet.*) . . . the whole day long.

Piglet   The whole day long!

Frank *plays a verse of the song on his trumpet.*

Piglet *blows out the candles on the cake.*

Frank   The first day I met Joe he was hacking at the ice on the puddle.

Piglet   Hello.

Joe   Hello, Frank.

Piglet   My name's Piglet.

Joe   No – your name is Frank. Frank, thank you. You're not a pig, are you?

Piglet   I heard Mickey Douglas saying I was.

Joe   Where's the ring on your nose?

Piglet   I have no ring.

Joe   Then you're no pig.

Piglet   What are you doing?

Joe   I'm hacking at the ice.

Piglet   What would you do if you won a hundred million trillion dollars?

Joe   I'd buy a million Flash bars. Or a million macaroons.

No – a million Flash bars. No – a million Triggers.

*As **Piglet** hacks at the ice:*

Frank   The sky was the colour of oranges. Someone had painted the sky orange. Far as the eye could see. Orange.

Frank *plays the trumpet.*

Piglet   I have a hide-out!

Frank   We had a hide-out. Me and Joe. It was the best hide-out in the world.

Piglet   Any of you dogs try and escape into our hide-out, youse is dead.

Frank   Shoot them, Piglet!

Piglet   Banzai! Banzai!

Frank   Aaargh!

Piglet   Banzai, you yellow sons of Nippon.

Frank   Me and Joe made that hide-out. He was my best buddy.

Piglet (*writing*)   'This hide was builted by Joesup Purcell and me and anybody what tries to get into it is deaded by guns – so stay out or die. By order!'

Scene Two

Frank   Joe made most of it. I got the sticks. Joe was the best. Philip Nugent – he thought he was the best.

Piglet   Ha ha ha.

Frank   What a laugh.

Piglet   Philip Nugent the best.

Frank   What a laugh!

Piglet   Ha ha ha ha!

Frank   Joe was the best.

Piglet   The best!

Frank   Philip and the blazer.

Piglet   The auld blazer.

Frank   And the tie!

Piglet   The tie!

Frank   The dirty auld stripey tie!

Piglet   The dirty auld stripey tie!

Pause.

Frank   But the comics – the comics, Piglet!

Piglet   Best ever.

Frank   The comics!

Piglet   Best comics in the world.

Frank   *Dandy Beano Topper Victor Hornet Hotspur Hurricane Diana Bunty Judy* –

Piglet   And *Commandoes*!

Pause.

Frank   I said to Joe:

Piglet   We've got to have them, Joe.

Frank   We cleaned him out – I admit it. Philip didn't mind. I know he didn't. It was his mother. If she'd stayed out of it, there'd have been no trouble. But she couldn't, could she?

Piglet   Always poking her nose in.

Frank   Poking the nose – every time.

Piglet   Just because she lived in England.

Scene Three

Knock knock.

Piglet   Open up, Ma, I'm home.

Knock knock.

Piglet   Open up, Ma, I'm home.

Ma   I'm going to hang myself.

Piglet   Knock knock! Open up, Ma, I'm home.

Ma   I'm going to hang myself. Come back later, Piglet.

Piglet   Ma, are you finished hanging yourself, yet?

Ma   No, I can't do it right.

Piglet   Well, isn't that what they say in this town, Mum? Those pigs – they can do nothing right.

Ma   That's what they say, son.

Piglet   You might as well let me in then.

Ma   Very well then, son. Would you like some tea, son?

Piglet   Yes, I'll have some potato skins and an old turnip, please.

Ma   There you are.

Piglet   I met lots of people up the town.

Ma   Did you, Piglet?

Piglet   Yes I did.

Ma   And what did they say to you?

Piglet   They said to me, 'When's the next breakdown, Piglet?'

Ma   And what did you say, Piglet?

Piglet   I said, 'Boys, what's breakdown?'

Ma   And what did they say, Piglet?

Piglet (*munching into bread*)   They say, 'It's when you're took off to the garage.'

Ma   Ha ha – aren't they a laugh.

Scene Four

Knock knock!

Frank   I said to Joe.

Piglet   You're my blood brother.

Joe   Yup!

Piglet   We'll never part.

Joe   Never part.

Piglet   Ever.

Joe   Never.

Frank   And we never would have either. Only for a certain nose.

Mrs Nugent   I've warned you once and I won't warn you again! Stay away from my son!

Piglet   Yes, Mrs Nugent. (*Aside.*) Auld fucky fuck.

Frank   I admit it. We did give her son Philip a bit of a hiding. Well, not so much Joe. Mostly me. He was in a bad state when I was finished with him. I thought that was the end of it. But it wasn't.

Knock knock.

Mrs Nugent   Mrs Brady, what I want to know is – where are the comics? Do you know how much they cost? Do you? Do you? How do I know it was Frank! Oh for God's sake! Maybe it wasn't him. Maybe it wasn't Frank! Of course it was Frank. (*Surveying the house and sniffing contemptuously.*) Pigs! Live like pigs. Pigs.

Piglet *snorts.*

Frank   When she was gone I said to Ma:

Piglet   Are you in there hanging yourself, Ma?

Frank   But she didn't answer. And in I went.

Piglet   There you are, Ma!

Frank   Sitting by the fire.

Piglet   Sitting by the fire.

Frank   Only where's the fire?

Piglet   What fire do we want? Isn't that right, Ma?

Frank   We need no fire.

Piglet   Ma?

Frank   Ma?

Piglet   Ma?

Scene Five

Piglet   Joe?

Joe   Frank.

Piglet   Are you there?

Joe   I'm here.

Piglet   It's sad, Joe.

Joe   One thing's for sure – you and me's buddies.

Piglet   That's for sure, Joe.

Joe   Frank.

Piglet   Joe.

Scene Six

Frank   The next day I met Philip and his mother coming down the street.

Piglet   Hello, Philip.

Philip   Hello, Piglet – I mean Frank.

Piglet   Yes. Frank's my name. Hello, Mrs Nugent.

Mrs Nugent   Yes.

Piglet   Yes what?

Mrs Nugent   Yes nothing.

Piglet   Oh.

Mrs Nugent   Let me past, please.

Piglet   Oh, I'm sorry, I forgot to tell you.

Mrs Nugent   Forgot to tell me what?

Piglet   There's a new tax.

Mrs Nugent   A new tax?

Piglet   Yes – The Pig Toll Tax. Now you have to pay.

Mrs Nugent   Don't be ridiculous.

Piglet   I'm sorry but someone has to do it – ha ha!

Mrs Nugent   Let me past, please!

Piglet   You have to pay!

Mrs Nugent   Let me past!

Piglet   You have to pay!

Mrs Nugent   Let me past!

Piglet   Sorry!

Mrs Nugent (*at the end of her tether*)   Let me past!

Piglet   OK.

Pause.

Bye, Philip. Bye, Mrs Nugent.

Frank The thing is – I liked Philip. I really liked him. I had a name for him. Mr Professor I called him.

Piglet Mr Professor.

Frank Any time I saw him I used to think: I wonder where he's going now? Off to investigate the boiling point of water . . .

Piglet The boiling point of water.

Frank . . . or the secret life of the ant.

Piglet The secret life of the ant.

Frank Something like that. I really did like him. It was a pity the way things turned out in the end. But there's nothing you can do about that, is there?

Pause.

Frank Who arrived next only a fellow with a bike. Hello, I said.

Piglet Hello.

Bike Man Hello hello.

Piglet Hello hello hello.

Bike Man Hello hello hello hello.

Piglet Hello hello hello hello.

Bike Man Where are you off to?

Piglet I'm collecting the tax.

Bike Man Tax?

Piglet The Pig Toll Tax.

Bike Man Tax?

Piglet The Pig Toll Tax.

Bike Man Pig Toll Tax?

Piglet It's my tax.

Bike Man   Your tax?

Piglet   Invented by me.

Bike Man   Have I to pay it?

Piglet   No – Mrs Nugent only.

Bike Man   I see. That's a good laugh.

Piglet   Laugh?

Bike Man   Yes. You can't beat a good laugh.

Piglet   It isn't a laugh.

Bike Man   What?

Piglet   It isn't a laugh.

Bike Man   Ha ha. You're a gas man and no mistake.

Piglet   I don't know what makes you think it's a laugh.

Bike Man   I'm as well go on.

Piglet   Good luck now, man with the black bike.

Scene Seven

First Woman   Hello, Piglet.

Piglet   Hello, ladies.

Second Woman   Hello, Piglet.

Piglet   Hello, ladies.

First Woman   How's your mother, Piglet?

Piglet   Never better! She went off to the garage this morning.

Second Woman   The garage?

Piglet   Aye. She had to get the ankle tightened.

First Woman   Is that right, Piglet?

Piglet It is.

Second Woman It is indeed.

Piglet But she'll be back on the road by Christmas.

First Woman Isn't she great? Some that goes into that garage is never heard tell of again. Isn't that right?

Piglet Oh it is.

Second Woman Never a truer word.

First Woman But not your mammy. Isn't that right, Piglet?

Piglet That's right, ladies.

First Woman Come Christmas she'll be back on the road.

Piglet Bright as a button.

Second Woman And ready to roll.

Piglet She will!

First Woman She will!

Piglet For the party of a lifetime.

Second Woman Party?

Piglet Yes, indeed my friends!

First Woman (*astonished*) A party in the House of Pigs?

Second Woman We heard nothing about a party, Piglet?

Piglet The Uncle Alo Party!

First Woman (*quizzically*) The Uncle Alo Party?

Piglet The Uncle Alo Christmas Party!

Second Woman The Uncle Alo Christmas Party!

Piglet Uncle Alo's Christmas Party!

First Woman So he's coming home!

Second Woman Your Uncle Alo!

Piglet   Yes, indeed! My Uncle Alo!

First Woman   Hip! Hip!

Second Woman   Hooray!

Piglet   Hip! Hip!

First Woman   Hooray!

Piglet   Hip! Hip!

Second Woman   Hooray!

First Woman   His Uncle Alo's coming home!

Second Woman   After all these years.

First Woman   Will we get an invite? Oh no, we're not mad enough!

Piglet   I'll see what I can do, ladies.

Second Woman   Of course you will, won't he, ladies?

First Woman   Indeed he will! Won't you, Piglet?

Piglet   You bet, ladies!

Second Woman   Well good-night now, Piglet.

Piglet   Goodbye, ladies.

Scene Eight

The kitchen: Sacred Heart picture.

Frank (*car horn*)   Parp! Parp!

Piglet   Ma!

Ma   Piglet!

Piglet   No more garages now, Ma!

Ma   That's the end of garages, Piglet.

Piglet   Garages – good luck!

Ma   I think I'll make a few cakes.

Piglet   Good luck, garages.

Ma   A few wee cakes for Alo.

Piglet   We don't care what they say, Ma.

Ma   Will I make a few cakes, Piglet?

Piglet   OK, Ma.

Ma   No, I won't.

Piglet   OK, Ma.

Ma   Yes, I will.

Piglet   OK, then, Ma.

Ma   No, I won't.

Piglet   Yes, Ma.

Ma   No, I won't.

Piglet   OK then, Ma.

Ma   I think I will.

Frank   She did.

Ma   La la la la la la. Will I make some more cakes, Piglet?

Piglet   There's no more room, Ma.

Ma   I know what I'll do, I'll make a few more.

Piglet   Where will we put them, Ma?

Ma   Or a few butterfly buns?

Piglet   Yes, Ma.

Ma   That's a good idea.

Frank   I met Philip and his mother on the street a few times after that but I couldn't be bothered with them. I was too busy thinking about Alo. Around that time I thought of a new name for the house –

Piglet   House of Cakes.

Frank   If you came in, there they were. On top of the
washing machine. And some on the wardrobe. There were
ones with icing and without, all decorated with hundreds and
thousands and marzipan and different kinds of designs. I had
a hard job keeping all the flies away from them.
Bzzzzzzzzzzzzzzzz!

Piglet   House of Cakes! Da dan! Come on now, flies! I'll not
warn you again.

Piglet *goes around swatting flies. Ends up on the ground.* **Da** *blows on
the trumpet.*

Da   I can't play it! They're right, son. Your father can't play
it! What am I going to do? What am I going to do? (*Drunk.*) I
was playing the trumpet when the halfwits of this town were
scraping the bog off their boots. Do you hear me? (*Desperate.*)
Do you hear me?

Da *blows the trumpet.*

Da   You name me any man in this town that can play the
trumpet, go on! Can Mickey Douglas play it? Charlie
Lawrence? Harry Connolly? None of them! But I can play it.
Benny Brady can play it! (*Frantic.*) They can't take that away
from me!

Da *blows the trumpet.*

Da   I used to be able to play it. Do you remember? (*Plays on
trumpet.*) 'I dreamt that I dwelt in marble halls' ... I had a da
too son. He left us, me and Alo. In the House of a Hundred
Windows. Annie? Annie, please.

He picks up the trumpet and begins to play. **Ma** *is stirring a cake
mixture.*

Ma   Do you know something?

Piglet   What, Ma?

Ma   Your da loved me once. (*Stirs.*) I slept on his shoulder
... (*Stirs.*) ... once.

Scene Nine

Piglet *goes to the window.*

Piglet   Joe! There you are!

Joe   Hello there, Francie! Do you hear Tango McFee barking?

Tango   Wuff! Wuff! Wuff!

Piglet   Indeed I do, Joe.

They do a medley of barking.

Joe   Do you know what he's saying when he does that?

Piglet   No, I don't. What is he saying?

Joe   How the hell do I know? I don't know dog language.

They laugh.

Frank   Knock knock. I couldn't take my eyes off him!

Alo   There you are soldier. He's got as big as a house.

Frank   I said, 'Alo,' but it didn't come out. He had a red hankie in his breast pocket and the crease of his trousers would cut your hand.

Alo   Another glass of your best malt! Where's the bold Benny?

Frank   But Da never came.

Alo   Sure we'll start anyway. (*Sings.*) Underneath the arches . . .

Piglet   Underneath the arches . . .

Alo   Ah yes, how time passes! I'll never forget the day I left this town for the streets of London! So here's to the health of all in this room!

All   Hip hip! Hooray! Hip hip! Hooray!

Alo   Don't sit under the apple tree with anyone else but me!

Piglet   Anyone else but me, anyone else but me! (*Pause.*)

They do a verse of the song.

Alo   Mary – marry me! Underneath the arches!

Piglet   Ha ha ha! Isn't Alo a laugh!

Alo (*drunk and desperate*)   It's no laugh!

All   Ha ha ha!

Alo   I've always wanted you! I've always loved you!

Piglet   Hooray for Alo!

Frank   Da was there a long time before anyone noticed.

Piglet   Good man, Alo! Hip hip! (*Silence.*) Hooray! (*Pause.*) At it again. Poor old Alo – at it again. How long's it going to go on, Alo? Marry me! Never had the guts to ask her out straight. Alo did well! Good man, Alo! Camden Town! Alo did well!

Piglet   It's getting late? It is. Good-night. Good-night now! Good-night now! Good-night now! (*Sings.*) 'Don't sit under the apple tree with anyone else but me . . .' Alo. Alo.

Alo   It's getting late. Maybe it's time I was in my bed. Goodbye.

Piglet   Goodbye, Alo.

Frank   And that was the last I ever seen of him.

Da *is stumbling with the trumpet.*

Da   Alo! Alo!

Da *puts down the trumpet.*

Frank   Oh – and Ma. She went back to the garage. I never saw her again after that because . . .

Scene Ten

Piglet   There you are, man with the black bike.

Bike Man   Here I am.

Piglet   I'm off up the town.

Bike Man   Off up the town, he says.

Piglet   And I'm never coming back.

Bike Man   Never coming back, he says.

Piglet   No more Piglet!

Bike Man   You're an awful man!

Piglet   I'm an awful man!

Bike Man   You're more fun than a barrel of monkeys.

Piglet   I'm more fun than a barrel of pigs.

Bike Man (*considering*)   Aye – or pigs aither. You could have pigs right enough.

Piglet   Good luck, man with the black bike. You won't be seeing me ever again!

Bike Man (*looking down*)   Well feck it and double feck it – me good trousers is all grease. Him and his fecking blathering.

Piglet   Oh yes – I'm gone, I'm afraid. (*Skips.*) 'I am a little baby pig . . . Dublin – ninety miles – sixty miles – thirty miles – (*Finishes song.*)

Piglet *walks around looking at the city.*

Piglet (*trying out*)   Hello! Hello! Hello!

Newsboy   *Herald* or *Press*! *Herald* or *Press*! (*Pause.*) *Herald* or *Press*! *Herald* or *Press*!

Piglet   Is that all you can ever say, boy?

Newsboy   *Press* or *Herald*! *Press* or *Herald*!

Piglet   Is that all you can ever say, boy?

Newsboy   *Herald* or *Press*! *Press* or *Herald*!

Piglet   Is that all you can ever say, boy?

Newsboy   *Herald* or *Press*! *Herald* or – aargh! Me leg!

Piglet   That's all you've been saying since I came here. (*Mocks.*) *Herald* or *Press*! If you've nothing better to say I'm going home.

Newsboy   *Herald* or *Press* (*Etc.*) I hate this place!

Piglet *goes into a shop.*

Shopkeeper   A present for your mother, eh?

Piglet   I want that one there with the shamrocks.

Shopkeeper   That's a nice little song. Your mother will like that.

Piglet   That's the one for me.

Shopkeeper
   By the side of a clear crystal fountain
   There stands a lonely churchyard closely by
   There's a tombstone decorated with primroses
   In the memory of a loved one passed away.

Piglet *grabs the plaque and runs.*

Piglet   Goodbye now, Mr Shopkeeper. I'm off to see Ma!

Mrs Nugent   Piglet! You're home! They were all looking for you!

Piglet   Well, here I am now, Mrs Nugent! Me and my famous present!

Mrs Nugent   It's dreadful the way it happened.

Piglet   No it isn't. It cost nothing, Mrs Nugent.

Mrs Nugent   Please God she's happy where she is now.

Piglet   Who?

Mrs Nugent   Oh Piglet!

Piglet   Who!

Mrs Nugent   Oh Piglet! Come on and I'll bring you home.

Knock knock.

Mrs Nugent   I'm sorry, Piglet.

Piglet   Go away, Mrs Nugent. Just go away. Knock knock.

Da *is drunk.*

Da   Did anyone see my trumpet? I can play it. Trumpet, where are you? There you are! We couldn't find you anywhere, Francie. Annie's gone. Into the river – of all the rivers, Francie. Rats the size of that. It wasn't always like this. We said the rosary on the rocks.

Sound of the sea.

I played the trumpet. I sang in the parlour. I bought her lovely barley sugar. I told her I love – I told her I love – (*Gags.*) We said the rosary on the Bundoran rocks, son, the first day of our honeymoon. I think it was the first time she had seen the sea. Outside the window of the boarding house that was all you could hear. Ssssh. All night long. We said the rosary on the rocks. We said the rosary on the rocks.

Sound of the sea made by **Piglet**.

Scene Eleven

Frank   I wasn't sure if Philip Nugent would be going to music that day but I waited at the corner anyway.

Piglet   La la la la. (*Sudden.*) Hello!

Frank ˙ He broke into a trot but I ran after him.

Piglet   There you are, Philip.

Philip (*lisp*)   Yes, here I am.

Piglet   The moon – ninety million miles, Philip – imagine! The secret life of the ant! Tsk! Tsk!

Philip   Yes.

Piglet One hundred degrees centigrade – isn't it astonishing?

Philip Yes.

Piglet Yes it is.

Philip Yes!

Piglet Say it's astonishing, Philip.

Philip It's astonishing.

Piglet It certainly is, Philip! Philip?

Frank I had news for Philip.

Piglet Philip – I have news for you.

Philip News for me?

Piglet Yes! News!

Philip News?

Piglet Yes – news!

Philip I don't understand.

Piglet About the Pig Toll Tax – remember?

Philip Oh!

Piglet You see? Now you understand!

Philip Yes! Yes I do!

Piglet Pig Toll Tax! (*Pause.*) Did you ever hear anything so stupid in all your life! Imagine having to pay a tax to get past on the street. Philip – the street belongs to you as much to me!

Philip That's what my mother says.

Piglet And she's right. But you have to say this, Philip. It was a good laugh. Wasn't it? You have to say that.

Philip Yes it was.

Piglet No it wasn't. (*Pause.*) It was a very good laugh.

Philip It was a very good laugh.

Piglet   Philip – how would you like to see my secret collection of comics?

Philip   I have to go home.

Piglet   There's all about ants and water and planets in them. You name it, they're in it. And Romans. You don't want to see them?

Philip   Yes I do.

Piglet   Well, let's go then – I have them hidden in the chicken house.

Frank   Was it dark inside that old chicken house. All you could hear was the chicks. Maybe ten thousand.

Both   Burbleburbleburble.

Philip   (*echo*)   It's so dark. I can't see anything.

Piglet   You can't see anything?

Philip   No.

Piglet   Are your eyes open?

Philip   Yes.

Piglet   And you still can't see?

Philip   No.

Piglet   Then you can't see this!

Piglet *swings the chain.* **Philip** *screams.*

Piglet   It's no use, Philip. I'm afraid there's just too many bad things and that's all there is to it.

Philip   Don't hurt me!

Piglet   I'm sorry, Philip, but you have to take your medicine.

Joe   (*echo*)   Put it down, Frank!

Piglet   Take it like a good boy, Philip!

Joe   Put it down, Frank!

Piglet Joe! You don't understand!

Joe Give it to me! Give it to me!

Piglet I'm sorry, Joe!

Joe Now look what you've done!

Piglet I'm sorry, Joe. I won't do it again!

Joe You know what they'll do? They'll put you away.

Frank He told Philip to say he fell off a tree.

Joe You ever do that again! (*Pause.*)

Piglet I won't, Joe. I promise! You hear me, Joe! I promise! I promise! I promise!

Joe It's OK! Let go of me! It's OK.

Piglet I promise!

Joe OK OK! That's the end of it!

Piglet Yes – never again!

Joe You promise?

Piglet Yes!

Joe That's the end of it.

Piglet That's the end of it?

Frank (*darkly*) And it would have been too (*Pause.*) only for Mrs Nugent.

Joe Let's ride out to the river, Frank.

Piglet Joe – look at the sky.

Joe The sky – what about it?

Piglet It's orange.

Joe So it's orange. So what if it's orange.

Piglet It reminds me of the day you and me were hacking at the ice.

Joe   What would you do if you won a million billion trillion dollars?

Frank   I wanted to say, 'I'd buy a million Flash bars' ...
Poor old Philip! He looked so sad! But then – Knock knock –
the Nugents are all off to the seaside.

Piglet *takes a leap.*

Piglet   Welcome to the Famous House of Philip Nugent! So
this is what you've been up to, Philip! The dirty auld stripey
auld tie! Hmm – I say, boy, what is your name? My name is
Philip Nugent!

Piglet *dances in front of the mirror.*

Piglet (*breathless*)   I'm so happy I'll dance and dance and
dance!

Mrs Nugent (*echo*)   You know why he's doing it.

Piglet   Who was that?

Mrs Nugent   You know why he's doing it!

Piglet   Who was that?

Mrs Nugent   He wants to be one of us! (*Chuckles.*) He wants
to be one of us!

Piglet   No!

Mrs Nugent   He does.

Piglet   No!

Mrs Nugent (*ever so softly*)   Like Philip.

Piglet   It's lies!

Mrs Nugent   It isn't.

Piglet   It's a lie.

Mrs Nugent   It isn't!

Piglet   Nugent! It's a lie! Say it's a lie!

Mrs Nugent   Yes!

Piglet   It's a lie – isn't it! Isn't it – pig!

Mrs Nugent   SILENCE!

Piglet   Right, today we are going to do pigs. I want you all to scrunch up your faces like this. Very good. Now repeat after me: I am a pig.

Mrs Nugent   I am a pig!

Piglet   Again.

Mrs Nugent   I am a pig.

Piglet   And now you, Philip!

Philip   I am a pig!

Piglet   That's very good! (*Pause.*) Just to recap then, everybody! What do pigs eat?

Philip   They eat turnips and potatoes and any old rubbish they can get their hands on.

Piglet   They do indeed. And what else do they do?

Philip   They run around the farmyard.

Piglet   And what else?

Philip   They do pooh.

Piglet   Mrs Nooge?

Mrs Nugent   They do pooh.

Piglet   They do indeed! Come on then, everybody! Let's do our pooh lesson. That's it. Everybody down! Now – after me! Ugh! Ugh! Phew – this is hard work! (*Pause.*) Uh-oh! Who's that? Mrs Nugent! Yikes! The real Mrs Nugent. (*Pause.*) Hello, Mrs Nugent! Was it no fun at the seaside?

She screams.

Mrs Nugent   Get out of my house! Get out of my house!

Piglet   Really – Mrs Nugent!

Frank   NEE NAW NEE NAW!

The **Sergeant** *enters.*

Scene Twelve

Sergeant   Get into that van and not a word out of you, you hear me? (*Pause.*) You hear me?

Piglet   Oink.

Sergeant   By Christ, if you were mine, I'd break every bone in your body.

Piglet   Oink.

Sergeant   Man, but you're the cur!

Piglet   Oink!

Sergeant   If you don't shut up, I'll put you across that room and don't think I wouldn't.

Piglet   You would!

Sergeant   I would!

Piglet   I know you would!

Sergeant   You can be sure I would!

Piglet   Of course you would!

Sergeant   I would! Ah Jaysus, Mary and Joseph will you quit this, son. It's no way to behave. It's no way to go on.

Piglet   I know it's not.

Sergeant (*tired and weary*)   I'm not able for this any more. I've seen enough sadness. (*Pause.*) Your mother and me. We danced a few steps. Me and her – way back.

Piglet   Before the rats.

Sergeant   Living's hard, son.

Piglet   It's hard enough without people going oink! Oink! Oink! Oink!

Sergeant   There you are, father.

Priest   Here I am, sergeant. So this is the fellow we've been hearing so much about? You come along with me. That's the baby Jesus. He'll always be there when you need him.

Piglet   Hello, Baby Jesus. What good are you? You're a dead loss.

Piglet *is clattered by the* **Priest**. *Then* **Piglet** *kneels down to pray.*

Frank   And then I thought . . .

Piglet   I'm going to be good and then I'll get out to see Joe!

Priest   Step together, swing your arms. (*Sings.*) Michael row the boat.

Piglet   Am I doing good work, father?

Priest   You're going to win the Piglet prize!

Piglet (*digging furiously*)   Am I doing good scrubbing, father?

Priest   That's the best scrubbing I've seen all year!

Piglet (*hammering furiously*)   Am I doing good digging, father?

Priest   I haven't seen better digging in many a long day!

Piglet (*scrubbing furiously*)   Am I doing good hammering, father?

Priest   You just keep that up, Piglet, and the prize is yours for ever.

Piglet   And then can I see Joe?

Priest   Then you can see Joe.

Piglet   Waa-haay! Back, you sons of Apache dogs. We're riding out, Joe. I'm up here! Can you see me, Joe? I'm coming in to land. Nnngyeow! Here I am, Joe. And this is where I'm gonna stay.

Silence.

Piglet   Am I doing good work, father?

Priest   You're doing good work, Piglet.

Piglet   Am I scrubbing hard, father?

Priest   Hard's not the word, Piglet.

Piglet   Am I doing good digging, father?

Priest   Digging's not the word, Piglet!

Piglet   Am I doing good hammering, father?

Priest   Any day now we'll be letting you go!

Piglet   Hooray!

The **Priest** *gives* **Piglet** *a letter.*

Frank   Joe wrote:

Piglet   'Dear Francie, why did you break into Nugents'?
Signed Joe.' 'Dear Joe, thank you for your letter. I will tell
you all about Nugent when I get back. Signed your fond
blood brother, Francie. PS Saddle up, we're ridin' out!'

Piglet *jumps up.*

Piglet   Yee-ha! Saddle up, Joe. We're riding out! Goodbye
father, goodbye scrubbing, goodbye digging, goodbye
hammering, goodbye Baby Jesus.

Scene Thirteen

Frank   I don't know how long I was in there. Two years
maybe. (*TV voice.*) 'After two years of hellish torture Frank Pig
stepped out once more into a world that had no place for
him.' Oh yes, it had.

Piglet   Hello, ladies!

First Woman   Piglet! You're home.

Piglet   I am indeed!

Second Woman   Look at Piglet! He's home!

Piglet   Home, she says.

First Woman   Do you know what, Piglet, you've got as fat as a –

Piglet   As a . . .

First Woman   Don't say it. For the love of God, say nothing!

Piglet   Ladies – please!

Second Woman   Did you miss us, Piglet?

Piglet   I missed all my old friends, ladies. I couldn't stop thinking about the old pig days. Will you ever forget them?

First Woman   Oh now, don't be talking, Piglet.

Piglet   The old pig days.

First Woman   They were hard to beat.

Piglet   Ah well. They're all over now.

Second Woman   They are indeed, Francie.

Piglet   You can't be a pig all your life. Isn't that right, ladies.

First Woman   It is indeed.

Piglet   It is.

Second Woman   Ha ha

Piglet   Ho ho.

First Woman   Ha ha.

Piglet   Hee hee.

First *and* **Second Women**   Ha ha.

Piglet   Well goodbye now, ladies. Musn't dawdle!

First Woman   Goodbye, Francie!

Piglet   Bye!

Second Woman   Bye!

Piglet   Bye-ee!

First Woman   Bye-ee-ee!

Piglet   Bye-ee-ee-ee! Hello! Man with the black bike! Hello!

Bike Man   There you are!

Piglet   Here I am!

Bike Man   You were away!

Piglet   I was!

Bike Man   Now you're back!

Piglet   I am!

Bike Man   And where were you?

Piglet   I was in the jail.

Bike Man   Jail, be cripes! Would you credit that? What for, me son?

Piglet   Fiddling the tax!

Bike Man   Fiddling the tax!

Piglet   Fiddling the tax!

Bike Man   Fiddling the tax!

Piglet   No.

Bike Man   What?

Piglet   That's all over.

Bike Man   You're a great man for a laugh.

Piglet   I don't know why you think it's a laugh.

Bike Man   I see.

Piglet   You'll be hearing no more about it.

Bike Man (*uneasy*)   Oh.

Piglet   Yes.

Bike Man   I'd best be off home.

Piglet   Tax? (*Shakes his head.*) The end.

Bike Man   I'll be off then.

Piglet   Right so.

Bike Man   Ta ta now.

Piglet (*calls*) Hey! Hey! Man with the black bike! (*Pause.*) Did you ever see? (*Pause.*) Did you ever see such an orange sky?

Bike Man   I can't hear you.

Piglet   The sky! Look at it! Look at it!

*The **Bike Man** tries to look at the sky to keep **Piglet** happy, then there is a clatter and he falls across his bike, trying his best to struggle to his feet.*

Bike Man   What do you have to ask me about skies for? I know nothing about skies. Why do you have to ask me? Buck him and skies. Ah Jaysus, me good trousers.

Piglet   My trouble days are done. (*Pause.*) A million Flash bars, please.

*The **Bike Man** stumbles off, dragging his bike.*

Scene Fourteen

Frank   KNOCK KNOCK!

Piglet   Is Joe in?

Joe's Ma   He's not in.

Frank   KNOCK KNOCK!

Piglet   Is Joe in?

Joe's Ma   He's not in.

Piglet   I'll call back later.

Frank   KNOCK KNOCK!

Piglet   Is Joe in?

Joe's Ma   He's not in.

Frank   KNOCK KNOCK!

Piglet   Is Joe in?

Joe's Ma   He's not in.

Frank   KNOCK KNOCK!

Piglet   Is Joe in?

Joe's Ma   He's not in.

Frank   KNOCK KNOCK!

Piglet   Is Joe in?

Joe's Da   You were told – he's not in.

Scene Fifteen

Frank   What made me sad was – I knew he was in. (*Pause.*)
I went round to the puddle to see if it was frozen over. Sure
enough it was. There was hard twisty paper growing out of
the misty ice. I broke off a bit of a twig and hacked away at
it. When I looked up there was this kid standing there like
something off a Christmas card with a big stripey scarf and a
hat with tassels on it. He said:

Kid   You're dead, mister.

Piglet   Why?

Kid   That's our puddle.

Piglet   Your puddle?

Kid   Yup. Me and Alfie.

Frank   Oh.

Kid   We're in charge of it. Guess you'd best be riding out,
mister.

Piglet   It used to be our puddle – me and Joe.

Frank   I just looked at him standing there with his rosy
cheeks and two silver snots on his nose and everything seemed

so good. I said to myself: It's so good being here I could stand here for ever. I said to him:

Piglet What would you do if you won a million billion trillion dollars?

Kid (*on one knee hacking at the ice*) I'd buy a million Flash bars.

Scene Sixteen

Frank I knew Joe was in. But I wasn't going to start any trouble. I knew he'd have a reason. KNOCK KNOCK!

Piglet I'm looking for Joe.

Joe's Da (*ignoring him, calling over his shoulder*) Looks like rain!

Neighbour It does!

Joe's Da The farmers won't like that!

Neighbour They won't!

Joe's Da Indeed they won't.

Piglet I'm looking for Joe.

Joe's Da You can't please the farmers.

Neighbour The farmers can't be pleased!

Joe's Da Rain one minute! Shine the next!

Neighbour They'll see they're well looked after!

Joe's Da Never seen a poor one yet!

Neighbour Rain or shine there's no pleasing them.

Joe's Da Long as they have the shillings!

Neighbour That's all they care about.

Joe's Da That's all, he says.

Neighbour Ha ha.

Joe's Da Ha ha.

The door clicks shut.

Piglet   I'm looking for Joe.

Voice (*vague*)   Frank! Hello, Frank! (*Pause.*) Frank!

Frank   I looked round but there was no one there.

Scene Seventeen

Frank   And then I went off up to the school.

Master   Ah what the hell are you fiddling at, for the love and honour of St Joseph! Can't you pay attention like a Christian?

Piglet   Me and Joe's going to the hide-out today.

Master   You have a cake and Jim wants half. Then Joe comes in and he has to get a share. How much does each get now?

Piglet   None – because I'd give it all to Joe.

Master   If this keeps up I'll go down to your father.

Piglet   He doesn't be at home now. He be's in the pub.

Master   The English did terrible things to the people long ago. There was a man from this very town and do you know what they did? They dragged him out of his house and hung him from a tree because he wouldn't tell.

Piglet   The bollocks.

Master   What did you say? What did you say?

Piglet   I said he was the bravest man ever lived in this town, sir.

Master   You did not! You're a liar, Brady!

Piglet   Sir, I'm not, sir!

Master   Sir, you are, sir!

Piglet   Sir, I'm not, sir!

Master   I'll break this across your back if there's any more lip out of you! It'll be a long time before you or any of yours dies for Ireland.

Piglet   Sir, we're dying every day in Maguire's slaughterhouse.

Master (*losing it*)   One of these days you'll go too far – do you hear me?

Piglet   I'm sorry, sir.

Master   Now where were we? (**Piglet** *snorts*.) The Vikings were known for their fearsome brutality and when they came to the village they spared no one. They burned down the huts and split all the young men open.

Piglet   Well done, Vikings.

Master (*gone mad*)   Shut your mouth! Do you hear me? I'll give you what's coming to you!

Piglet   OK.

Master   If you don't want to come back to school, Brady, why don't you stay at home?

Frank   So I did.

Da *rolls around in his greatcoat, drunk.*

Piglet   Knock knock! Open up, Da, I'm home.

Da   I want to tell you.

Piglet   Knock knock! Open up, Da, I'm home.

Da   We said the rosary on the Bundoran rocks, son . . .

Piglet   Knock knock! Open up, Da, I'm home.

Da   . . . the first day of our honeymoon.

Frank *lays out* **Da***'s suit in the armchair.*

Da
  'I dreamt that I dwelt in marble halls
  With Vassals and Serfs at my side

And of all who assembled within those walls
That I was the hope and the pride.'

Frank *plays the trumpet.* **Piglet** *snorts.*

Da (*sings*)   That you loved me still the same . . .

Piglet   Oink! Oink!

Da   I'm your father, son.

Piglet   Oink!

Da   I deserve better than this.

Piglet   Oink!

Da   Please, son!

Piglet   You put her in the garage.

Da   No!

Piglet   You put her in the garage.

Da   It's a lie.

Piglet   You put her in the garage!

Da   Stop it! Stop it!

Da *plays the trumpet.* **Piglet** *repeats 'Oink Oink!', then he slinks away. Trumpet faintly in the distance.*

Piglet   Joe! Hey Joe! (*Breathless.*) I got you things, Joe. Look! I got you fags. You don't want fags? What about this – *The Eagle*! Once more Dan Dare outfoxes the Mekon! Look – *The Rawhide Kid*. We're riding out, Joe. Whaddya say? Riding out Joe, eh?

Frank   KNOCK KNOCK!

Piglet   Is Joe in?

Joe's Da (*stone cold*)   Gone away.

Piglet   I'm looking for Joe.

Joe's Da   He's gone away.

Piglet   Is Joe there?

Joe's Da   Back Monday.

Piglet   Gone away?

Joe's Da   The country.

Piglet   Gone to the country.

Joe's Da   Back Monday.

Piglet   I'll call back Monday. (*Pause.*) I'll call back Monday. (*Urgent.*) I'll call back Monday.

Dead silence.

Frank   KNOCK KNOCK!

Piglet   It's Monday.

Joe's Da   Back tomorrow.

Piglet   Right! Tomorrow it is!

Frank   So I called back the next day – but he wasn't there. He wasn't there the next day either. He wasn't there any day. Sometimes when it got dark I stood in the alleyway across from his house to see if I could see him moving about upstairs. I thought maybe I could give him a signal. Sometimes it rained but I didn't mind. I just stood there.

Voice (*distant*)   Frank! Hello, Frank!

Piglet   Who's there? (*Pause.*) Who said that? (*Pause.*) Who was it?

Scene Eighteen

Frank   You say to yourself: I can wait for ever. I can wait till the world turns to dust. I can wait until the seas dry and branches crumble to ash. But you can't. There's only so long you can wait. KNOCK KNOCK!

Piglet   I have to see Joe.

Joe's Ma   He's not here.

Piglet   I have to see Joe.

Joe's Ma   He's not here.

Piglet   I have to see Joe.

Joe's Ma   He's not here.

Piglet   Where is he?

Joe's Ma   He's gone to music!

Piglet   Music!

Frank   I didn't know Joe went to music.

Piglet   Music?

Frank   Joe never went to music.

Piglet   What do you mean – music?

Joe's Ma   I told you – music.

Piglet   I never knew.

Frank   He never said.

Piglet   With who?

Joe's Ma   Please!

Piglet   With who?

Joe's Ma   Nobody!

Piglet   With who?

Joe's Ma   The nuns.

Piglet   The who?

Joe's Ma   The nuns!

Piglet   With who?

Joe's Ma (*unable to hold back any longer*)   Philip Nugent.

Piglet   Look – crows.

Joe's Ma Crows?

Piglet On the roof.

Joe's Ma Where?

Piglet There.

Joe's Ma There?

Piglet And there.

Joe's Ma There?

Piglet And there!

Joe's Ma There?

Piglet Yeah. What do they think they're looking at? (*Roars.*) What are you looking at? You better shut your mouths, crows. You better shut your dirty rotting stinking mouths. That's all they ever do, isn't it? – that's all you ever hear. Kakakakaka. Kakaka. Shut up!

Scene Nineteen

Piglet Hello, Philip.

Philip Hello.

Piglet That's a lovely music case. It's one of the nicest music cases in the town. No! It is the nicest music case in the town.

Philip Thank you.

Piglet Philip – can I have it?

Philip It's not allowed.

Piglet Philip – can I have your music? Thank you.

Philip Please –

Piglet Thank you, Philip. You have a lot of good books in here. Look at all these. *Bluebells in Spring. Study in F.* I love all these books. Can I put them out on the ground?

Philip   You'll make them wet! I'll get in trouble!

Piglet   I was just looking at them, Philip! For heaven's sake!

Philip   I'm sorry.

Piglet   It's all right, Philip. Philip – do you know something?

Philip   What, Frank?

Piglet   I love the way you say, 'What Frank?' I say, Algernon Carruthers, old boy! That's a good laugh isn't it, Philip?

Philip   Yes, Frank.

Piglet   It is indeed. Isn't it, Philip?

Philip   Yes, Frank.

Piglet   Ho ho ho. Say ho ho ho.

Philip   Ho ho ho.

Piglet   It's a great laugh! (*Silence.*) Philip?

Philip   Yes, Frank?

Piglet   I'm sorry about giving you the hiding.

Philip   It's OK, Frank.

Piglet   I'll never do it again. And do you know what, Philip?

Philip   What Frank?

Piglet   I'll never break into your house again.

Philip   Thanks, Frank.

Piglet   It's OK, Philip. But Philip?

Philip   Yes, Frank?

Philip   Joe and me. It's just me and him. (*Pause.*) I'm sorry.

Philip   Yes, Frank.

Piglet   Maybe one day. Maybe one day you can be a blood brother too. OK?

Philip   OK, Frank.

Piglet   You do understand – don't you? That's the way it's gotta be.

Philip   I understand, Frank.

Piglet   Thanks, buddy. Shake hands.

Philip   Can I go now, Frank?

Piglet   Sure. Here – I'll help you with the music books. (*Pause.*) Now.

Philip   Goodbye, Frank.

Piglet   Goodbye. (*Pause.*) Maybe one day, Philip – huh?

Frank   It was hard for me to say all that to Philip. But I had to put him right. There was enough lies in the world. That was what I thought. I didn't want him thinking he was all in with Joe just because they went to music. It wouldn't be fair. Sometimes when we rode out to the lake me and Joe sat by the campfire in Fort Apache and we gave ourselves Injun names. You could be . . .

Piglet   Swift Deer Running . . .

Frank   . . . or . . .

Piglet   . . . Bird Who Soars.

Frank   After I put Philip right about everything, I was Bird Who Soars. I went out across the rooftops and in between the bending aerials. The sky opened and said: Come on, Bird Who Soars.

Piglet   I don't know Sky.

Frank   And soon everything's gonna be just like it used to be. When I was orange and all was well, says Sky.

Piglet   That's right, Sky . . .

Frank   . . . I said. Then I went home and I found Da asleep again. Every night now he was asleep.

Piglet   Now look here, flies! I really have had enough of

you. You needn't think you can come in here any old time
you like acting like you own the place.

Frank   Buzzzzzzzzzzzzzzzzzzzzzzz.

Piglet   Take that! And that! See how you like that, my
flying friends. You don't like it at all, do you? Well then clear
off! Don't you worry, Da – I'll put manners on them.

Da   Francie?

Piglet *locates the trumpet and polishes it affectionately, then presents it
to* **Da**.

Piglet   There you are now, Da. Play a tune. You can play 'I
dreamt I dwelt in marble halls.' (*Silence.*) You can play
anything. (*Silence.*) You can play 'Paddy McGinty's Goat' – just
play it! (*Silence.*) Just play it! (*Pause.*) Your forehead is like ice.
I'll go up the town and get you something. Ha ha! Ha ha! I'll
just get some money out of my piggy bank. (*Busies himself with
piggy bank, but there is nothing in it.*) It's gonna be just like the old
days. (*Pause.*) It's gonna be just like the old days. It's gonna be
just like the old days, Da!

Frank   Buzzzzzzzzzzzzzzz.

Piglet   Will youse fucking flies mind your own business,
please! I'll show them! I'll clean this house from top to
bottom. I'll look after us. We'll see who's pigs. It's up to me
now! (*Shakes empty piggy bank furiously. Breathless.*) I'll earn the
shillings. I'll do it – I'll show them, Da! (*Pause.*)

He turns the piggy bank upside down but it is still empty.

Scene Twenty

Frank   KNOCK KNOCK!

Piglet   Is Mr Maguire there?

Maguire   You're looking at him.

Piglet   Maguire the pig man?

Maguire   Maguire the butcher, the pork on the plate. If it's a start you're after what do you know about pigs?

Piglet   That's a good laugh, Mr Maguire.

Maguire   A good laugh?

Piglet   What do I know about pigs!

Maguire   And what do you know!

Piglet   What do I know!

Maguire   What do you know!

Piglet   Oh ho, Mr Maguire!

Maguire   We'll soon see what you're made of! Come on!

Sound: inside the abbatoir.

Maguire   Do you see this little fellow? I'll take him in my arms. What do you think of him now?

Piglet   He's a lovely little baby pig.

Maguire   Stroke him.

Piglet *snorts.*

Maguire   Never harmed a soul.

Piglet   No.

Maguire   Never harmed a soul.

Piglet   Not one.

Maguire   And never will.

He cuts the pig's throat with one upward thrust of a knife. Deathly scream.

Maguire   D'you see that? Blood on your coat.

Piglet   You killed him.

Maguire   What do you think about that!

Piglet   Poor little piglet.

Maguire   What do you think now? Will you be staying?

Piglet   But Mr Maguire! Look at this other little fellow! Now he's all sad!

Maguire   He's not for killin'!

Piglet   Mr Maguire, it isn't fair!

Maguire   Put him down.

Piglet   You sent away his friend and now he's all alone. Don't worry, I'll look after you.

Maguire   You'll do as I say.

Piglet   Give me the knife.

Maguire   He's not for killin'.

Piglet   Give me the knife!

Maguire   You haven't the guts.

Piglet   Look what I have for you, piggy!

Death squeal as he slays the baby big. Dull thud.

Maguire   Be the hokey!

Piglet   He's happy now.

Maguire   You're not so bad.

Piglet   Can I stay, Mr Maguire?

Maguire   Any lip out of you –

Piglet   Yes, Mr Maguire.

Maguire   Start Monday.

Piglet *snorts.*

Scene Twenty-one

Piglet   Ladies – did you hear the news? I have lately been appointed to a position of some importance!

First Woman Piglet – you haven't!

Piglet Oh but I have! I'm in Mr Maguire's employ.

Second Woman Piglet! How wonderful for you!

Piglet Now if you'll excuse me I have a number of items which I wish to purchase. Young lady – could I have twelve fly-papers, two bottles of Domestos, two bottle of Jeyes Fluid, three mousetraps, three tins of floor polish and a pack of Rowntree's fruit pastilles, please.

Second Woman You're doing a bit of shopping, Piglet.

Piglet Yes – I'm in charge now, ladies.

First Woman Is that right.

Piglet It is indeed.

First Woman The floors are a divil to keep clean.

Piglet A fright to the living world.

Second Woman Never mind the flies!

Piglet Would you stop!

First Woman Would you stop!

Piglet They will when they hit these. (*Holds up fly-papers.*)

Second Woman Dear, oh dear, aren't you a character, Piglet!

Piglet Well ladies, I must be off.

First Woman To do the polishing.

Piglet To do the polishing.

Second Woman And polish off the flies!

Piglet Now you're talking, ladies!

First Woman How's your father? (*Pause.*)

Second Woman We haven't seen him in many's the long day.

Piglet   Have nothing to do with that Mr Sheen, ladies. It's a dead loss.

First Woman   A dead loss.

Piglet   Windowlene for me. Bye, ladies.

Women   Bye!

Piglet   Bye-ee!

Women   Bye-ee-ee!

Scene Twenty-two

Parp! Parp!

Frank   The car came round the corner. Joe's folks got out. I hid in the alley. 'Joe,' I said.

Piglet   Joe! Joe! Joe's going to get out now.

Frank   But he didn't. Someone did. But it wasn't Joe.

Mrs Nugent   They really have become great friends, Joseph and Philip.

Scene Twenty-three

Frank   On the way home I sneaked into the dance.

Music: Elvis – 'Be-bop-a-lula'.

Piglet   The old shaky-shakies.

Piglet *dances.*

Piglet   Any of youse for a dance, girls? Yeah! Yeah!

Girl   Sorry – we don't dance with pigs.

Piglet   Dance?

Girl   No thanks – we don't dance with pigs.

Piglet   Dance?

Girl   No thanks – we don't dance with pigs.

Piglet   Dance?

Girl   No thanks – we don't dance with pigs.

Piglet   Why'd'n you bring your knitting? Haw! Haw! Haw! (*To* **Dancer**.) You dunted against me when you were going past.

Dancer   I didn't dunt against you.

Piglet   Did.

Dancer   Didn't.

Piglet   Did.

Dancer   Didn't.

Piglet   Did.

Dancer   Didn't.

Piglet   Take that! Let's see you dance now. Wee! Wee! Wee! Wee! Wee! Wee! Hey bouncer! Take this!

Bouncer   You're dead.

Piglet   I'm a rasher sandwich. (**Bouncer** *hits him on the head.*)

Piglet *arrives home.*

Piglet   Hello, Da, I'm home. Will I do a bit of cleaning, Da? I will. No, I won't. Yes, I will. OK, I will. Am I doing good cleaning, Da? Am I doing good scrubbing/baking/ sweeping/polishing/digging/hammering . . .

He builds up on this routine until he is dancing.

Piglet   Dance? Dance? Dance?

Joe   Hello, Frank.

Piglet   Joe!

Joe   We're riding out.

Piglet   Joe, what are you doing in here?

Philip   One hundred degrees.

Piglet   That's right, Philip.

Maguire   Kill the pig.

Piglet   Yes, Mr Maguire.

Alo   Don't sit under the apple tree . . .

Piglet   Alo!

Piglet   Uncle Alo, cha cha cha! Uncle Alo, cha cha cha!

Ma   Will I make some more cakes, Piglet!

Piglet   Yes, do Ma.

Ma   Have you got some cakes, Piglet?

Piglet   Yes, Mum, I've lots of cakes.

Ma   Do you need some more?

Piglet   No, I've lots.

Ma   Lots and lots?

Piglet   Lots and lots.

Frank   KNOCK KNOCK!

Piglet   Is Alo going to be pleased! What a party we're going to have. Do you think we have enough cakes here, Da? You don't. Maybe I'll make some more. Phew! Boy, I'm sweating. Da – are you sweating? Oh, Da – you're as cold as ice. I'll get your coat.

Knock knock.

Piglet   Now I know what. As soon as Alo comes in the door you start playing – right, Da?

Knock knock.

Piglet   Parp! Parp! 'Don't sit under . . .' Oh, what fun this is going to be! Sssh! I think I hear him coming now!

Knock knock.

Piglet   Here he is! Da, get ready! One two three!

The door bursts open with a crash.

Sergeant   Dear God and His Blessed Mother.

Piglet   Where's Alo? (*Weeps.*) Where's Alo?

Sergeant (*standing over* **Da**)   Oh sweet Jesus. Look at him.

Piglet   Alo! Where are you, Alo! Mary – Alo loves you!

Sergeant   Easy now! Easy!

Piglet   Please, Mary. Please. 'Don't sit under the apple tree . . .'

Sergeant   Easy now! Easy!

Sound of the waves.

Scene Twenty-four

Piglet   Yoo hoo! I'm flying. I can see all the way down there. Hello, roofs. Can you see me? I'm waaaay up here. It's Piglet. It's Bird Who Soars. No, it isn't. It's Pig who Soars. Pig who flies high into the sky and away over the roofs of the town. It's warm and then it's cold.

Frank   One day the priest from the school for pigs came to see me but he had a wasp's head.

Piglet   Go away! Go away!

Father Alien   Woo! Woo!

Piglet   Please go away. You're not the real priest. If you were the real priest you wouldn't have a wasp's head.

Father Alien   Woo! Woo!

Piglet   Oh please! Oh God, please!

Frank   The next morning he was gone and the sky was orange. I could fly for ever. I was Bird Who Soars again. I spun sideways and the black hole that was in my stomach was full of light. I flew down to the puddle and landed on a branch and just watched them hacking at the ice. 'Hello there,' I said.

Piglet   Hello there. Are youse hacking at the ice?

First Kid   Hi! Hi boys – did youse hear that? A talking bird!

Second Kid   Fawk me!

Frank   I was lying there for weeks. Or maybe months. Then I got up and this fellow says to me:

Patient   You needn't think you'll pull the wool over my eyes, you Cavan cunt. Youse wouldn't spend Christmas, not if it was to save your lives. Go on – get out of this hospital.

Piglet   I'm not from Cavan.

Patient   Shut your mouth! You are!

Frank   They took me down to a room and asked me about dreams.

Psychiatrist   Did you have any dreams?

Piglet   I did.

Frank   I said I did.

Psychiatrist   What about?

Piglet   Wasps.

Frank   I said, 'Wasps.'

Psychiatrist   Wasps.

Piglet   And priests that were really aliens.

Frank   And priests that were really aliens.

Piglet   And aliens that were really priests.

Frank   And aliens that were really priests.

Piglet   Am I good at this?

Frank   I said to them, 'Am I good at this?'

Psychiatrist   Oh, yes.

Piglet   Let's do some more.

Psychiatrist   Oh, ja.

Frank   Then they took me down to the Time Travel Room. It was just like Adam Eterno in Philip's comics. They strapped me to a chair and they scribbled away. I didn't care what they scribbled. I was off.

Piglet   Nnnnnnngyeow! Hello there, Egyptians. Youse are doing fierce hard work at them pyramids. Have a break. Have a Kit Kat – that's what I say! Well, got to be off, can't stay, I'm a busy man. Nnnnnnngyeow! Excuse me, Romans, would you mind leaving that Christian alone please. Yes – now! Excuse me, lion – buck off! Nnnnnnngyeow! Through the wastes of space and time. Nnnnnnngyeow!

Frank   It was hard to beat that chair. Only me got it.

Frank *operates a drill.*

Piglet   No, please.

Surgeon   Can you move your head a little, please?

Patient   Pull the whole lot out! The whole bleddy lot! Then maybe he'll stand a man a drink! (*Laughs.*)

Piglet   Wee! Wee! (*Sings.*) Be-bop-a-lula.

The drilling stops as **Piglet** *sings.*

Joe   Come on, Piglet, we're riding out!

Piglet   Joe!

Joe   Oy-yee-yoy-yo!

Piglet   Joe! Where's Joe? Tell me – where's Joe?

Doctor   Ssh now. (*Pause.*)

Piglet   We're riding out. Aren't we, Joe? Oy-yee-yoy-yo! I know we are, Joe. (*Pause.*) I know we are.

Doctor Wake up! Wake up!

Piglet (*snorts*) I'm cured! Look – real feet! Be-bop-a-lula!

Doctor Easy, Frank. Easy now.

Frank They put me making baskets and painting pictures with all the madmen.

Madman Baskets! You can't beat them for holding things!

Piglet Now you're talking!

Madman Messages, papers – the lot!

Piglet Baskets!

Madman And fruit!

Piglet Fruit!

Madman Baskets – you can't beat them!

Piglet You can't beat them!

Madman Not with a stick!

Piglet Every time!

Madman Don't talk to me about women!! You know what they do? Hah? Take you down a long garden path and in behind a tree. Then what do they say – do you remember the day you rang me on the telephone and I laughed and you laughed and Mum laughed and then we all laughed! That's women for you!

Piglet Women!

Madman Don't talk to me! You have none of that with baskets!

Scene Twenty-five

Doctor Well – I guess this is it.

Piglet Goodbye, doc.

Doctor   Goodbye, Frank.

Piglet   Doc, I like you saying that.

Doctor   Saying what?

Piglet   Frank.

Doctor   Isn't that your name?

Piglet   It's my real name, doc.

Doctor   Frank Brady.

Piglet   That's right, doc. (*Pause.*) Goodbye then, doc.

Doctor   Goodbye.

Pause as **Piglet** *looks around, holding a basket.*

First Woman   There you are!

Piglet   Here I am.

Second Woman   Home from the garage.

Piglet   Home from the garage, she says. (*Listens.*) Flies? Flies
– I know you're there! You don't fool me! Come out, flies!

First Woman   They're all gone, Piglet. Not a one to be
seen!

Piglet   Ladies – you've cleaned the whole house for me!

Second Woman   Indeed we have! From top to bottom!

Piglet   It's clean as a new pin!

First Woman   Flies! You won't be seeing them again!

Piglet   Ladies – a million thanks! But now it's time for me
to saddle up – I'm ridin' out!

First Woman   Goodbye, Piglet!

Piglet   Bye! Bye!

First Woman   Bye! Bye!

Sound: galloping hooves.

Piglet   Joe? (*Pause.*) Joe?

Dead silence.

Frank   There was no sign of him. I waited.

Piglet   I'm waiting.

Frank   He never came. All you could hear was:

Piglet   Ka ka ka.

Frank   I went down the diamond.

Piglet   How much is that jacket in the window?

Shopkeeper   Which one?

Piglet   That one.

Shopkeeper   This one?

Piglet   No, that one.

Shopkeeper   This one?

Piglet   Elvis.

Shopkeeper   Elvis?

Piglet   Elvis Rashers. Be-bop-a-lula, she's my baby. Wait till Joe sees this. And I don't mean maybe!

Piglet *wanders about trying out words of song and a few steps, saying hello to all and sundry.*

Piglet   Joe? Wait till Joe sees this.

Piglet *approaches* **Maguire***'s.*

Maguire   Ah, for the love of Christ.

Piglet   Elvis, Mr Maguire.

Maguire   Ah, for the love of Christ.

Piglet   It's number one on 'Top of the Pops'.

Maguire   You're back.

Piglet   Will you have me?

Maguire   Thousands wouldn't.

Piglet   Thanks, Mr Maguire . . .

Maguire   Half the wage.

Piglet   Thanks, Mr Maguire.

Maguire   Ah, for the love of Christ. A white bucking jacket. Take that brock cart and get round to the hotel.

Piglet   Right you be, Mr Maguire. Mr Maguire, I'm off.

Scene Twenty-six

Piglet *with a handcart.*

Frank   Hello there! Yes indeed! Hello, stone. Excuse me, please. Hello there, man! Bones for the dog? Yes, indeed! Hello, farmer! Did you get the hay in yet? That's good. Wuff! Wuff! Sorry dog, I don't know what you're talking about. I don't know dog language. I say – she looks like rain.

Piglet *stops and smokes.*

Frank   The Mystery of Joe.

Piglet   Where are you, Joe? (*Pause.*) Where are you, Joe? (*Pause.*) We're riding out! (*Pause.*) Joe. Are you there?

Frank   KNOCK KNOCK!

Piglet   It's always raining.

Joe's Da   What do you want?

Piglet   Every time I come.

Joe's Da   What do you want?

Piglet   It rains.

Joe's Da   What do you want?

Piglet   Joe.

Joe's Da   He's gone.

Piglet Ho ho! You old trickster, you!

Joe's Da You won't be seeing him again!

Piglet That's a good laugh.

Joe's Da It's no laugh. I don't know what makes you think it's a laugh.

Piglet You old bag of laughs! You're more fun than Harry Worth! It's just like the old days, Joe's da! (*Silence.*) Where is he then? (*Silence.*) Where is he? (*Silence.*) Where is he? Tell me! Be-bop-a-lula. Tell me!

Piglet *does a little dance and sings: 'Bee-bop-a-lula, she's my baby.'*

Piglet Tell me – you have to! You must tell me!

Silence.

Frank I didn't have to turn. (*Pause.*) She was there. (*Pause.*) Even in the rain.

Silence.

Scene Twenty-seven

Joe I'd buy a million Flash bars.

Silence.

Frank I went out to the river. I counted all the people who were gone on me now. 1. Da. 2. Ma. 3. Alo. 4. Joe. When I said Joe's name – that was the best laugh ever!

Piglet Joe? Joe gone? That's the best laugh ever!

Frank I lay on the grass with tears running down my face.

Piglet Joe gone!

Frank Looking up at the orange sky. (*Pause.*) The orange sky. (*Pause.*) Except for one thing. (*Pause.*) It wasn't orange.

Silence.

Voice (*dead whisper*) Frank. (*Pause.*) Frank.

Piglet Joe!

Voice I'm over here, Frank.

Piglet I'm coming, Joe.

Voice Over here.

Piglet Where?

Voice Over here.

Piglet I can't see you.

Voice No – over here!

Piglet (*distraught*) Where? Where! Where are you, Joe? Where!

Voice (*barely audible*) I'm down in my house. Come on down and see me. Come on.

Frank There was a light on in the front room. Joe's da was handing round glasses. (*Sings.*) Don't sit under the ...

Piglet (*hammering on door*) Open the door! Do you hear me! Open door!

Joe's Da You! It's three o'clock in the morning.

Piglet What's the party for? Is Joe home?

Joe's Da I don't know what you're talking about!

Piglet Just tell me – is it something to do with Joe?

Joe's Da Joe's not here.

Piglet He is.

Joe's Da Son, he's not.

Piglet He is.

Joe's Da He's gone away.

Piglet No, he's not.

Joe's Da Yes, he is. He's at school in Bundoran!

Piglet (*pause*) It's her, isn't it?

Joe's Da Who? What are you talking about?

Piglet It's all right. I know it was her. I know you wouldn't do it. You're Joe's da. It's her.

Joe's Da Look, Frank – go home.

Piglet (*whispering*) It's OK. I know! (*Pause.*) There was never any trouble till she came round. (*Pause.*) Isn't that right?

Joe's Da (*wearily*) Yes!

Piglet You go back into the party. (*Does a little dance and sings: 'Be-bop-a-lula.'*) Elvis Rashers. She's my baby. Go on (*calling after him.*) Don't worry – soon it'll be like the old days again. And I don't mean maybe. (*Pause.*) A million Flash bars, please!

Scene Twenty-eight

Piglet *howls like a coyote.*

Piglet We're riding out, Joe. Joe! We're riding out!

Piglet *howls like a coyote.*

Piglet There you are.

Bike Man Here I am.

Piglet The Pig Toll Tax!

Bike Man The Pig Toll Tax! Eh? The Pig Toll Tax!

Piglet Ho ho!

Bike Man Ha ha!

Piglet Ho ho!

Bike Man Hee hee!

Piglet The Pig Toll Tax!

Bike Man Now you said it!

Piglet   The black bike!

Bike Man   The black bike!

Piglet   I need it.

Bike Man   That's a laugh. Ho ho!

Piglet   It's no laugh. I don't know where you get the idea it's a laugh.

Bike Man   What are we going to do with you at all?

Piglet   I don't think you're going to do anything with me. I won't be here. I'm off on this bike.

Bike Man   Hey! Hey! Stop thief! My bike! My bike!

Trumpet music.

Piglet   Parp! Parp! Hello there, dandelions! I do believe I shall have to take your heads off with a cut of my stick. Good day, my man! Could I have one dozen cough-no-mores, one dozen Flash bars, sixteen macaroons and a bottle of Mr Sheen. Mr Sheen – oh no. Windowlene for me, please, if you don't mind! Not a bad day. Indeed it is not! I'd say it'll pick up. Oh, indeed it will! Parp! Parp!

Woman   Damn it sowl will you watch where you're going!

Piglet (*brakes suddenly*)   Oops!

Woman   Did you hear the news?

Piglet   About Joe?

Woman   Ah Joe! Joe Stalin! The end of the world!

Piglet   Nobody tells me nothin'.

Woman   Come ten o'clock there won't be a bullock standing.

Piglet   It's a terror.

Woman   There's no end to what they'll do.

Piglet   No end.

Woman   Go on communists.

Piglet   Go on communists.

Woman   Dirty rotten baby-boilers.

Piglet   And priests.

Woman   And children.

Piglet   And nuns.

Woman   And now us.

Piglet   Me and Joe.

Woman   Bye!

Piglet   Bye! Bye-ee! Yee-haa! Ting a ling a ling. Here I
come, Joe! We're riding out! Let's saddle up and ride! Philip,
sorry but you can't come, I'm afraid. Just me and Joe. Will I
make some more cakes? Yes, I will. Oh no, I won't. Yes, I
will. Whiz! Down the hill and over the dale! Excuse me
chickens, if you don't mind. Bwawk! Bwawk! Mrs Nugent? I
really wouldn't know where she is. Sorry, I can't help you
there. I'm sorry, Mrs Nugent, but if you have some plan up
your sleeve about me and Joe, you can forget it! Oh yes!
You're old troublemaking days are over. Bwawk! Bwawk!
Honestly chickens!

Music section.

Piglet   Da dan! The house of a hundred windows. I'm
coming, Joe! I'm riding in! Yee-haaa!

Finale of music.

Frank   I arrived at the school and slipped in.

Piglet   Aiee! A hundred sleeping bogmen boys! Howyiz boys,
did yiz get the hay in yet? Don't mind me, boys. I just want
to see Joe Purcell. Me and him's riding out. Sorry boys, you
can't come. Saddle up, Joe! We're riding out! Be-bop-a-lula!
Oy-yee-yoy-ee-yo! Blood brother, Joe. Bogmen – mind your
own business.

Sound: alarm bell.

Piglet   Saddle up, Joe! We're riding out!

Priest   What's going on? What the hell's going on?

Piglet   Hello hello!

Priest   Don't hello me. Don't hello hello me.

Piglet   Joe? Where are you, Joe?

Priest   You behave yourself.

Piglet   Take 'em to Missouri.

Priest   I'll not warn you again.

Piglet   Joe!

Frank   Joe! Joe! (*Pause.*) So – it was all over. I'd found him at last. All I had to do was walk over to him and we were gone for ever and that's what I would have done. (*Pause.*) I would have done that. (*Pause.*) I didn't want Philip Nugent there! (*Urgent.*) Why did he have to be there? Why did he have to be there? (*Pause.*) Joe just stood there. (*Pause.*) With him.

Priest   Is this fellow a friend of yours or is he not?

Silence.

Frank   Then Joe came over to me. Joe knew what was wrong. He knew everything about me.

Joe   What do you want?

Frank   That was what he said. (*Pause.*) No, it wasn't.

Long pause.

Joe   What do you want?

Frank   That was what he said.

Silence.

Joe   What do you want me for?

Piglet   Joe, it isn't a laugh.

Joe   A laugh? I don't know where you get the idea it's a laugh. Are you deaf or something? (*Pause.*) Do you hear me? What do you want me for?

Pause.

I've never seen him before in my life.

Silence.

Piglet   I'm sorry for causing trouble, father.

Priest   Be on your way now.

Piglet   I will indeed.

Priest   Goodbye, then.

Piglet   Father?

Priest   Yes?

Piglet   I'm lucky you didn't call the police!

Priest   Yes.

Piglet   You know what they'd do?

Priest   It's time I was in my bed.

Piglet   Take me downtown!

Priest   Good-night!

Piglet   Well – good luck now! (*Pause.*) I'm off on my travels. (*Silence.*) Yes, indeed. (*Silence.*) Yup! (*Silence.*) Whee-hoo! Yes-sir! (*Silence.*) You hear, Joe old buddy? We're ridin' out! Let's go then! All aboard! Bwawk! Bwawk! Joe's gone away, chickens. Isn't that right, Mrs Nugent? We won't be riding out any more – isn't that right, Mrs Nooge. (*Alarmed.*) Now I'm never going to see him again.

Trumpet music and silent section on bike.

Frank   I rode all the way back to the town. There was an orange glow in the sky as I headed over the hill.

Piglet   Yee-haaa! Yup it's me, folks! Ol' Piglet's home! Hello there, street! Yeee-haaa! Ladies!

First Woman   Piglet!

Second Woman   Were you away?

Piglet   Ladies! Ladies! You do make me laugh! Of course I was away! I was off seeing my old buddy Joe! Can't stop to talk! I'm off again! Hey! Hey!

Bike Man   My feet's covered in blisters. And the Blessed Virgin Mary coming!

Piglet   What a day it is now that I'm home! What you should do is cycle off out into the country and have a look at that sky! That's what I'd do if I hadn't to go round to Maguire. Look at it! Just look at it! It's so bright it'd blind you! If you like I'll go with you later! Yes! We could both go – you and me, the bike men, off to see the sky! What do you say!

Bike Man (*fading off*)   It's a sad state of affairs. It'll be a bitter day for this town if the world comes to an end.

Piglet   It's always sad when things come to an end.

Bike Man   Our Lady's coming.

Piglet   What does she want?

Bike Man   It's to do with the communists.

Piglet   She'll settle them.

Bike Man   She'll shift them good and quick.

Piglet   No better woman.

Bike Man   I'm off to take my cash out of the post office.

Piglet   Just in case.

Piglet *begins his Elvis act.*

Piglet   Awopbopaloobopawopbamboom. Our Lady – she's coming. Our Lady – she's coming! Mrs Nugent – I'm coming!

Scene Twenty-nine

Maguire   Where the hell were you?
Awopbopaloobopawopbamboom. You think you can stroll in
any time the notion takes you, is that what you think?

Piglet   I was away, Mr Maguire. I was off to see my buddy
Joe. It'll not happen again. That's one thing you can be sure
of, Mr Maguire.

Maguire   What you'll do – you'll do what I say. Don't
think you'll make a cod of me! You hear me? You hear me
now?

Piglet   I hear you, Mr Maguire.

Maguire   Now get round to that hotel.

Piglet   Yes, Mr Maguire.

Piglet *takes the cart.*

Piglet   We're riding out, Joe! Yee-haa!

First Woman   Hello there, Piglet!

Piglet   Ladies!

Second Woman   Off on your travels again!

Piglet   Off once more!

First Woman   Where to this time, Piglet?

Piglet   To see my old friend Mrs Nugent!

Second Woman   Mrs Nugent.

Piglet   Mrs Nugent.

First Woman   Mrs Nugent.

Piglet   That's right.

Second Woman   Did she not pay?

Piglet   Pay, ladies?

First Woman   The Toll Tax!

Piglet   Oh! The Toll Tax!

Second Woman Do you remember?

Piglet Will I ever forget!

First Woman Piglet, you're a scream.

Piglet She'll have to pay.

Second Woman She will indeed.

Piglet (*darker*) She'll have to pay.

First Woman Piglet – you're such a laugh, you really are.

Piglet It's no laugh, ladies.

First Woman Ha ha!

Second Woman Ha ha!

Piglet I don't know why you think it's a laugh. (*Pause.*) I don't know why you think that.

First Woman Piglet – what are you doing with that knife?

Second Woman What are you doing with that knife?

First Woman Piglet!

Second Woman Piglet!

Dead silence. **Piglet** *goes off singing 'I Am a Little Baby Pig . . .'*

Scene Thirty

Frank KNOCK KNOCK!

Piglet Mrs Nugent.

Frank I'm coming in.

Piglet I'm coming in.

Frank Mrs Nugent.

Mrs Nugent Go away!

Piglet Mrs Nugent. I'm coming in.

Frank   I'm coming in, Mrs Nugent.

Piglet   Mrs Nugent, I'm coming . . .

Mrs Nugent   You can't come in!

Piglet   I'm coming in.

Mrs Nugent   You can't come in here!

Frank/Piglet   I'm coming in!

Mrs Nugent   Help!

Frank/Piglet   Mrs Nugent – I'm coming in.

Mrs Nugent   Please help me.

Frank   You try to cry out and you don't know how.

Piglet   You try to cry out and you don't know how.

Frank   Isn't that right, Mrs Nugent?

Piglet   Now you know.

Frank   Cry out.

Piglet   You can't.

Frank   Cry out.

Piglet   You can't.

Frank/Piglet   You can't. (*A scream.*) You can't. (*Silence.*) That's what it's like for dumb people. (*Silence.*)

Frank   The secret life of the ant.

Piglet   The secret life of the ant.

Scene Thirty-one

Piglet *wheels* **Mrs Nugent** *about in the cart.*

Bike Man   Hello! (*Pause.*) Hello hello!

Piglet   Hello!

Bike Man   Not long now, Frank.

Piglet   She's on her way.

Bike Man   She is indeed.

Piglet   Any minute now.

Bike Man   The miracle of all miracles.

Piglet   The miracle of all miracles.

Bike Man   In this happy holy town.

Piglet   I must be off.

Bike Man   To pray this day.

Piglet   Soon as I bury me brock.

Bike Man   God reward your labours.

Piglet   Thank you, man with the black bike.

Piglet *goes around with the cart.*

Piglet   Hello there, kids. Can I play?

Kid   Feck off, man. You're too big.

Piglet   Please let me play.

Kid   Get that auld cart out of the way.

Piglet   What would you do if you won a million billion trillion dollars?

Kid   Hm. I'd buy a million Flash bars!

Piglet   Whee-hoo!

He goes off with the cart.

Maguire   Where the hell were you?

Piglet   Tricking about.

Maguire   Trick about in your own time!

Piglet   Mr Maguire – where's the lime?

Maguire   Beside you, are you blind as well?

Piglet   Mr Maguire, the world is sad.

Maguire   Sad?

Piglet   The way it all comes to an end.

Maguire   Buck you and sad.

Piglet (*to cart*)   Why'd you have to go poking? Why? Yee-haa! Come on, Mrs Nooge. We're riding out! (*Sings.*) 'I am a little baby pig . . .'

Sound of a siren.

Sergeant   Stay where you are, Brady! (*Pause.*) Son, what have you done? The neighbours saw you leave. Please tell us, son.

The **Sergeant** *approaches.*

Sergeant   I knew your mother.

Piglet   Before the rats.

Sergeant   Son, please make it end.

Piglet   For ever and ever.

Sergeant   Where is she, son?

Piglet   Could she be here? No. Could she be here? No.

Francie *behind bars.*

Piglet   Ladies! Look where they're taking me now! This is what I get for not paying my Pig Toll Tax.

Sound of the sea.

Piglet   The Mystery of Joe. (*Silence.*)

Silence. Sea – hush hush. The trumpet sounds.

Piglet   Are they coming to hang me, sergeant?

Sergeant   No, Frank.

Piglet   Where are they? What's keeping them?

Sergeant   I'm afraid there's no more hanging, Frank.

Piglet   Sergeant – what's this country coming to?

Sergeant   You'll be going away for a little while, Frank.

Piglet   To make baskets?

Sergeant   Yes.

Piglet   You can't beat them. Baskets!

Sergeant   Do you remember the old days, Frank?

Piglet   The old pig days, sergeant?

Sergeant   No, Frank, just the old days.

Frank   They were good days.

Piglet   They were good days.

Frank   Good old pig days.

Piglet   Good old pig days.

Frank   Pig days.

Piglet   Pig days.

Piglet *snorts.*

Scene Thirty-two

Frank *in lost Eden hacking at the ice.*

Piglet   What's going on here?

Frank   Nothing.

Piglet   Nothing!

Frank   Just hacking.

Piglet   Ah, you can't just be hacking!

Frank   I'm thinking what I'm going to buy with my million billion trillion.

Piglet   So you're going to win a million billion trillion?

Frank   I am.

Piglet   A million billion trillion?

Frank   Same as Joe.

Piglet   Give me a bit of that stick there. (*Hacks.*)

Frank (*looking up*)   I just want to watch the orange sky.

Piglet (*looking up*)   The sky's not orange, Frank. (*Pause.*)

Frank   I know. (*Pause.*) But you know something?

Piglet   What?

Frank   It once was.

Piglet (*warily*)   Yeah.

Frank   Right over the town. Orange. (*Long pause.*) If I won a million billion trillion dollars – you know what I'd do? (*Silence.*) I'd paint it. (*Pause.*) Far as the eye could see, I'd paint it. (*Pause.*) Orange. (*Pause.*) Everything would be OK then, wouldn't it? (*Pause.*) I know it would. (*Pause.*) Wouldn't it? Wouldn't it? (*Pause.*) Tell them, Joe! Tell them!

Frank *gets up from the puddle.*

Trumpet music.

Slowly the sky begins to turn orange.

Patrick McCabe was born in County Monaghan in 1955. He has published a children's story, *The Adventures of Shay Mouse* (1985), and four adult novels, *Music on Clinton Street* (1986), *Carn* (1989), *The Butcher Boy* (1992) and *The Dead School* (1995). *The Butcher Boy* was the winner of the *Irish Times*/Aer Lingus Literature Prize in 1992, was shortlisted for the 1992 Booker Prize, and has been made into a film by Neil Jordan for release next year. His play *Frank Pig Says Hello* based on *The Butcher Boy*, was first performed at the Dublin Festival in 1992. His new novel *Breakfast on Pluto* is to be published in 1998. He lives in Sligo with his wife and two daughters.

Hard to Believe

by Conall Morrison

Hard to Believe was commissioned by the Bickerstaffe Theatre Company and the Cultures of Ireland Group. It was first performed at the Andrews Lane Theatre, Dublin, on 11 March, 1995:

Performed by Seán Kearns

Directed by Conall Morrison
Produced by Lynn Cahill
Designed by Marie Tierney
Lighting by Cormac Sheridan

An attic. A chair. A bottle of gin. Boxes, bags, suitcases. Old, dusty clothes hanging like ghosts.

Music: Second movement, Schubert, Piano Trio in B flat major Op. 99

Foster   Aah. Music to top yourself to.

Scuttle yourself . . . sad but happy.

Oh, I've always been a cultured man. Too fucking right, I have. Most people wouldn't know a crotchet from a hatchet, but me, oh yes, I had it from the cradle . . . the music of my parents: a constant bloody soundtrack to my life . . . washing the dishes, cleaning your teeth, scored by Schubert if you were lucky, Schoenberg if you weren't. My parents' music. I'm only just coming to understand it.

Music ends.

But I'm mainly an ideas man. Bright boy, free thinker, original, y'know. Too original for some of the muppets I had to work with, but well, their loss . . . tossers.

He takes off funeral gear and dries himself.

It wasn't a bad turn-out at the graveside, as bad turn-outs go. Most of my mother's relatives are dead; the disinherited were disinclined to show up; but as well as the diggers and the priest, splashing his sprinkler about, as if we weren't drenched enough already, there were a few grave fanciers, the cemetery dog, and a couple of my mother's decrepit ole neighbours who could have saved themselves some upcoming expense by jumping in on top of the coffin. I'm sure my mother would have been glad of the company.

Oh yes, and we were graced by the presence of the lovely Monica, my ex-girlfriend, standing at a safe distance. And skulking behind her, Mr McIvor, my ex-colleague. How kind of him to show up, the bastard. So. All in all a respectable enough showing, in a miserable kind of way. I dunno, maybe the church service was packed to the rafters, maybe they were swinging from the chandeliers singing to the glory of the Lord. I dunno. I wasn't there for that bit.

He dresses in a skirt, pullover and women's shoes.

Mother! MOTHER!

These things are murder to walk in. (*Changes clothes.*) All this junk. A lifetime's collection of crap ... they'd have kept their own crap if they could have found a way of preserving it. Boxes, cases, bookends ... several bloody lifetimes. Oh, and it had to be kept locked up. We weren't allowed access to it, my brother and me, wasn't safe. Uh-huh. Aliens in the attic.

Copy book.

And they kept all my cuttings, all my jottings. John Foster, aged seven and a half, describing the lambs gambolling in the fields in spring. An early example of the author farting about with the facts. The only spring lamb I had ever seen had been gambolling about on my dinner plate.

Large bundle of newspapers.

To my more mature efforts. I tried to direct them to particular articles, y'know, hint that that was me, that was my work. But because my name was never on it, no smiling snap, they could never really understand it, and I could never really explain. So they just kept whole papers instead.

'What exactly is it you do, John?' Mother would ask in the early days. 'Mrs Golightly was pressing me hard because her Arnold works in the same neck of the woods and sees you going in every day. And there was me, unable to say ... I know we have to be cautious, but ...' That's the security forces for you, Mother, hush-hush, the less you know, safer you are. And with my background ... 'but it's only me. I'm your mother!' Well, Mother, I'm kind of a public relations officer ...

Newspaper.

Rats, the dog: he was mine. Now, say what you will: the Sistine Chapel, the Pyramids, Bach's Mass in B Minor ... no, no, no, chocolate buttons and glass beads. *This* was a creation, this was genius. Things had been going badly for a while: a sixteen-year-old shot with only a fully charged paintbrush in his hand, a twelve-year-old caught in crossfire with just one person shooting . . . the Army needed a lift.

There was I in Crossmaglen, quietly hoping the Injuns wouldn't attack before I finished my briefing, finished my drink and got the first horse out of town, when the door is nudged open and what looks like a yak enters. Fleabus, the regimental dog: so hairy you didn't know which end was up and named Fleabus because he acted as public transport for every insect in the country.

'Fleabus, get oot, y'useless hairy bollox, g'wan, y'big squirt of shite. He's a disgrace. We should have him shot and have Rats instated.'

Rats! Who he?

Rats, the camp favourite, a stray who had strolled in and stayed. There he was, patrolling up and down the barracks, waggling the remains of his tail; eager, loving, dedicated. Bingo. A star is born. A mere three weeks before I had him on tea-time TV.

'Rats, as number D7/767, is the longest-serving member of the British Army in South Armagh. Of uncertain parentage, Rats most resembles a corgi.' Royal connection, loved it, loved it. 'Here we see Rats accompanying fellow soldiers on patrol, where they're most at risk, providing another pair of eyes, vigilant and friendly.'

And because he was a local stray, that meant he was a *defector*, come over from enemy lines to comfort the beleaguered squaddies and maybe show them the secret highways and byways. Friggin' Crossmaglen Tonto. TV features, colour supplements, a radio interview with Walter Love:

'So Rats, what are your hopes for the New Year in the Province?' Woof. Presents flooding in. The book: *Rats. Story of a Dog Soldier.* So bloody popular they made a hand puppet out of him. (*Puppet.*) Y'wee beauty. '*Rats! Eyes bright!* Here comes Action Dog, running gallantly alongside a foot patrol, with a regulation shine to his nose after breakfasting in the officers' mess. Rats, twice wounded in action, is soon to be awarded a gold medal by the canine charity. Pro dogs!'

A beautiful ceremony on the BBC's Nationwide.

Sound of bagpipes.

As the pipes wailed, and Rats howled along, an NCO presented the medal:

'We are gathered here this afternoon to pay homage and tribute to this small, mighty dog, our one and only friend in the Crossmaglen area.'

Even when I decided it was time for Rats to retire before he bit Roy Mason's arse or shat on the regimental mat, a few well-placed phone calls and the eulogies poured in.

'An old soldier stands at ease. He has patrolled the murderous streets of Crossmaglen with his army chums and heard the crack of a sniper's rifle a thousand times.'

And a lovely picture of Rats with his medal reclining in a deck-chair.

'But if there's one thing he can't stand, it's cocky young pups who think they know it all. What they need is a bit of National Service. And look at the length of their fur these days.'

He retired to an ex-officers' farm in Kent. Oh, the poetry.

'On the wall behind the Grand Old Warrior were his two favourite pin-ups, Prince Charles and Prince Philip, resplendent in their uniforms. (*Sound of the last post.*) The light was fading at the going down of the sun and I asked the owner where he intended to bury the little hero when he faded away? 'Oh, I don't know – in some corner of a foreign field which is forever England, I suppose. I know, I know, we are in England, but you know what I mean.' (*Umbrella.*)

And when the awful day came, it was like a state funeral. Press, TV, military band, Churchillian rhetoric, Never before ... and unbridled grief as they lowered the coffin into the ground ...

That's what I did, Mother. I made people believe that Rats had more humanity than the entire population of Crossmaglen. I made people believe in a dog.

Sound of Rain.

It's always miserable at Irish funerals, winter or summer. Rows of red faces, battered about by grief and the rain. Someone should tell the weather there's a peace on. Or maybe the weather knows something. The neighbours, the crumblies, throwing odd glances at me, wondering why I wasn't at the mass; digging into the dust behind their eyes for the memories about the last Foster family service and what exactly happened then.

Monica leaves . . . but then who do I see sidling up the path, leaving his trail of slime behind him but Mr McIvor. Coming to gloat at the graveside was extreme, even by his standards, but there he was in his trilby, his ugly little smear of a moustache, and his gaberdine. Always an embarrassment to the profession. Talked shite, looked like shite. Friends for about a week, until he realised I had the ideas, I was moving, and that by comparison, he looked nailed to the ground. (*Umbrella down.*)

I hadn't seen him since my brother's funeral, eight years ago, when he shook my hand: 'Sorry for your trouble . . .' Sorry for your trouble. The pair of us professionally trained in community cant and yet he comes over to me as if I was ninety and he had just swallowed the Fenian phrasebook. If it hadn't been for the ruckus earlier on that day, I would have taken him away and had his balls on toast . . . but I had to settle for the firm handshake and 'jump up your own hole'.

Why won't you go to the mass, why won't you go, why won't you go just this once/look Mum, you know why/won't you go just this once, in the name of the good God, your only brother and you won't forget this arrogant, evil nonsense for one blessed day/look, I'll meet youse at the graveyard, there's no point/you will not, you'll not turn up like some passer-by/ what are you trying to do, make me feel worse, I already feel as if/you do my eye, how much do you care, how much, if you cared for him or cared for me, you'd come along/would you bloody listen/to what, to your beliefs? Believing in nothing? What kind of belief is that!? This is the only kind of help we're going to get, John this is the only way we're going to understand. How can you believe in nothing?

He puts on one of his mother's dresses.

Music: Bach's B Minor Mass. Agnus Dei. It is played in its entirety.

When my mother was three years old her mother caught TB. They were pretty poor, she was pretty weak, she knew she wasn't going to live long; so she set to and made clothes for her daughter for when she would be aged four, and five, and six, up until eleven, mapping out the young life she knew she wasn't going to see. And after his wife's death, my grandfather filed all the clothes away in a chest of drawers and told my mother not to be poking and prying, they'd come when they'd come. But sometimes, when he was out working on the farm, she'd sneak upstairs, open the drawers and dress up in the clothes of the years to come, imagining what was ahead, what her mother foresaw for her.

When she reached twelve and had outgrown the last contents of the top drawer, she refused the offer of new clothes from her father and squeezed into the old ones until she burst out of them and they fell apart. And then she kept all the scraps in a bundle in the attic, until moths and mildew destroyed the lot.

Cup and saucer.

Oh, it helped me to remember John, it helped me to remember . . . the threads of my life! Yes. Oh, I remember . . . the watery soup the year round and the Christmas goose killed with the razor blade; and the children in limbo, up a rung with every prayer; and the banshee screaming in the ditch because the devil was mad if a soul got into heaven; oh, the cattle markets and my father robbed blind every year; the lovely tassels on the priest's garments.

Stop your noise.

And the dead cardinals' hats hanging by threads in Armagh
Cathedral; and lighting candles to saints and the flames
flickering up like prayers; and the two cathedrals on the facing
hills like the twin horns of a dilemma; oh, the stained glass
windows with colours that were a wee glimpse of heaven; and
the money for masses for the living, the dead and the
haunted.

Stop footering with that.

The Far East and the nuns with men's names; and hand-me-
downs from England; and conniptions because of the priest
calling; and the black spot on my tongue that the Devil put
there for my lies; and my gleaming white dress for my first
communion; and very little money that Sunday because I had
few relatives; and the tea, the cups of tea. Here you, get that
kettle on, careful now.

Knitting.

And the angels' harps like the Gold Guinness sign; and the
Out-and-Outers with their green badges; and confessing my
sins which are the cause of Jesus hanging on the cross; and
God looking at me even when I was hiding in the cupboard;
and whitewashing the walls, inside and out; and God hearing
everything when I tried to sing and think bad at the same
time; and the baby that fell into the river, and floating the
bag of spuds down to see where the current took it; and the
notice in the paper to remember the martyrs of '16; put that
doofer down, I'm sick of telling ye; and young Latheran
Murphy trying to dig up her father's grave; and the priest's
big cold thumb on Ash Wednesday; and fighting for the music
lessons; and the ten miles on the bike to the convent; and St
Peter upside down on the cross; and that hound James Craig;
and the battle over the hemlines; and stigmata and Iron Nails
Rammed In; and my pioneer badge; and squinting at candles;
and St Thomas putting his hand in the wound; and the heat
of hell and the nature of eternity; and belted coats and berets
and boys and mortal sin.

Have you listened to a word I said?

And your father, handsome as they come; concerts and cycle rides; his parents long dead; oh, up round the Ards peninsula; apparently wind that would slice you; oh, terrible to be an orphan; and a quiet wedding, mostly my side; fingers off the photographs; and the hymns, people sang up; that's Aunty Kathleen, that's Uncle Declan; those suits were made to last.

Away you, up and get the wet battery changed and we'll listen to Athlone. And Father Prionsias, not a note in his head; baptised the pair of ye; a beautiful little gown, sick all over it; and crying through the concerts; oh and lazy at your catechism, the tears, the tears; sure aren't the answers laid out for you, it's not like your mathematics; oh, you thrand article, c'mon, Who is God, Who is God; mumbling through your rosary, your father little better for all his promises; Prionsias is your confirmation name we'll hear no more about it; that suit'll do you for years; you're a grand wee lad; and when it comes to the Total Abstinence Pledge, say twenty-one out loud and not be mumbling eighteen under your breath.

Think of the gifts: wisdom, fortitude, courage; you'll not know who you are, you'll be set up for life; oh, look at all the gorgeous wee suits, everyone in their best; that's a beautiful shirt on young Oliver Plunkett; and that's a nice coat on Mrs McRory; now that dress didn't cost nothing.

So, listen closely, speak clearly, and mean what you say, d'yhear me; He sees everything, He hears everything, and never forget, He knows what you're thinking . . . He knows what you're thinking . . .

Music ends.

Changes clothes.

I know what you're thinking, missus . . . you're thinking if I'm only charging that amount of money for that amount of laundry, I'm just gonna take them away in this van, give them a lick, a spit and a rub and then give it all back to ye.

Couldn't be farther wrong, believe me. They'll be spotless. You could have had the full bombscare in your underpants, we'll send them back as if you'd been dumping ice-cream.

And we don't just send back your clothes clean – sure a dog with a mallet up its arse could do that. We send them back improved, with a new lease of life.

Away home and get them gansies out now, ladies, get them shirts them pigs of husbands bring you back; turn them armpits into charmpits. Now, I know what you're thinking: with them prices, he's mad as a spoon, mad as a toolbox. Not at *all*; we just have your best interests at heart, we're the ones you can trust, we're the FSLS, the Four, Square, Laundry, SERVICE!

This is not intelligence. This is a crossed wire on our scanning system. This is the patter of Sergeant Bob Jones, an unshaven man in a purple tank top drumming up custom from the back of his van. We should be listening for crumbs from the tea-table, chats across backyards, angry calls in kiosks . . .

Right, that's it, that's enough for this round, thanks very much, pick up usual time Thursday, ladies. What? No, I will not wash your dog! G'wan, y'scut!

Right. Cough, we're off.

Camera.

Over there, look, coming out of number eleven. (*Click, click, click, click.*) New car; very flash; saving the giros; just turn round there mister . . . just . . . thank you.

Drogheda plates . . . uhuh (*Click.*) oh, look at that, wouldn't mind giving that a bit of deep interrogation . . . curtains closed, number 61; traffic light smashed . . . (*Click, click.*)

Chat from the van; happened now and again; the machinery wasn't as smart as today and when you're packing cameras and two men into a false ceiling, there isn't room for a pylon. When it worked, it worked. Little bits of info out of the squelch; park beside the chippie, or the street corner; the pub; in through the windows, the half-open doors; catching the people passing . . . drop the laundry, and pick up the gossip on the wind.

Then off, tootling through the estates like Postman Pat.

Sergeant Jones at the wheel, whistling, nodding, flicking his fag at the dogs. Upstairs, the two lads, secret and snug in the top bunk, watching, snapping away. New faces, who's meeting who, what car's going where; click, click, click, click, smile, you ugly inbreds, you're on Bandit Camera. (*Bag of clothes.*) I always tried to pull rank on clothes duty. I shouldn't have been sifting through sackloads of kaks, and I often managed to unload it on McIvor, but it had been my idea, and it was working, so occasionally I had to show willing.

Examines clothes.

Different size shirts from number 37's normal, possibly a second man.

A husband in gaol, but male clothes in for washing? Could be Uncle Joe up to stay, could be someone on the run.

A name-tag.

Gun oil on a pillow case.

Small traces of blood.

Women transported explosives about their person … ANFO smelt of diesel … gelignite … smelt of marzipan … Traces … ideas … little leads …

And it was while I was going through some of this … for the lab … that the idea struck.

Underwear.

Papers creamed themselves.

'Dressed to kill! Leading scientists have revealed that the static from nylon underwear when brought into contact with explosives can form a drop-dead combination. The bus-stop. The taxi. The packed street. Women Bombers Warned. No more bikini-line problem? No more bikini-line. Beware the storm in a D-cup.'

When you can't trust your own knickers, what can you trust? And after everything was scrutinised and logged, it was washed and primped and pressed, and sent back out on streets to pick up more dirt.

I liked listening to the tapes. There were edited transcripts but
I liked actually listening in on people's lives; some of it
helpful, most of it rubbish . . . kids shouting, football banter,
abuse across a street, all delivered in those accents honed for
conflict. And as the technology got better, after the days of
laundry vans and crossed wires, the range got better, and
people knew it. All over the province, people didn't know for
certain that what they said in their beds could be picked up,
but they didn't know for certain that it couldn't. Course they
were used to the idea. Up there in those big green towers,
listening to their every thought and word, was an old man
with a long beard wearing a white nightie.

(*Click.*) Oh God, me bollox . . . Here. Who's that he's with,
get him, I've seen him . . . c'mon, gottle of geer . . . (*Click.*)
awright. (*Click.*) And I've seen him somewhere, not from this
estate, though . . . here . . . did you fart! You dirty . . . oh
wait, check this out (*Click.*) Blue Ford, serious hurry, coming
out of Juniper Park, get it (*Click, click.*) mad bastard . . . here, I
don't like this . . . give them a knock down there. *Move*, Bob!
Jesus, he's swinging round in front of us . . . holy fuck, move,
Bob, *move*, fuck, fuck, two, armed, bail out Andy, bail out,
Jesus, bail out . . .

We had to pick up the cleaning bill on that one. Still, it was
good while it lasted.

Age fourteen. A van arrives late one evening at our house.
Some bags and suitcases are spirited up to the attic. My
brother and I knew something had been going on with all the
hushed phone calls, whispers about funerals, but Mr Nosey
Parker, Mr Nosey Parker, why don't you park your nose in
the fire, see how you like it then. And hell roast anyone who
goes poking about in the attic; those floorboards are far from
safe, I'll know if you've been up there. Limited knowledge of
child psychology, my mother.

A month later: an empty house, a stolen key.

Torch. From a suitcase he takes a bible, a razor, black robes, a journal.

And a box of photographs.

Old codgers, black jackets. 'Mr C. D. Trimble.' 'The Archery Club.' 'Ellen on the road to Hackballscross.' A whiff of familiarity off some of them. Jumpin' Jesus, that was me. 1904 . . . My father. Then some of these old black crows were probably my relatives, my grandparents. How did we just get these? If my grandparents were supposed to be over fifty years dead why did all this just arrive? 'Mr Smyllie.' 'The Visit of the Trapeze Artists, 1899.' 'Mrs de Courcy, Ballywalter. (*Journal.*) 'R. S. Foster, Ballyhalbert, Co. Down.' Double pages, single entry: 'My son is dead.'

He puts on the robes and becomes his grandfather.

(*Sings.*)
   Through all eternity to Thee
   A grateful song I'd raise
   But O eternity's too short
   To utter all Thy praise.

As God worketh oftentimes to save man from going down to the pit, so too my parents laboured hard. The crowning job of Christian parents is to know that the names of their offspring are written in heaven and they strive to have the lambs gathered at an early age into the folds of Christ. But Satan also labours hard and rams his darts into callow flesh.

   When in the slippery paths of youth
   With heedless steps I ran
   Thine arm, unseen, conveyed me safe
   And led me up to man.

I was, indeed, stumbling upon the rocky ground, when the Lord led me to the bedside of a beloved neighbour, Jas. McConnell.

While we loudly sang, 'The hour of my departure's come', he uttered his last words, 'Glory, Glory, Glory', and his mild eye closed on earth to gaze on all that was heavenly for ever. This death was, for me, a signal deliverance from the path of sin. I became deeply impressed with eternal things and prepared to receive the consolation of the gospel. Yea, this

was a happy time, when all at once the clouds burst in
meridian splendour, revealing the Godhead reconciled. Happy,
happy is he who passes out of darkness into light, shakes
hands with his sins and sells all for the jewel of the gospel.

> Soon as my all I ventured
> On thy atoning blood
> The Holy Spirit entered
> And I was born of God

And as a sign, one day as I sweated in the earthly fields, he
sent a human angel to me. As she walked past the hedgerow I
had no doubt but she was my divinely designated helpmeet;
these things are not ordered by chance but by a being who
numbers our hairs. The Lord led me to her door, and I
implored her father. We both feared God and wrought
righteousness and within a month I was married to his
daughter, Elizabeth. Within a year, a son was given to us,
Joseph, whose presence often made my heart a little heaven.

Takes out photograph.

But God expects service in return. The glow-worm sheds light
as well as the mighty sun; he expects from us what we can
perform and he excuses none. Although without formality of
training, my aim became the salvation of souls and I sought
for direct results in the conversion of sinners and edification of
believers. Christ crucified and a full salvation for all were
themes upon which I delighted to dwell. For many happy
years as a lay preacher, from Ballyhalbert to Glastry, from
Portavogie down to Cloghy, I strove to go forth in mighty
phalanx and sound the gospel clarion.

And I was often called upon to say prayers over newborn
farmyard stock, and to involve myself in the quarterly love-
feasts, and on occasion to reconcile troubled couples
whereupon I donned a black gown resembling the minister's
and took them over their marriage vows, often with
encouraging results. But Satan, seeing my earnest efforts and
sensing my strength, assailed not me, but my goodly wife. We
prayed and prayed but she became more ill.

She bade goodbye to her relations, and with her hand clasped in mine she whispered, 'Now. Where is the Nazarene, my true and never-failing friend?' And so saying, she closed her eyes. I wandered on to barren ground. I cried, 'Fruit, Lord, more fruit,' but I was unable to grasp the Seed of Life. A storm of passions tossed me. I rowed hard to get to land, but all in vain, till, drowning at last, I cried, 'Lord I perish,' and He came to my help.

He came with such glorious power and filled me with such presence as I had never felt before. I felt the Three One God overshadow me, producing such a heavenly awe and peace and felt a full, sweet assurance that he had taken possession of my heart. What better course for repairs than to bring the injured instrument to Him who made it and to whom the Harp with a thousand strings is so intimately known.

Were the whole realm of nature mine,
That were a present far too small;
Love so amazing, so divine,
Demands my soul, my life, my all.

Relieved with this, I resolved to visit Joseph, who had departed to train in music teaching in Belfast, to talk with him, rest and partake of the Turkish baths. I thought to surprise him, and journeyed up unannounced. On calling at his rooms, I found him in the company of a young woman. She left on my arrival, but on close interrogation he revealed she was of the Roman faith. I warned him to pray to the God who kept our eyes from tears and our feet from falling. I warned him to beware a well-laid plot for his soul. I warned him to keep the faith of his fathers, and I returned to Ballyhalbert with black clouds enshrouding my heart. We corresponded regularly. I exhorted him to return home – he told me of his strong bond of Christian affection. I asked him to think of his mother walking with the Lord – he told me he believed in the communion of peoples. And on a morning when I was up in the watch tower looking for my Lord, another letter arrived announcing his damned decision. I burned any others that came, weeping each time I watched my son's soul blacken and flame.

Saviour, to thee my soul looks up
My present Saviour thou!
In all confidence of hope,
I claim the blessing now.

Burns photo.

'Tis done! Thou dost this moment save,
With full salvation bless
Redemption through thy blood I have
And spotless love and peace.

Friend after friend, departs
Who hath not lost a friend
There is no union here of hearts
That finds not here an end.

Change.

Realised all I'd been told . . . was a lot of stories . . . mickey-
mousey-makey-uppy stories. Your poor father, orphaned at
such an early age. Grandma Foster, Rest in Peace; Granda
Foster, oh long dead, oh, big fat fucking fib. The one, holy,
catholic and apostolic church . . . the faith of our fathers. My
father maybe, but one step back down the line and we knew
the Pope wore the skullcap to hide the 666. And what was
my father really thinking when he scraped off his knees to
declaim, 'I believe in one holy, catholic and . . . was that
coming from his heart or his arse; an affirmation of a new
creed or a weekly show-trial speech with my mother over one
shoulder and my grandfather's hatred hovering over the other.

Clears up.

I began to pack it all away, the tooth fairy and Santa Claus,
and said nothing, the banshee and the bogeyman, through the
next few days, the man in the moon and my guardian angel.
Sunday morning, instead of mumbling the rhythm like
everybody else, every other week, like a dull poem I didn't
understand, I listened closely.

I believe in one God the Almighty Father, maker of heaven
and earth, Maker of all things, visible and invisible.

I believe in one Lord, Jesus Christ, The only begotten Son of God, Born of the Father, before time began. God from God, Light from Light, true God from true God. Begotten, not made, one in substance with the Father: and through him all things were made. For us men and for our salvation he came down from Heaven, Was incarnate of the virgin Mary by the power of the Holy Spirit, and was made man. For our sake, too, under Pontius Pilate, he was crucified, suffered death, and was buried. The third day he rose again from the dead, as the scriptures foretold. He ascended to heaven, where He will come again in glory to judge the living and the dead. He it was who spoke through the prophets.

I believe in one holy, catholic and apostolic church. I profess one baptism for the remission of sins. And I look forward to the resurrection of the dead, and the life of the world to come. Amen.

Copyright, Stephen King. Soon to be a major motion picture. I didn't believe a word of it. And who else did I believe in? The teachers in my school, or the people across town in the King's Institute?

Pearse and the boys, Carson, Craig? And I looked at my father, Joseph Foster, music teacher in a Catholic school, and didn't quite know who he was, didn't know what side he was on, and didn't really trust him an inch.

Oh yeah, the people we trust . . .

Broken phone.

Hiya Monica, did I wake you, love? Och, I'm just ringing because I'm bored and the only thing left on the telly is some beardy bollox talking about particle physics. No, I'm not on patrol, do you think we have a portable TV running off the cigarette lighter? I'm not supposed to, no . . . I'm in Goldilocks' house; yes 'her'; oh right, I'm gonna tell you her name so you can tell the Rotary Club about the sex-for-secrets slut your boyfriend's running. I shouldn't be saying a word, but two of the bears are up with the aul' boot as we speak and the bloody noise is unbearable. What? Jesus!

Oh yes, it's a fair cop. I'm on top of her as we speak and I just thought I'd give you a call to get the electric blanket on. Here, Goldilocks! stop biting the back of me balls would ya and say hello to me girlfriend Monica. Hello Monica, he's no slouch in the sack now is he, you're a lucky girl, now make sure you indulge his every sexual fantasy or I'll rob him off ya for good. Oh now girls, get off that phone, you'll be there all night ... oh, here ... upstairs, business concluded, that's fit young soldiers for ya; look love, it'll be late, half three, four; I'll creep in, you'll not hear a thing; trust me ... awright ni-night.

All right lads, both done your duty for Queen and country, eh? Paper bags are off are they? All right, cleaned up? Yeah? No matter how hard you shake your peg, there's always a drop runs down your leg, eh? Ha ha. Right, wait in the front room till I've debriefed Goldilocks. (*Pours gin.*)

Happy girl? Them two lads good enough for you?

Sorry I tucked into your gin.

What have you got?

And where is the house?

There's three bricked up in that street. Which is it?

No, more questions might smell a bit, leave it, we'll work out which one; you've got to be discreet, nothing more than gossipy.

And that's the word? Them goats did the post office?
Excellent.

That club is great, get you down there every night. Yes, we'll pay the dues, throw in a bit for a few gins too. No, no. I'm virtually a married man, that's not the kind of debriefing I do; thank you for the offer. Now call me, when you've got something new; there's another regiment arriving through next week and if you have something decent I'll bring two of the finest young squaddies as usual. You're happy. We're happy.

Yeah. Okay. Mwah.

Change.

Listen sergeant, this cute little student boy of yours, your bit
of bog rough, well you have two options: you manage to turn
our Jimmy Dean, get him working for us, or you get turfed
out. You start pumping him in a different way from what
you've been doing and maybe, just maybe, you've still got a
career. I don't want to hear about your childhood. I don't
want to hear about love, and I do not want to hear that you
were trying to run him as a source in the first place.

Puh. Box of farts.

These are very real family connections he has and as you're
tucking up with cocoa in your little Lisburn Road love nest,
start picking out the fluff, start getting the gen. Where does
his uncle always go off to? Who all goes where? What routes
do they maybe take: 'Oh, I've heard that's scenic, very nice.'
What kind of car do they drive? Build it up. Get more out of
him. Not my problem how, I don't wanna know; use your
charm. Yeah, try and keep it sweet . . . get drunk, take some
fun Polaroids. If he clams up or tries to back out, let him
know the polaroids are in An Post to *An Phoblacht* in the
morning. And you; you fuck up, you try and back out and in
the morning I send the shots of the pair of you creeping into
the flat to your brigade commander and to every tabloid I
can think of. But listen, it's a free country, you're over twenty-
one; you make the choice.

Change.

Have you read the background to this, sir, it's a fucking
outrage. If McIvor has spilt some piss I don't see why I have
to clear it up. If he chose to run a plank of wood as a source,
that's his lookout. That lad he picked, hatchet head . . . Straw
Man, doesn't have the cop on to do a double knot never
mind run as a double agent.

McIvor hears the army have pulled in some plooky
adolescent. He storms down there, and probably with no more
than a fiver and a packet of cheesy Wotsits he manages to

'turn' him. Big tickle. The poor bastard agrees to have some cartridges 'found' at his house in a raid, so he'll have to go on the run. Really? Brilliant. Did McIvor think the boys wouldn't work out who put it there, does he think they don't count this stuff in and out at night?

Anyway. Raid happens, slap, bang, and Straw Man's meant to go to a priest who McIvor was convinced was a link to an escape route. Not a bit of it; priest told him to fuck off. Lad's clueless. Wanders into Dungannon police station and asks for McIvor to find out what to do next. The cops arrest him, he's on the wanted list after the raid. Fair enough. McIvor has to wade in and half-way half-explain his half-arsed plan and the lad's booted out on to the street again. This time he's picked up by a patrol for the possession rap . . . proper order, not walking into a fucking cop shop.

And, of course, when he gets sent down, the crew in the Crumlin Road are convinced he stinks to high heaven, so they kick him stupid. And what does he do to save his skin? Tells them he's been trying to work as a double agent for them, and gives them a list of people he 'knew' had been co-operating with us. This list is pure fiction, it includes people like his bloody milkman. Mentally, the guy is not with us; he has left his brain in a bag at a bus-stop, he is lost somewhere in the Craigadick picnic area. And now he's out, still working for us, but rootin' tootin' and shootin' at anything that moves to prove his credentials with them. And you want to switch Straw Man to me; you want me to run him so he'll feel happier?! McIvor would go through the roof if he found out, and as it stands, we are not getting on. And if I refuse?

Change.

I've worked it through in my mind, I've walked it through so many times since. My brother leaves the house. For safety's sake he didn't normally call, but we had been counselling Monica. It had got heated. Hugh said he would leave us, go and get some take-away food. I gave him my car keys, told him to drive down, the garage door only opened half-way when . . . I've walked it through so many times in my mind . . .

'Mother, this is not the time ... I refuse to go, let's leave it at that, I am just not ... Monica, tell her ... she obviously cannot hear me ... of all times this is no time for me to get involved in a demeaning, hypocritical charade. I am sorry if it's hurtful, we have been through this. You do whatever it is helps you through the midnight hours and I'll do what helps me. I will meet you outside the church and I will put the bones into the earth and I will cry blood with the rest of you but I will not suddenly retract and retreat into this fantasy bullshit to help me blot out how awful this really is.'

Some bloody priest, his hands still warm from an altar boy's balls, spouting crap over the coffin. 'O God we humbly pray for the soul of your servant Hugh who you have called forth from this world. Bid him to be received by the Holy Angels and borne to the realm of paradise, so that he who has believed in you may not suffer the punishments of Hell, but come into possession of everlasting happiness.'

There were nearly blows in the funeral home. Through her grief my mother had one glimmer of optimism: that this might waken in me the need for God. Tough shit, Ma. Oldest trick in the book. You're weak, you're fucked up, you can't cope, you don't understand? Ring the Confidential Telephone, Paradise 6500.

But we'd been up and down this road so many times, so many rows and tears. Stakes were high: they were fighting for my eternal soul, no less, and I was fighting on the side of sanity. Last mass I went to was my father's funeral. And when I heard some white-haired old duffer try to transfigure my grief through his childish images, I said, that's it, from now on Ah'm livin' on Reality Row.

Puts on his brother's jacket. It does not fit.

My big brother. Smaller than me. Used to hack him off no end.

'But Monica, we know, do we not, we are reminded daily are we not, that John here is a rabid atheist, so he's not arguing from some Opus Dei position; he just feels, like me, that a human life is a human life from the moment of conception, whenever it quickens. And you're absolutely right, this futile debate that, oh, tick, tick, tick, three months past, bing! oh, he's got a soul, sorry, she's got a soul . . . it's rubbish! Souls schmouls, y'know. But as a woman, surely you can feel the undeniable life force that's growing within you and how wrong it would be to negate that. You and John have had a happy accident and you should celebrate it.'

Yeah. Bollox to the churches and their dodgy dogmas, but, well, I'm not one for throwing out the baby with the bath water. So to speak. Monica was all for a termination. I was agin it. And after my brother's death . . . a grandchild for my mother, a new baby to brighten our lives . . .

Music: 'Current Affairs' by the Test Department.

Time off work!? What I am gonna to, play golf? An idle mind is the Devil's workshop. I had to get back into the fray, finish off my latest press pack, put the finishing touches to the new volunteers' oath of allegiance I'd uncovered: I swear by Almighty God, by the Blessed Virgin Mary and her sufferings at the foot of the Cross, by the blessed Rosary and the Holy Beads, by the sacred Church in all ages and by our Holy National Martyrs, to fight until we die wading in the fields of the red gore of the Saxon tyrants, the enemies of the glorious cause of Nationality . . . et cetera.

Newspapers quite liked it; upstairs thought it was a bit much.

A tip-off that the Shramrock Bar is going to have a bomb planted in it, yet again. Me in the car with the hip-flask, the patrol inside the walls of the yard, waiting. Hours pass. The patrol – to a man – falls asleep. Sam, a local drunk, is shuffling past . . . feels an urgent need . . . wends his way in . . . scrabbles around for any kind of arsewipe to hand . . . some of the squaddies, hearing this, finally waken. Sam can't see a thing . . . lights a match . . . LOOK OUT! (*Sound of gunfire.*) Each man in the patrol had four magazines, with 20 rounds in each . . . they let it all go. The pub was trashed and Sam crapped himself all over again. Red cheeks all round, 'cause of dodgy information from Straw Man.

Tried to chime in with Mr Paisley's ecumenical phase; the
one topic that all the churches were really in agreement on –
his Save Ulster from Sodomy campaign. I leaked all they
could want to know about a loyalist homosexual army, a gift,
but nobody seemed to want to take it. What was wrong all of
a sudden? Didn't they believe me?

But it was Monica who came to my rescue; gave me an idea
that got the batting average up again. She went ahead and
got rid of the baby, without telling me, without telling her
family.

Oh, how it amused me, standing there at the Harbour
Airport, or Larne, sometimes Stansted or Stranraer, with my
file of photos and passenger list.

Her. Bring her in.

Sit down, Patricia. Have a cup of tea.

You must be feeling fairly shaky . . .

Not a pleasant experience . . .

Oh, we know where you've been, we know what you've done.
Big Ears listening on the phone line from the 'Woman's
Group' that helps girls from your estate get over and back
without friends or family knowing diddly. Shockin' business.
And how are you now? Bit battered, yeah? Bit broke? Just
spent a night with six other girls called Patricia? Yeah? Well,
listen, we want some help from you, some information, or, the
state you're in there'll have to be a phone call to the mammie
or the priesht to come and pick you up.

Funnily enough, when I got drunk one night and told Monica
about this wheeze, she left me. Fuck her. I'm now in a stable
relationship with two pieces of liver and a jamjar.

Down to my office, that night, bottle of gin.

Bottle and a gun.

Little scraps of information, little scraps of dog shit, they don't
tell me what I want to know . . . I want to know who sneaked
into my garage . . . and riddle me this . . . what is a shaggin'

soul then? Does a little rat of a human have a soul? Is my
brother's soul wafting around in the ether somewhere? Bollox.
Soul . . . my hole. One of them's floating down towards the
sea while the other's rotting in the ground, and if I had their
carcasses here I'd hug them and say, that's your lot, I'm
sorry, but that's your lot. But oh, Ma, I'm not as closed as
you think. I know I'm not just blood and gristle, I understand
this spirit malarkey. I've been reading up, I've been taking
measure.

Undresses. Drinks.

*Music: First movement from Three Movements for Orchestra, by Steve
Reich.*

We are so behind; press releases, surveillance . . . pathetic.
The Americans had people in the Kremlin, and I don't mean
they walked in the door, I'm saying they went through the
walls. All the way from Washington, travellers, astral-bloody
travellers. Up from the Pentagon, clipping the Azores, up
through France, Germany, gliding over Prague, Warsaw,
dipping down over Minsk, Orsha, Smolensk . . . Moskva, in
through the windows, into the offices, into their enemy's heart.
Some of them could only look about, observe, read, but one
of them could turn pages, open doors. This isn't Patrick
fucking Swayze, this is real. They brought back details, the
SP, the goods.

And no religious guff, Ma, not a thurible or a cassock in
sight; ordinary people, with only a talent for concentration,
and visualisation, and a desire to do it.

I am going to scour this city. I am going to soar and swoop
until I have looked in every clubhouse and shebeen, every
back room, every taxi rank, every bus shelter, every chip
shop, every shithouse, every back-kitchen two-up-two-down
hole in the ground until I hear somebody congratulate
somebody on a job well done.

And if my astral gun doesn't work I'm going to fly right back
and get my real one and fly down there in my Vauxhall Astra
and blow holes in the side of his head.

Step One. Relax. (*Drinks.*) Relax. (*Drinks.*) Breathe, breathe, breathe and . . . visualise . . . visualise . . . if I could only see your face, you bastard . . . breathe . . . breathe . . . visualise . . . the bloody garage, no, relax, relax (*Drinks.*) visualise yourself, yourself, it's yourself you're going to let go . . . breathe, breathe, breathe . . . a noise . . . breathe, a noise, a voice . . . visualise, breathe . . . voice again, FUCK OFF . . . breathe, breathe, breathe, get out, get out, breathe, breathe, let yourself go, breathe, JESUS CHRIST! McIvor! You bastard! Let me about my brother's business! (*Shoots. Music ends.*)

They took away my gun; they took away my office; they took away my job. I found myself in Southampton . . . in Netley Military Hospital . . . in my underwear . . . being poked, and prodded, and asked stupid questions. I'll come clean, I'm a hit man for the Legion of Mary. Astral travelling? I'm Uri Gallagher, the Irish medium. Fuck off. Scared of ideas, scared when they see a glint of genius, just when I was about to maybe make a breakthrough, open up a whole new realm of approaches: sectioned, slammed up, 'for my own good'. Found by a colleague on a desktop packing a pistol and a bottle of gin. Occasional excesses of zeal in my counter-terrorism techniques. Breaches of professional confidence, the passing of code-names et cetera with non-military personnel, as testified to by Ms Monica Lennox. Thanks, baby. Glad I could trust you. Slung out on a dunghill; the golden boot up the arse; pissed on and pensioned off, thirty years too early.

Oh, I still work in security. We specialise in supermarkets. On my patch I have every angle of every shelf covered by mirrors. I've blocked off some of the walkways to control traffic flow. Couple of ex-servicemen as store detectives. A few pensioners from the Neighbourhood Watch scheme who do a few hours for me, pottering about with their trollies, eyes pealed. And loads of cameras, some real, some not. The crooks aren't sure they're being watched . . . but they can't be sure that they're not.
I fucking hate it.

I stayed away; tried to settle down to Sainsbury's and snobbery, and the *Daily Telegraph*; keep it all at bay. But Mother fell ill and back I came.

There she was, nodding in and out of consciousness and, opportunist that I am, I tried to explain, kind of hoping that her dozing self would take it all in and finally see it my way.

Dresses in a nightgown. Rosary beads.

You see, Mother, I have prided myself on not falling for any of this nonsense, religious or political. Look at you there with your rosary beads and your *Irish News*. And when I realised it was *all* fabricated, that everybody was peddling their stories to prove their points of view, that there were no facts, nothing you could really believe in ... then I decided the only way to keep that fact clearly in front of my eyes was to become one of the people who was helping to make it all up, one of the fabricators, see it from inside the machine. D'y'see. It's very simple. And that meant there was nothing sectarian about me, Mother; I was able to hate all sides at the same time.

Too complicated ... hmmm; well, old habits die hard. One last dirty trick, one last little assault in my personal battle for hearts and minds.

Music: Ravel's Trio in A minor; No. 3, Passacaglia.

I went to the church this afternoon, Mother. I tried. You would have been proud. Pray your way out of it was always your solution, d'you remember. If your faith is failing, pray for help. I could never really see the logic of that: I no longer believe, so I'll pray to the being that I no longer believe in. But I tried, I had a go, you would have been proud. It didn't work ... I had a shot though. But as I passed the bookrack on the way out, I found a wee publication called 'When my brother died. A little book to help parents and children come to terms with bereavement'.

Booklet.

'Next day Father Pat came to see us. My Dad said, "Father, we all feel angry with God. We can't see why He let this happen to us."

'Father Pat just smiled and then said, "Just think, God gave you the happiness of being with that wonderful boy for twelve years. Wasn't that a marvellous gift to you? You all love Tom very much, but not as much as God loves him. Now he is with God and he is loved and happy.

"I want you all to try and do something. First, I'd like you to trust God. Nobody understands why he allows some things to happen, but we do know that he loves each one of us with a love stronger than we can imagine.

"Secondly, I'd like you to thank God for Tom, and for all the love there is in this family.

"And thirdly, I'd like you to think about Tom often, and always remember him with love."

'I couldn't take all this in, but Mum wrote it down for me, so that I could think about it. Now years later, I feel better about Tom and know that he is safe with God.'

Now, at last, eight years later, does that square with your experience, Mother? Does that answer your questions? Does that help? No, it's not enough, is it? It's not enough.

Music ends.

(Sings.)
> Jesus wants me for a sunbeam
> To shine for Him each day
> In every way try to please Him
> At home, at school, at play.
> A sunbeam, a sunbeam,
> Jesus wants me for a sunbeam
> A sunbeam, a sunbeam,
> I'll be a sunbeam for Him.

Dersses in the funeral clothes.

Today, at Mother's funeral, there was no one to hector me to go to the mass. I sat outside in the car, like a guilty schoolchild unable to enjoy his ill-gotten gains, thinking aloud about, oh, victory and defeat. The odd well-wisher: 'The ceremony's about to start, do you not want to come in, are you unwell?' And because no one was really bothered, a one-man protest that nobody really knew or cared about, I began to suspect that it was only the fights that had mattered to me, and in the fights I'd maybe lost what was worthwhile . . . and I felt completely bloody forlorn.

Ashes to ashes, dust to dust; clump. Thanks very much for coming, thanks very much for coming, here he comes, thanks very much for coming. Mr McIvor.

'Mr Foster. Sorry for your trouble. Dreadful. That's you an orphan, eh? When both your parents die, no matter how old you are, you still feel like an orphan. Dreadful. Listen, I believe you're still over in England and I didn't know how long you'd be back for, if I'd get a chance to see you, so I hope you don't think it improper but I brought this along. I thought you might like to see it. Now that your mother is dead and that. Oh, and don't mind the "Confidential", sure we're old hands the pair of us, and things are loosening up a wee bit, with the times, y'know . . . wee bits of information are being leaked out. Here, on me, have a piece of the Peace Dividend. All the best now.'

Envelope.

Transpires, a few years ago they discovered that it was most likely Straw Man who booby-trapped my garage. My double agent; licence to kill to keep his cover; wanted out of agency work and figured the best way to do it was to try and kill me, the bloke who was running him. Straw Man. As effective as ever.

Went back to the church, sat down . . . listened to someone practising on the organ . . . and squinted at the candles . . . focused on the red light . . . smelt all the cold stone in the air . . . thought about the stories in the stained glass windows . . . thought about feeling at home here many years before . . . and tried to suck the whole atmosphere into myself, tried to condense it.
And only managed to feel very damned foolish. I strolled round the place, stopped at the Marian altar where a wee

woman was arranging flowers, and then left, making myself look straight ahead as I passed the book rack.

So here I am, back up in the attic, up in the watch tower, the man of the house, on my own ...

Lights candles. Dresses up in all the clothes.

Music: closing moment of B minor Mass.

> You are all going to help me,
> You are all going to help me,
> You are all going to help me,
> I am going to learn your manky music if it kills me.
> Hugh ...
> Mum, you're going to help me ...
> Dad ... you never fitted ...
> Grandfather ... you're going to help me, you can forgive can't you ...

What did you have? What did you have?

Bible. Anima Christi.

> Soul of Christ, sanctify me.
> Body of Christ, save me.
> Body of Christ, inebriate me.
> Passion of Christ, strengthen me.
> O Good Jesus, hear me.

Music ends.

> O Good Jesus. (*Undresses.*)

There is no fucking point. I have trashed it, I have drowned it, I have strangled it, it's been throttled by bloody creeds and lies and trench warfare ... Peace? Peace of piss. A little bit of remission is nothing to a terminal case like me; far too much internal bleeding and scarring, far too full of pus and shite; they'll have to get new models and start again, I've killed off whatever there might have been.

Still. Cheer up, John Foster, you can still atone ... blood for blood ... (*Strops Grandfather's razor.*) That's the way of it, isn't it, that should initiate you, yes. Yes, Grandfather, this will

please you better won't it . . . the blood of the lamb, blood
back through the family, blood for an errant son, a brother's
blood, the blood of my defeat, Mother, the history of a
working life written in blood, yes, blood will have blood they
say, oh yes, d'y'see, d'y'see where Christ's blood streams in
the firmament . . .

It's only fitting, don't you think . . .

O Lord, into your hands I commend my spirit.

Goes to cut himself. Then:

No fucking way. I haven't earned that. Nothing so noble as
blood sacrifice. Let his death be fashioned after his deeds.

*Shaves insides of wrists; pares wires; attaches them to light socket and
Elastoplasts them to his wrists.*

Oh, the Americans knew what they were doing. We're so
behind.

Turn of the century, fierce rows between two rival electrical
companies over who would light up New York. One company
sold AC, alternating current, the other sold DC, direct
current. AC was the only really plausible force; it could travel
upwards, it was powerful, used correctly it was perfectly safe.
DC didn't travel vertically at all well. DC knew they were on
to a loser. How to get people to buy DC? Make them afraid
of AC. Invent a machine called the electric chair and bribe
the authorities to power it with AC current. When the switch
was pulled, the condemned flipped, smoked and flamed for
several minutes before blessed release. Did the trick. People
didn't touch AC for years. Gotta be impressed.

Right. Our Father, who art in Heaven, hallowed be thy
name. Thy kingdom come, thy will be done as it is in Heaven
. . . Our Father, who art in Heaven, hallowed be thy name,
thy kingdom come, thy will be done . . . no, bollox.

Hail Mary, full of grace, the Lord is with thee. Blessed art
thou amongst women blessed be the fruit of thy womb,
Jesus . . .

Music: closing moments from the Schubert piano trio.

When I was standing at the Marian altar, gawking, the wee lady said, 'Are you devoted to the Immaculate Conception?' I thought, the act? the person? Do you mean Jesus? She said, 'No, he's not the Immaculate Conception?' I thought he was. I thought he was conceived immaculately because Mary and Joseph didn't, y'know . . .

'Oh, they didn't, but she's the Immaculate Conception.'

You mean her parents didn't?

'Oh, they did, but God intervened and made her Immaculate, stopped her from getting Original Sin.'

Is that true?

'Oh, yes.'

You don't believe that, do you?

'Oh, I do surely, there's no doubt about it. And what's more, when Pope Pius the Ninth pronounced it to be true, he introduced the new concept of infallibility to prove it. So there you are. God bless you, love.'

Trumped to the last.

The story of my bloody life.

Hard to believe, huh?

Music ends.

Pulls light cord.

Black.

Conall Morrison is originally from Armagh. He has lived in Edinburgh, where he directed numerous plays, and Liverpool where he studied drama. He now lives in Dublin where he is an Associate Director at the Abbey Theatre. His own plays *Rough Justice* and *Green, Orange and Pink* have been produced in various English theatres. His adaption of Patrick Kavanagh's novel *Tarry Flynn* was premiered at the Abbey.

Printed in the United Kingdom
by Lightning Source UK Ltd.
131595UK00001B/10/A

9 780413 722706